A Critical Study of
SANGITA MAKARANDA
of Narada

A Critical Study of
SANGITA MAKARANDA
of Narada

Dr. (Mrs.) M. Vijay Lakshmi
Faculty of Music & Fine Arts
University of DELHI

FOREWORD BY
Prof. G. H. Tarlekar

GYAN

Published by

GYAN

Gyan Publishing House
5, Ansari Road
Daryaganj, New Delhi-110002
Phone: 011-47034999, 9811692060
E-mail: books@gyanbooks.com

Distribution Network
gyanbooks.com
India, USA, Canada, UK, Australia, France

ISBN: 978-81-212-0526-9 (HB)

Reprint in India, 2024
First Published, 1996

Printed at: Gyan Press, Delhi.

A Critical Study of Sangita Makaranda of Narada
Author: M. Vijay Lakshmi

To

Shri S. N. Iyer—

An engineer, social worker

And an artist.

My source of inspiration

And guiding spirit

—That is my father.

CONTENTS

FOREWORD

The work Saṅgītamakaranda is ascribed to Nārada. The name of Nārada occurs in the Veda, the Purāṇa, the Śikṣā and works on Saṅgītaśāstra (Please see pages 15 and 16 of the Introduction to Vol. II of Saṅgītaratnākara edited by me and published by Maharashtra Raj Sahitya Samskruti Mandal), Nārada, the author of Śikṣā deals primarily with Sāmagāna. As stated in the Nāṭyaśāstra, Nārada is Gandharva and as such, expert in Gāndharva. Saṅgītamakaranda treats Saṅgīta which includes vocal music, instrumental music and dance. The book contains two main chapters called Saṅgītādhyāya as Nṛtyādhyāya, each one having four *pādas* (parts). As there is no other manuscript available, the scholars have to depend on the Baroda edition based on a single manuscript and seek references from other sources to remove the inaccuracy. Dr. Vijay Lakshmi in her book *A Critical Study of Saṅgītamakaranda* has divided it in ten chapters giving information about the cultural heritage of India, chronological record of historical events, works, etc. After this, she deals with Nārada, the author of Saṅgītamakaranda, his style, his treatment of *nāda, śruti, svara, grāma, mūrchanā, tāna*. Then follows the Nirūpaṇa of Saṅgītadeha. The 7th chapter deals with Rāga classification, 8th with Prakīrṇaka in which the musical instruments and merits and demerits, etc., find place. The 9th chapter deals with dance and the 10th with *tāla*.

Nārada classifies Rāgas into male, female and neuter Rāgas. He gives Gāndhāragrāma. Bharata has not mentioned it perhaps due to its deficiency in regard to consonance. The *druta* and *anudruta* in the case of the *tālas* are found in the *deśī tāla*. As regards the *mūrchanas*, has Śikṣā follows Nāradapurāṇa which gives 7 *mūrchanas* of gods (*devas*), 7 of manes (*pitṛs*) and 7 of sages (*ṛṣis*). The names Agniṣṭoma etc. which are connected with sacrifice are mentioned by Nārada and others, says Dattila.

Later, in the Saṅgītasamayasāra of Pārśvadeva, we find the names of *śrutis* in all the three *spatakas*. The word *turuṣka* in the name Turuṣkatodi may refer to śaka. Dr. Vijay Lakshmi has ascertained the date of Saṅgītamakaranda as belonging to 7th to 9th century. Looking at the term *deśīrāga* in this work, one is reminded of the Bṛhaddesī of Maṭaṅga which also emphasices *deśī* music. The date of Maṭaṅga is also understood by scholars to be 7th to 9th century.

Her study of Rāgas mentioned by Nārada includes the comparison with available similar Rāgas. This part of her book is significant in regard to the study of Rāgas. It is essential to find out the justifiable basis of the classification of Rāgas as male, female and neuter. The significance of the names of *śrutis, rāga* time relation and *rāga-rasa* relation need to be studied critically with the help of modern scientific knowledge.

The efforts of Dr. Vijay Lakshmi in studying Saṅgīta-makaranda critically would certainly help the students of Saṅgītaśāstra.

April 19, 1996
Pune, 411005

Prof. G. H. Tarlekar
Ex-Professor (Sanskrit)
Arts and Science College,
Dhule (MAHARASHTRA)

PREFACE

In ancient India, Sanskrit language played an important role. The literary works and works on all subjects were written in the Sanskrit language. Therefore, to study about the origin and development of a subject of this ancient country, the knowledge of Sanskrit is of great help for those who prefer in depth study of the subject.

This applies to music too as the ancient works on music are in Sanskrit and even at present most musical terms are in Sanskrit.

From my childhood, I was brought up in an atmosphere which was dominated by the Sanskrit language. Our daily prayers were in Sanskrit. Slokas were set in tune and we used to recite them. From my school age till graduation, Sanskrit language was my favourite subject. As the vocal music was one of my specialised subjects as well as a hobby, I came in contact with the musical works in Sanskrit. I realised that my research work should be on the text of some Sanskrit works only.

'Sangita Makaranda' of Narada seemed to be the most interesting and uncommon work on which no work has been done. Though it contains many unique principles of music prevalent at the time of the work, yet no author or critic has discussed about the work at length.

There are many such works on music in Sanskrit which remain untouched. They should be considered for research work. However, this type of work is very difficult, and tiresome at times. But by divine grace, somehow I have been able to finish this work 'A Critical Study of Sangita Makaranda of Narada'.

I have visited Pune, Baroda, Calcutta, Madras and

Thanjavoor (Tamil Nadu) to get the photocopies of manuscripts of all the works of Narada.

It was my late father's (Shri S. N. Iyer) wish that I do some loyal service to the Sanskrit language, and keep the mantle aglow, afresh for ever. It remains to be seen how far I have been successful in fulfilling his wishes.

The present work 'A Critical Study of Sangita Makaranda is based on my thesis presented for my Ph.D. I express my sincere regard and thanks to Prof. (Mrs.) Krishna Bisht, Dean, Faculty of Music & Fine Arts, Delhi University, for her guidance and help.

I am indebted to my colleagues who have encouraged and helped me to bring this work in book form. My heart felt thanks are due to my son Shri M.S. Rajan without whose help this work would not have seen the day light.

January 1, 1996 Dr. (Mrs.) M. VIJAY LAKSHMI

INTRODUCTION

'Sangita Makaranda' is attributed to Narada. It is a small and complete work on Music and Dance. Sangita might be translated as Music in English, yet it has a wider meaning than music. It comprises vocal, instrumental music and dance also. According to Bharata, it is a part of Dramaturgy. Therefore Sangita is supposed to comprise all the forms of performing arts.

There are numerous manuscripts in Sanskrit on various subjects which still remain untouched waiting for seeing light, and it might be added that in a precarious, decayed condition. Though at present, the value of the manuscripts are realised and they are preserved in various libraries and institutions, yet publishing them is a very difficult work.[1] The manuscripts mostly are in Sanskrit either in Devanagari script or the local scripts are used. Therefore, one should know the language as well as the subject to decipher the contents of the manuscript, edit them properly and explain the subject accurately. Most of the ideas, terms and the practice are out moded and proper links and relevance of the subject to the present times are not easy to establish.

The Sanskrit works on music starting from the ancient to medieval period also face the same consequence. The foreign influences, due to the invasions, made the music of ancient times most incomprehensible at times and cannot be interpreted in term of modern music. Yet this much can be said that our music still follows the old traditions, accommodating the changes, which are time-oriented and a natural process in all subjects.

'Sangita Makaranda' is a work on Deshi Music based on supposedly, Tantra concept. The terms used in music evolve around the male-female concept of the universe, which is the basic concept of Tantra—Purusha and Prakriti. The Raga classification, Mridanga and its sound, evolution of Nada, Svara, Shruti, Tala, etc., confirm the above statement.

'Sangita Makaranda' is a work based on the Murchana system of Ragas. There are seven Murchanas appearing from each one of the three Gramas. Except the two Sadharana notes, no other Vikrita note is used in the formation of Ragas.

This work 'A Critical Study of Sangita Makaranda' of Narada is an effort to throw some light on the special and extraordinary features related to music, which are expressed by the author Narada. At the same time I have presented a comparative study of the works by three well-known authorities, viz., Matanga, Nanya Bhupala and Sharngdeva. Their works are 'Brihaddeshi', 'Bharata Bhashyam' and 'Sangita Ratnakara' respectively.

The work 'Sangita Makaranda' belongs to a period not later than ninth century A.D. which has been established through a thorough study of internal and factual evidences and according to the opinions of several reputed scholars of today.

I have selected this particular work 'Sangita Makaranda of Narada', because it serves as a link between 'Brihaddeshi' and 'Bharata Bhashyam'. The chapter on Deshi Ragas of 'Brihaddeshi' is not yet available, so it is not possible to ascertain about the Deshi Ragas described by Matanga.

Moreover, this work has not been given the due attention, it deserves. There are several such Sanskrit works on music belonging to various periods. 'Oumapatam', 'Sangita Chudamani', 'Sangita Narayana', are some of them. As at present, Sanskrit is not a very familiar language to all, and there are only a few people who know Sanskrit and Music equally well, to interpret the Sanskrit works on Music. This work is a small effort of mine in this direction, which I hope will be appreciated by the readers; music lovers and students.

1

Our Cultural Heritage

The ancient culture and literature of India, inferior to none in variety or extent, are superior to many other so called ancient cultures in originality, grandeur and infinitely above them all in glory. The faculty of arts as well as science might surpass any nation in colourful and practical imagination, unique splendour and highly advanced theories. The fact that a much advanced civilization dawned in India and progressing still further, while the rest of the world was struggling and groping in the darkness to achieve the same, is getting established gradually.

According to western historians, the only weak point of India is history. Due to lack of historical records of past events and periods, India is misplaced among the other recognised ancient nations and their civilizations. Arthur A. Macdonell says— "History is the one weak spot in Indian literature. It is in fact non-existent". Max Müller is of the view that this absence of historical literature among Hindus indicates their being a nation of philosophers. "Greece and India are indeed the two opposite poles in the historical development of the Aryan man. To the Greek existence is full of life and reality; to Hindus, it is a dream, delusion.[1] While Greek or other people belonging to western countries are more practical and give much importance to their day-to-day life, Hindus are more concerned with the 'goal', i.e., *moksha* ; deliverance from this worldly life—salvation.

Life is nothing but a dream to them—the acts committed by them are not their own, but are driven to the act. Therefore, they associate no importance to the activities of life.

At the same time, their tradition demands the anonymity of any act. The Vedas, mantras and shastras are not the work of any human being. They are the revelations of God to the Hindus. Therefore, it is meaningless to find fault with Indians for not maintaining the history or historical events in chronological order. They do not believe that various religious books—the Vedas and Puranas; the legendary authors—Manu, Vyasa, Bharata, Narada, and other sages belong to any particular time or period. According to the Hindu philosophy, these scriptures and the sages are beyond the boundaries of the time-bound world.

The literature of the Vedas is termed as 'Shruti', meaning "what has been heard", that means they are not the work of man. According to the tradition, the Vedas are eternal (*nitya*), beginningless (*anadi*) and not made by man (*apourusheya*).

The Sage Vyasa is not the author of Vedas, but the arranger or the compiler of Vedas, Puranas and many other works ascribed to him. His name 'Vyasa' itself means 'arranger or distributor'. The recurrence of many 'Vyasas' stands for the different individuals who remodelled the Hindu religious scripts and it has nothing to do with the authorship. The name itself seems to be a post filled in different periods by different individuals.

There are many such ancient scriptures related to various branches of knowledge; science and arts. There are numerous works on various faculties—starting from religious rituals to legal practices, arithmetic, astrology, the Gandharva Veda (music) and so on. The remarkable point about these works based on various subjects is, they neither specify the period of the work nor the authorship. Indians however, preferred sheer anonymity than publicity which according to them is rather demerit. Humility is recognised as a merit of the first degree and to ascribe that "*I* have done it" or "It is *mine*—is pretty arrogance and self-denouncement is the first step to salvation.

The history of ancient Indian music virtually faces the same problem—tracing its exact time or origin. For that matter, no country can claim to know the origin or the time of the origin of the music which was there even before man learnt to speak.

Yet, this is certain that the most ancient living music of the world is Indian music. The survival of Indian music after such struggles, foreign invasions and multiple influences, is in itself a proof of its adaptability, undying quality and everlasting strong basics.

Many schools of music were flourishing side by side and probably each school had different works of music to establish its own theory. Vedic and Loukik, Gandharva and Gana Margi and Deshi, music based on Jatis only, and then comes the Grama Ragas and Murchana based music, yet another school of music to fulfil the demands of Tantric practice. Basically music developed with the religion and helped the human beings to reach a higher plane thereby attaining the salvation. Music has two aspects—spiritual and cultural from the very beginning. In the same way, the schools of music also differ accordingly. Spiritual music has many branches to fulfil the requirements of various rites and rituals of numerous religious traditions—Vedic, Tantric, Pauranic—depending on the periods.

In Puranas, i.e., Vayu, Vishnu and Markandeya as well as the Tantras, we shall get enough materials about Shruti, Svara, Murchana and Grama. The term 'Gandharva' stands for music in the Puranas and Tantras. The names Vashista, Yajnyavalkya, Narada, Kashyapa and Panini are mentioned among the early musicologists. Nandikeshwara is famous for his work on the structure of language as well as for a treatise 'Nandi Bharatam' or 'Bharatarnavam' on music. Maheshwara Sutras, the fourteen aphorisms of the origin of the Sanskrit language are explained by Nandikeshwara and are called as Nandikeshwara Karika.

The various forms and systems of music found in India did not come from a common source. Hence, a common generalised theory to explain all the musical facts and terms belonging to various periods is impractical. Beginning from the Vedic music (according to some scholars, Gandharva system of music is as old as the Vedic music, and this conception cannot be neglected as baseless) to Narada, Bharata and Matanga there are atleast three or four schools of music—Vedic, Gandharva, Narada, Bharata, Nandikeshwara and Matanga.

Prajnananda classifies those schools under six categories:

1. Vedic or the Saman;
2. Gandharva Narada;
3. Druhina Brahma;
4. Muni Bharata;
5. Nandikeshwara and
6. Matanga.[2]

According to him, there was a novel school of music known as 'Gandharva' devised by the Gandharvas, Narada, Tumburu, Vishwavasu, Chitrasena and others. The Gandharva music was in practice along with the Vedic music and the Marga music (later development) collected materials from both the Vedic and Gandharva system of music.

In 'Harivamsha Purana'—an appendix to the Mahabharata, mention is made of famous 'Chalikya' music based on Shad Grama Ragas. It is stated that Narada along with Krishna and his son learnt Deva Gandharva Chalikya music from the heaven in the Court of Indra[3], and brought the music to the earth.

The name 'Narada', mentioned in Harivamsha belongs to Gandharva Narada, who expounded the Gandharva school of music with three Gramas, based on seven Grama Ragas. Hence the music is called as Gandharvam after the Gandharvas, who are demi-gods with inclination towards music and dance, especially after the founder member 'Narada'.

It is also stated in the 'Harivamsha Purana' that Narada taught the Gandharva Grama to "Bhaimas". Narada has been honoured as an authority on music. Even Bharata accepts that he has followed Narada as far as Dhruva Geetis are concerned—

ध्रुवासंज्ञानि यानि स्युर्नारदप्रमुखैर्द्विजैः।
गीताङ्गानि तु (नीह) सर्वाणि विनियुक्तान्यनेकशः।।[4]

Therefore, a school of music started or established by Narada is very much feasible though there is little evidence available in black and white. There are several musical works ascribed to him or to his name. The Gandharva school of music based on 'Shad Grama' Ragas (according to 'Harivamsha Purana') might have flourished before 'Natya Shastra' of Bharata and the Vayu and Vishnu Puranas, because the term 'Gandharva' is used for music. The fact that Gandharva's contribution to Indian music was great, is highlighted by naming the music as Gandharva Veda. It is further more stressed by using the term Gandharva Shastra by reputed ancient treatises of music.

A unique problem of ancient Indian mentality is its preference for anonymity in all fields—religious, scientific, cultural and so on. Music is no exception and the same rule applies to it too. There are various schools of music and each of them lays claim to the same ancient treatises and authors. All performing arts claim to have the same origin and the same legendary authors such as—Shiva, Brahma, Bharata, Narada, Tumburu and Nandi to prove their antiquity. The very same practice still persists as every Gharana links itself some how or other with Tansen, the renowned artist.

Often the recurrence of the same name misleads and creates confusion in deciding the period of the works and authors. However, the authors of ancient treatises are some mythological or legendary figures. No art, literature or epics and sacred chants were created by human beings. Every other astrological book has appeared from divinity and sages. Vedas are *apourusheya* and came from the mouth of God. It might be named as humility of Indians and respect to elders by dedicating every act to the elders without mentioning one's own name.

In a nutshell, it can be said that Indian mental makeup is something unique. Anonymity of name is sought to show one's humility, which is preferred by most Indian authors, than giving his own name, which is considered to be vain glorious. To respect the elders, it is considered proper to write under their names. The followers of one school of a subject always took shelter under the name of the founder. Some names are misleading as they stand for some particular authorship. Vyasa stands for the author of Puranas, Mahabharata and Vedas. Whoever writes on these subjects, takes the name of Vyasa and loses his individual name.

Sometimes, to prove the authenticity and antiquity, the names of divinity or some well-known ancient names of the sages are used. There is another view about the similarities of names occuring in Sanskrit literature frequently. The works on music (Sanskrit) extend over such a long time period, the similarities in names are bound to occur because of the Indian customs to repeat the names of their forefathers. Allain Danielou opines, "The difficulty is to distinguish between numerous authors of the same name. We know of at least ten Bharatas, authors of different works, six Somas or Someshwaras, five Narayanas, four Damodaras etc. Among the existent works, we have two Sangita Ratnakaras, three Sangita Narayanas, four Bharata Shastras, four Ragamala's and so on".[5]

With this foundation we seek to study 'Narada' as the author of 'Sangita Makaranda' and several treatises.

REFERENCES

1. *Ancient Sanskrit Literature*, p. 9.
2. *Music, its form, function and value*, p. 36.
3. *King of Devas*.
4. Natya Shastra, p. 288.
5. *The History of Indian Music*, p. 11.

2

Narada : The Author

The name Narada is well-known in Indian music. He is a mythological figure, a Sage, a Gandharva, and an author of many religious, social and cultural literature. There are at least four or five Naradas. A Sage Narada, who authored Saman hymns, Puranas and Samhitas, a Gandharva Narada who brought music to the earth, a Narada, the author of 'Naradiya Shiksha', a Narada, the author of 'Sangita Makaranda' and yet two more Naradas to whom 'Panchama Sara Samhita' and 'Raga Nirupana' are ascribed.

Thus Narada is a many-sided personality and a very controversial figure as far as his contributions to a variety of subjects and various faculties of learning are concerned. Therefore, the facts and data collected from different sources— treatises, Puranas and works on music regarding Narada are elucidated as follows.

Narada is a familiar name in the Hindu mythology. Almost all the Puranas, Upanishads and ancient religious works on music have something to say about the famous sage; Gandharva and a staunch devotee of Lord Narayana.

He is described as the son of Brahma, a blessed celibate and a roving communicator, similar to Goddess Saraswati, depicted with a Veena. In mythological (religious) stories, he is a mischief-monger creating utter confusion and chaos, but his mischiefs always end in a happy note.

We find a description of Narada in the 'Dictionary of Mytho-logy and Religion' as follows—"A Rishi to whom some hymns of the Rigveda are ascribed. He is one of the 'Prajapatis' and also one of the great 'seven Rishis'. The various notices of him are somewhat inconsistent. The Rigveda describes him as of the 'Kanva' family. Another authority states that he sprang from the forehead of Brahma, and the son of Kashyapa and one daughter of Daksha".

"In some respect, he bears the resemblance to Orpheus. He is the inventor of the Veena (Mahati) and was the chief of the Gandharvas or the heavenly musicians. Gandharvas and Apsaras were in the profession of 'Gandharva' music, dance and instrumental music. They were always adept in music. 'Gandharva' is said to be a division of the nine divisions of ancient India[1]".

'Narada has the appellations'-'Kalikaraka' (strife maker), 'Kapi-vaktra' (monkey faced), 'Pishuna (messenger or spy)'.[2] The name of Narada is referred to in several connections, in various Puranas and Vedas.

"In Atharva Veda, Narada is a mythological seer. The 'Maitreya Samhita' refers to him as a teacher. He appears in the 'Aithereya Brahmana' along with Parvati as the priest of Harishchandra, as teaching 'Somaka Sahedevya' and in'Samavidhana Brahmana' as a pupil of Brahaspati. The Chandogya Upanishad mentions him with Sanat Kumar[3]."

Narada is named as a son of Prajapati in Vayu Purana. According to Vishnu, Vayu, Bhagavata and Brahma Puranas, Narada is a Mauneya Gandharva presiding over the mouth of Madhava. He is also mentioned as an author of a work on the divine architecture.

The Deva Gandharvas are classified under two categories—the Mauneya and Pradheya. Mauneyas are those who are born to the daughter of Daksha named Muni and to Maharshi Kashyapa, who are sixteen in number. Narada belongs to the Mauneya Gandharva group.

"देव गन्धर्वा द्विविधाः केचित् मौनेयाः, केचित्
प्राधेयाः कश्यप पत्न्या दक्ष सुतायां
मुनि नागकायां जाताः मौनेयाः षोडशाः ...।
इत्येवं महाभारतादि पर्व पंचषष्टितामाध्याय उक्ताः यथा।
भीमसेनौग्रसेनौ च सुपर्णो वरुणस्तथा।
गोपति धृतराष्ट्रश्च सूर्यवर्चाश्च सप्तमः।
सत्यवागर्कपर्णश्च प्रयुतश्चाभि विश्रुतः।
भीमश्चित्ररथश्चैव विख्यातः सर्वविद्वशी।।
तथा शालिशिरा राजन् पर्जन्यश्च चतुर्दशः।
कलिः पंचदशस्तेषां नारदश्चैव षोडशः।
इत्येते देवगन्धर्वा मौनेयाः परिकीर्तितः।"

वाचस्पत्यम्, पृष्ठ २५२७-२८.

Narada is a Maharshi as well as a Gandharva or demi-god. Rather it is proper to say that the name Narada stands uppermost and is related to many faculties of learning and arts as well.

The following is about Narada in "New Catalogues catalagorum of Madras University":

1. Narada—grandson of Yajnika Kika Sarman and father of Sankarabhatta, a Siva dasa (author of 'Manava Sulabha Bhasya').
2. Narada—eponymus author on music reference to in 'Mahabharata' Shanti Parva 210-21, 'Natva Shastra' XXXII 484 (as expounder of Gandharva Veda).

   Ibid. (on Dhruvas)

   By Dattila Matanga and Abhinava Gupta.[4]

The earliest work which deals in Loukik music as a part of its subject is 'Naradiya Shiksha'. It is more concerned with Vedic music and is ascribed to Narada. But the following sloka specially indicates that Gandharva Narada is totally alien to the Vedic music and Gandharva community could not sing the Vedic music for lack of knowledge of Svara concept of the same.

तुम्बरु नारदवसिष्ठविश्वावस्वादयश्च गन्धर्वाः।

सामसु निभृंत करणं स्वरसौक्ष्म्यात्तेऽपि हि न कुर्युः।[5]

which also shows that Gandharva music was prevalent even before the period of Shikshas and Sage Narada and Gandharva Narada are different personalities. Then comes 'Natya Shastra' which also deals in Gandharva Veda. Bharata shows his indebtedness to Narada for the subject 'Gandharva', i.e., music.

"गान्धर्वमेतत् कथितं मया हि यत्पूर्वमुक्तंत्विह नारदेना"[6]

He says "I have explained the Gandharvam which is already said by Narada", shows that Narada—the 'Gandharvam' was already there before Bharata. Bharata has described 'Gandharvam' in the process of dealing in the dramatics. His 'Gandharvam' is related to dramaturgy and is not an independent form of art. Dattila, who is earlier than Matanga quotes Narada, and Matanga too mentions the name of Narada regarding the three Gramas. Abhinava, the commentator of 'Natya Shastra', refers to Narada in Vol. II with regard to the etymology and the meaning of the word Gandharvam—

प्रीतिवर्धनमिति नारदीयनिर्वचनमपि सूचिते।"

Krishnamacharyar, the famous author of the work entitled 'History of Classical Sanskrit Literature', draws the picture of Narada as a Hindu mythological bard with a Veena. He is the son of Brahma and is the first to be initiated in the art of music. He says, "Besides being cited as authority in the "Tantras", 'Natya Shastra' mentions that Bharata took Narada and Svati with him when he got leave of Brahma, for his first performance at "Dvajamaha".[7]

Again, according to Krishnamacharyar, Narada took his views on music from 'Naradopanishad' (not available) and the principles therein were developed by him in his 'Naradiya Shiksha'.

Sureshchandra Banerji describes Narada as follows—"Narada an authoritative writer on Smriti, who is supposed to have flourished between 100-300 A.D....." "To a Narada is ascribed also the work on music called 'Sangita Makaranda', 'Naradiya Shiksha', 'Panchama Sara Samhita' and 'Raga Nirupana' ".[8] This clearly shows that he is also of the opinion that there are several Naradas starting from the author of Smriti in various periods, ranging from pre-Vedic period to the tenth or more accurately upto fifteenth century A.D. Various persons bearing the 'non-de-plume' of Narada, or originally named as Narada come under this category. As it is said about Bharata, that Bharata is a general name for a person related to 'Natya Veda', the name 'Narada' also stands for a person connected with music. Narada and music are inseparable. Music is named as Gandharvam and according to many authorities Gandharva Veda was brought to the earth by Narada (a Gandharva).

According to Prajnananda, Narada is one of the Gandharvas among Tumburu, Vishwavasu, etc., who has expounded the Gandharva music. Gandharva music is as old as Vedic music. Margi music was a later development.

This fact is very well established in 'Naradiya Shiksha' of Narada which deals in both Vedic and Loukik music side by side. Regarding Narada, Prajnananda's views are worth mentioning. 'Narada—I, really brought a renaissance especially in the field of music, making a link between two times of music'.[9]

According to him too, there are four Naradas each one an author of different work. Narada-I is the compiler of 'Naradiya Shiksha' which deals with the metres of the mantra's texts as well as the Vedic songs and recitations. He has also dealt with Gandharva music in short.

Narada-II has 'authored' the 'Sangita Makaranda'. The 'Panchama Sara Samhita' and 'Chatvarimshchatta Raga Nirupanam' are attributed to Narada-III and IV respectively.

Therefore, Narada of 'Sangita Makaranda' comes after Narada of 'Naradiya Shiksha', i.e., second in order. Narada of 'Naradiya Shiksha' is accepted to be the first and foremost by all the scholars. 'Naradiya Shiksha' is given priority over the 'Natya Shastra' itself because of its subject (Vedic music).

Narada of 'Naradiya Shiksha' is the one who is mentioned by the other ancient authors—Bharata, Dattila, Nandikeshvara besides several puranas also in the context of music (Gandharva).

The Gandharva type of music described in 'Naradiya Shiksha' is older than Marga type of music. Narada is one of the Gandharvas, who propagated the Gandharva school of music. Music has been named as 'Gandharvam' or Gandharva Veda in the Puranas, epics, Tantras and other later treatises.

The aforesaid facts and descriptions of Narada from various sources are information about 'Narada' the name in general and not particularly applicable to any distinct Narada of any particular work. Gandharva Narada who brought Gandharva school of music to the earth and the author of musical treatises is our main concern (of this present work) because 'Sangita Makaranda' is a work on music. Sage Narada and mythological Narada are excluded and so are the Naradas, the authors of many other religious works unrelated to music, i.e., 'Narada Pancha Ratra', 'Narada Bhaktisutra', 'Narada Samhita' and so on.

After the Narada of 'Naradiya Shiksha', the second place goes to Narada of 'Sangita Makaranda'. There are two other Naradas to whom 'Panchama Sara Samhita' and 'Chatvarimshachatta Raga Nirupanam' are ascribed. There is yet an another Narada to whom a work 'Raga Sagara' is attributed with Dattila which is said to be of a later period.

These are the facts about Narada in a nutshell—Narada is a name connected with various religious works, various faculties of learnings, mythological anecdotes and Gandharva Veda (music). He is described as the son of Brahma, Gandharva singer with a Veena, propagator of Gandharva music, the one who brought music from the heaven. He is an authority on Tantras; a staunch devotee of Shiva and Shakti cult; yet he is the follower of Vaishnava cult and the propagator of the 'Pancharatra Vidhana' as well.

Indologists consider the 'Markandeya Purana' as the oldest and most important Purana. Reference of Narada as the main propagator of ancient music occurs in this Purana, and he is a familiar figure with the readers of this Purana. However, Narada is familiar to the laymen as well and he is identified as a sage singer with a Veena wandering in the universe and spreading the name of Narayana.

If the Sage Narada is the author of hymns, Samhitas and Puranas, there is a mythological Narada who used to sing the praise of Lord with a Veena, to whom the principles of Gandharva Vidya or music may be attributed.

In the sphere of music, Narada is the most ancient authority after Brahma, as it is believed that Narada is the first music disciple of Brahma and Saraswati and brought music to the earth from the heaven with him. This is accepted and mentioned by Bharata the earliest author on music Dattila, Matanga and onwards.

The Works Attributed to Narada

In India, there are a number of treatises related to the methodology and rituals as well as related to day-to-day life, i.e., laws concerned with the social life. Starting from Vedic hymns the list of works attributed to Narada are many and on various subjects.

Narada, the name is very popular and adopted by various authors belonging to different periods. The works bearing the name of Narada as the author are too many to be accounted for in this present work. The works of Narada can be mainly classified under two categories.

(i) General religious and scientific (astrology, archaeology), works

(ii) Works concerned with Gandharva Veda (Music).

'Naradiya Purana', 'Narada Smriti', 'Narada Pancharatra', 'Brihannaradiya', 'Naradopanishad', 'Narada Bhakti Sutra', etc. come under the first category. These works are not much related to the music or 'Sangita Makaranda', yet they provide some background for the name Narada and his vast and many-sided knowledge.

1. Naradiya Purana or Narada Purana

This is one of the eighteen Mahapuranas, accepted as sixth in order by the Vayu, Vishnu, Markandeya, Matsya, Skandha, Bhagavata, Agni and other Puranas. It is given the seventh position by the Kurma and Siva Puranas.

A study of 'Narada Purana' (version Venkateswara edition) shows that its title 'Narada Purana' is not maintained throughout the work. In the first edition (1905 A.D.) the colophones of some chapters name it as 'Brihannaradiya' instead of 'Narada Purana'. The second edition (1923 A.D.) entirely leaves out the name 'Narada Purana' and stick to 'Brihannaradiya'. However 'Brihannaradiya' is a Upapurana and not a Mahapurana. The whole 'Naradiyashiksha' appears as a part of 'Narada Purana' from the 15th sloka onwards in 'Narada Purana'.

Narada Smriti

This work also named as 'Narada Dharmashastra',[10] describes about the ethics, religious codes and conducts, applicable to day-to-day life similar to that of 'Manusmriti'.

Narada Pancharatra

'The Narada Pancharatra' is one of the oldest, if not the very first specimen of Vaishnava literature in Sanskrit. The only work which can contest the palm of seniority with it is the Bhagavata Purana".[11] It contains five parts called Ratras. Each Ratra has 15, 8,15,10,11 chapters respectively making 59 chapters in all. There are some verses devoted to music as follows:

श्री व्यास उवाच
अथ गंधर्व राजस्तु भगवानाज्ञया विधेः
संगीतञ्च जगौ तत्र कृष्णरासमहोत्सवम्।।[12]

The second and third sloka of the first Adhyaya (in continuation of the above sloka) also describes about music.

Naradopanishad

This work does not come under the eighteen well-known

Upanishads. This name is mentioned by Krishnamachariyar in his work—'History of Classical Sanskrit Literature'. He mentions therein that Narada was indebted to 'Naradopanishad' for his theories and principles of music written in 'Naradiyashiksha'. According to Krishnamachariyar, that particular work 'Naradopanishad' was published from Bombay.

Narada Bhaktisutra

This work is in the form of Sutras (short and meaningful sentences) about the art of devotion. Here Narada has expounded the theory of devotion and recitation (*kirtan*) of Lord's name. This work is divided in ten parts with 84 sutras. There are countless works ascribed to Narada and bear the name of Narada. They are not concerned with music or Gandharva Veda, yet there are some references of music at random related to the rituals, ratras and worship of some deities. Mostly the instruments to be used in the rituals are mentioned in these works.

Now the works on music attributed to Narada are—'Naradiya Shiksha', the earliest work on music (available) ascribed to Narada. It seems that this Narada is the one referred to by Bharata, Dattila, Matanga and others. However, there is controversy about this priority of 'Naradiya Shiksha'. Though Narada has been credited with the propagation of Gandharva Veda, (Music) and every authority on music shows his indebtedness to Narada, yet no extensive work on music bearing the name of Narada is available at present or mentioned by anybody in any work so far.

Krishnanachariyar finds an ancient Narada—author of 'Naradopanishad'. He says, "Narada was indebted for his views on music to 'Naradopanishad' (ed. Bombay) and the principles enunciated therein were developed by him in his Shiksha. Neither this 'Naradopanishad' is available nor included in the list of Upanishads.

Naradiya Shiksha

'Naradiya Shiksha' deals with the music of the Samaveda. In other Shikshas, i.e., of Sounaka, Vyasa and Apisali, etc.,

Narada is referred to as an authority. Bharata follows the opinion of Narada on *sama svara* and quotes a verse from 'Naradiya Shiksha'.

"आचार्यास्समभिच्छन्ति पदच्छेदन्तुपंडिताः
स्त्रियो मधुरमिच्छन्ति विकृष्टमितरे जनाः।।[13]

This verse may be general adage practically used by all. In 'Naradiya Shiksha', Bharata's name does not occur even once, while Bharata says plainly that he is indebted to Narada for the Gandharvam.

The whole Shiksha is reproduced from Naradiya Purana or vice versa. The reference of Narada by Bharata proves it to be an ancient work, earlier than Bharata. The special feature of 'Naradiya Shiksha' is the mention of Gandhara Grama and its Murchanas (names). The comparison between Vedic and Loukika Svaras is an indication that it is a link between the post-Vedic and the Vedic music. It is the earliest record of musical division and terminology.

'Naradiya Shiksha' is divided into two parts, each containing 8 Kandikas or chapters with 238 slokas. In the first part or Prapathak, the author describes about notes, Gramas, Murchana, Tana, Grama Ragas, Vedic and Loukik scales and things related to Gandharva music.

The second part or Prapathak deals with Vedic music, its rules and regulations. In the musical field 'Naradiya Shiksha' serves as a connective link between the Vedic and post-Vedic musical traditions. While the Vedic music is meant for the Vedic scholars and priests and to be utilised for rituals and spiritual purposes, Loukik music is meant for common man, which is termed as Gandharva for the spiritual attainment but with a little difference. It might be said that Gandharvam is used in Tantric rituals and other types of worships. Gandharvam is defined as follows in 'Naradiya Shiksha'.

"गेति गेयं विदुः प्राज्ञा धेति कारू प्रवादनम्
वेति वाद्यस्य संज्ञेन गांधर्वस्य विरोचनमिति।।"[14]

The archaic language as well as the subject prove its antiquity over other works including 'Natya Shastra'. Though some scholars are of different opinion on the treatment of Grama Ragas and Gandhara Grama which are not mentioned in 'Natya Shastra', such elaborate discussion is not necessary. Naradiya Shiksha's priority over 'Natya Shastra' is maintained.

In chronological order 'Sangita Makaranda' of Narada comes next to 'Naradiya Shiksha' among the works of Narada. But it will be taken up late for obvious reason. 'Panchama Sara Samhita' is discussed below:

Panchama Sara Samhita

This is a short but important work on music by Narada which follows the Raga-Ragini system of classification of Ragas. O. C. Ganguli is the first writer to mention and describe about the Raga Classification of 'Panchama Sara Samhita' in his work 'Ragas and Raginis'.[15] He gives an account of this work thus—"Panchama Sara Samhita (sometimes called "Panchama Samhita") composed by an author called Narada deserves notice. It survives in two Mss. One in the collection of the Bangiya Sahitya Parishad, (the copy bearing a date 1700 Saka-1778 A.D.). The second Mss belongs to the Asiatic Society of Bengal in Calcutta with a colophon dated 1440 A.D. (1362 Saka)."[16]

This latter manuscript can be seen at Asiatic Society. It bears the number G.5040. It is hand written in Bengali script, on a sort of yellow hand made paper. The manuscript contains nine leaves. At present it is available in print as an appendix of the monograph. "Fundamentals of Ancient Indian Music and Dance by Suresh Chandra Banerjee. It is published by the L.D. Institute of Indology Ahmadabad, 1976.

The text of 'Panchama Sara Samhita' is printed as the appendix of a small book 'Naradiyashiksha', translated by Suresh Chandra Banerjee (Published by Rabindra Bharati University).[17] It consists of ancient Ragas including the derived ones—Kalyani, Poorvi, Ramakali and Pahadika. The reason must be as suggested by the author that the Ragas described by him were the current ones in the regions to the north of the Vindya mountains, Rajputana Cutch and the areas adjacent to the sea.

"मेरोरुत्तरतः पूर्वे पश्चिमे दक्षिणे तथा
समुद्रकच्छे यं देशास्तत्रामेषां प्रचारणा।"[18]

The most important feature of the work is the contemplative verses (Dhyana slokas) of the melodies giving the iconographic pictures of the six Ragas and thirty-six Raginis, said to have emanated from the abode of Brahma to offer their prayers to Him.

"आगता ब्रह्म सदसि ब्रह्माणं समुपासते"[19]

In the other manuscript belonging to Bangiya Sahitya Parishad 116 Ragas are mentioned. (This manuscript is not seen by the writer). Suresh Chandra Banerjee has given both the versions in his appendix.

"गोपी गेतुमारब्धमेकैक प्रियसंन्निधौ
तेन जातानि रागाणां सहस्त्राणि च षोडशाः।"[20]

The time theory of the six Ragas and thirty six Raginis are given systematically. It is also ascertained that Ragas should be followed by their own Raginis while singing. Raginis of other Ragas should not be sung after an alien Raga and the rules may be are not applicable if the king orders to sing a particular Raga.

Chatvarimshachatta Raga Nirupanam

This is a small treatise on music ascribed to Narada. O.C. Ganguli opines that this work belongs to the sixteenth century. "The first text bears the name of 'Chatvarimshachatta raga nirupanam', attributed to Narada whoever may be the author, wrote under the cover of a name revered in musical history, he must have belonged to the sixteenth century".[21]

The paper manuscript of this work is preserved in the Tanjore Palace Library (No.6651). in 14 (20 including cover) leaves. This work is somewhat longer than the Panchama

Sara Samhita published by Arya Bhushan Press, Bombay by M.S. Sukanthakar in 1914. It is not available at present.

In 'Chatvarimshachatta Raga Nirupanam', the author introduces the Janaka (parent) Raga system, with ten Janaka Ragas. Each Janaka Raga has five wives and four sons. Each son has a wife making a total of 140 Ragas. The title indicates the number of Ragas dealt in the treatise. It is a novel system, an improvement on Raga-Ragini system. It might be possible that the author wished to link both the systems of Raga-Ragini and Janaka or accommodated the upcoming Ragas with in the Raga-Ragini system. Major masculine Ragas are—Shri, Vasanta, Panchama, Bhairav, Kaushika, Megha, Natta, Narayana, Dipaka and Hansaka. The contemplative verse of each masculine Raga is given and then five wives for each Raga is enumerated.

Raga Sagara

This work is named as 'Dattila Narada Samvada' too. It is written in three chapters and deals with Ragas, Shrutis and Svaras. There are references to the name of Sharngdeva, or it is better to say that many verses are copied down from 'Sangita Ratnakara'.

"ननु रत्नाकरे शार्ङ्गदेवेन विकृताः स्वराः"[22]
"देशीरागेषु ग्रथितः शार्ङ्गदेवसूरिणा"[23]

In the very beginning, Narada mentions the names of eight male Ragas which are identical to that of 'Sangita Makaranda'. But afterwards the work deals with the mela system of classification followed by meditative verses of Ragas.

This text was discovered by Dr. V. Raghavan, who mentions in his paper, " Some names in early Sangita literature". The manuscript of 'Raga Sagara' is lying at the Oriental Manuscript Library, Madras. O.C. Ganguli in the footnote of his book 'Ragas and Raginis', has mentioned that the text in two copies are available in the Madras Oriental Library Catalogue Vol. XXII, No.13014-15. But at present only a transcription done in 1947 is available as the Manuscripts are in bad condition. The transcription in 53 pages ends with following colophon.

इति श्री रागसागरे नारद दत्तिल संवादे
राग ध्यान विधानं नाम तृतियस्तरङ्गः

According to O.C.Ganguli, this is the earliest available text dealing with the iconography of Ragas. In the very beginning Narada answers to a question put by Dattila regarding music. After that he gives the eight names of major melodies—

"भैरवश्चापि भूपालः श्री रागः पटमंजरी
वसन्तौ मालवश्चापि बङ्गालो नाटकास्तथा
एते अष्टरागास्सर्वत्र पुंस (रा) गा इति कीर्तिताः।"

This classification of Raga-Ragini system, i.e., eight Ragas and three Raginis each might be the earliest according to many scholars. This classification is older than the conception of six Ragas and five or six Raginis each. This former classification of eight Ragas and three Raginis is found in 'Sangita Makaranda'; which is supposed to be the earliest text explaining the Raga-Ragini system. Raga Sagara is in puranic style narrated between Narada and Dattila. It speaks about on different kind of Ragas, their forms and attributes. Yet by judging through the names of Ragas and the mention of Mela system, it is a later work than 'Sangita Makaranda' and the author Narada of 'Raga Sagara' is definitely a different person than the author Narada of 'Sangita Makaranda'.

Sangita Makaranda

There is a work named Sangita Makaranda yet not by Narada. It is an exhaustive treatise on music and dance written by the court poet—Veda, in the royal palace of Shaji, the father of the Maratha King Shivaji. The king was known as Makaranda Bhupa. Veda was the tutor of Sambhu, elder brother of Shivaji. He belonged to earlier seventeenth century. The manuscript is available in the Tanjore Library. It bears the date of 1650 A.D. and is in a decaying condition.

There are two manuscripts: 1. 10725, 2. Collection No. B.L.6641 (paper) and 11511 (palm leaves) respectively. The earlier one is in Devanagari while the later one in Telugu script. This work comprises many later forms of modern dances.

Sangita Makaranda (of Narada)

This is a small work compared to 'Sangita Ratnakara' or 'Sangita Raja', concerned with our work here. It is attributed to Narada as per the internal evidence. Another work with the same name 'Sangita Makaranda' by the court poet Veda is entirely different from this work.

'Sangita Makaranda' is divided into two parts: 'Sangitadhyaya' and 'Narityadhyaya' with four chapters each. It has 560 slokas. Though the work is neither elaborate nor explanatory, it throws light on some novel aspects such as Shruti, (names), types of Nada, Raga classification, etc.

REFERENCES

1. *A Classical Dictionary of Hindu Mythology and Religion, Geography, History and Literature*, pp. 218-19.
2. *Bharatiya Sangita Ka Itihasa*, p. 225.
3. *Narada Purana — A Critical Study*. A thesis submitted by Damodar Nambiar, p. 396.
4. *New Catalogues Catalagorum*, vol. 10, p. 52.
5. *Naradiya Shiksha*, p. 72.
6. *Natya Shastra*—32, 484, 33.3.
7. *History of Classical Sanskrit Literature*, p. 829.
8. *A Companion to Sanskrit Literature*, p. 75.
9. *Music, its form, function and value*, p. 91.
10. *The Institutes of Narada* (small) by J. Jolly, 1856.
11. *Narada Pancharatra*—Introduction.
12. *Ibid.*, p. 99.
13. नारदीय शिक्षा, पृष्ट २३, नाट्य शास्त्र, पृष्ट ४५१
14. नारदीय शिक्षा, चतुर्थ कण्डिका, पृष्ट २७,
15. *Ragas and Raginis*, p. 43.

16. *Ibid.*

17. According to Mr. N. Ramanathan (Madras University), the addresses:
    1. Administration Officer, Rabindra Bharati University
    6/4, Dwarakanath Tagore Road Calcutta-700 007
    2. The Registration, 56, ABT Road, Calcutta 700 050.

18. *Panchama Sara Samhita.*

19. *Ibid.*

20. *Ibid.*

21. *Ragas and Raginis*, p. 57.

22. *Transcription*, pp 4 and 17.

23. *Ibid.*

3

The Time

In the Hindu mythology, the different aspects of life and learning are associated somehow with the God-Almighty. At the same time — the creation, preservation and destruction are threefold managed by the Trinity — Brahma, Vishnu and Shiva respectively.

Creation is assigned to Brahma. Therefore, music is also created or has originated from Brahma and Saraswati, the wife of Brahma got it and taught the music to her son Narada. Narada on his part brought it to the world after training the divine dancers, Gandharvas, Kinnaras and so on. According to Tantra, Nada is the outcome of the perpetual meeting of Shiva and Shakti, dance and music originated from Lord Shiva Himself.

This is a part of Indian mythology which does not care a bit for dates and periods. To a Hindu, every treatise bearing the name of a sage as its author is sacred and timeless, i.e., exceeds the boundaries of time. Yet the historians, modern and western scholars demand that a work should be apportioned in its proper period to enable them in studying the gradual and systematic development of civilization, arts and culture of that particular country.

There are various works in different branches of subjects

in India which are yet to be dated. India has access to an enormous variety of subjects from medicine to technology, art and architecture, astronomy to political science, faculty of law, finance and many other subjects. These subjects have many old treatises written upon them. Yet, they are still to be discovered and brought to light to get due attention from the scholars throughout the world. The works on music too belong to this category. Indian music is the only oldest type of music which is still flourishing. Though there are many ancient works like 'Naradiyashiksha', and 'Natya Shastra', 'Dattilam', 'Brihaddeshi', etc., the invations and influence of foreign forces have created many voids in the field of music.

Yet another factor which adds to the assimilation of facts is the ancient tradition of India. India always preferred and followed the oral tradition of imparting the knowledge in any subject. The subjects were never maintained in writing. The Vedas and music were strictly oral, we have a very few works of those days on any subject, compared to other countries. Though the fact remains indisputable that India was far advanced in culture and civilization, while the other so called advanced countries were groping in the dark.

'Sangita Makaranda' is one of those valuable works, which provides some novel ideas in exposing some factors about Gandharva music independent of dramaturgy.

'Sangita Makaranda' ascribed to Narada is a small work without bearing any date. Controversy shrouds over its date and period, as the work does not provide any hint about its time, or the name of the author. Narada has no definite history of birth and lineage. 'Sangita Makaranda' is not quoted as a work by any later author, though the name Narada is mentioned by everyone.

'Sangita Makaranda' is placed by many scholars in seventh or eighth century, a work prior to 'Sangita Ratnakara', which is a landmark in Indian musicology of the twelfth century (latter half). Therefore, it is better to start with 'Sangita Makaranda's' precedence over 'Sangita Ratnakara'. These are some points to establish its antiquity over 'Sangita Ratnakara'.

'Sangita Makaranda' is a short work written in two parts —Sangitadhyaya and Nrityadhyaya, each divided into four padas. Its presentation is very simple and the subject matter is arranged at random. Many verses appear in both works— 'Sangita Ratnakara' and 'Sangita Makaranda'. It might be the copyist inability to decipher the original manuscript (due to its condition). It might be the interpolation by the copyist. The subjects and terms are only mentioned at times without any explanatory definitions.

On the other hand, the 'Sangita Ratnakara' is an extensive work on music consisting of seven chapters, each of them is dealt with masterly elaboration. The arrangement of topics however, are systematic and scientific.

According to R.K. Telang, "The style of the book ('Sangita Makaranda') is very simple like that of Bharata's Natya Shastra." But the 'Sangita Ratnakara' is written in highly polished Sanskrit. The arrangement of subjects is scientific, seems to have been written after the art of music had attained a very high stage of development in all its branches.[1] However, the language of 'Sangita Makaranda' is even much more simpler than the 'Natya Shastra'.

The names of the ancient scholars and authors provided by Sharngdeva (as is customary) are not included in the similar list of scholars provided by Narada. Sharngdeva mentions the names of Nanya Bhupala, Abhinava Gupta, Rudrata, Paramardi, Somesa, Lollata, Udbhata, Shankuka and so on.

As far as Narada of 'Sangita Makaranda' is concerned he does not mention any of those names, and his names are totally different and ancient. He has mentioned the following names in the second pada of both Sangitadhyaya and Nrityadhyaya of 'Sangita Makaranda'.

"हरि, ब्रह्मा, मतंग, कश्यप, विश्वकर्मा हरिश्चन्द्र
भरत, कमलास्यक, चंडी, व्याल, शार्दूल, नारद, तुम्बुरु,
वायु, विश्वावसु, शौरी, आंजनेय, अंगद, षण्मुख
भृंगी, देवेन्द्र, कुशिक, कुबेर, मात्रागुप्त, रावण, समुद्र

सरस्वती, बलि, यक्ष, किन्नरेश, विक्रम"[2]

Above names occur in the second chapter of Sangitadhyaya. In the second chapter of Nrityadhyaya, some of those names are repeated with addition of Kohala and Durga Shakti. They are as follows :

"सदाशिव, हरि, ब्रह्मा, भरत, कश्यप, मतंग, दुर्गाशक्ति,
शार्दूल, कोहल, हनुमान, तुम्बुरु, अङ्गद, नारद"[3]

Though the treatment as well as the order of the topics handled in 'Sangita Ratnakara' are quite different from that of 'Sangita Makaranda', many identical verses describing the merits and demerits of musicians, Vaggeyakara appear in both 'Sangita Makaranda' and 'Sangita Ratnakara'. It is very difficult to say whether Sharngdeva or Narada has copied from either.

The deciding factor in favour of the priority of 'Sangita Makaranda' is the mention of the Gandhara Grama with its arrangement of notes, unavailable in 'Naradiya Shiksha'. Sharngdeva explains the Gandhara Grama as it is described in 'Sangita Makaranda', as follows—

"यद्वा धस्त्रिश्रुति षड्जे मध्यमे तु चतुश्रुतिः ।
रिमयो श्रुतिमेकैकां गन्धारश्चेत् समाश्रितः
प श्रुति धो निषादस्तु धश्रुतिं सश्रुतिं श्रितः ।।४।।
गान्धार ग्राममचष्टे तदा तं नारदो मुनिः
प्रवर्तते स्वर्ग लोके ग्रामोऽसौ न महीतले।।५।।"[4]

Since no other works of Narada are available, which have the arrangement of notes of Gandhara Grama prior to 'Sangita Makaranda', and Sharngdeva himself has quoted Narada as the authority over Gandhara Grama and his similar description of Gandhara Grama prove that 'Sangita Makaranda' is an earlier work to 'Sangita Ratnakara'.

Many reputed scholars and authors differ about the time of 'Sangita Makaranda' and an unanimous decision still has not been taken. Approximately the work is placed between seventh and eleventh century and almost everyone is of the opinion that it is prior to 'Sangita Ratnakara' of Sharngdeva. The work 'Sangita Makaranda' comes after 'Brihaddeshi' of Matanga and before Nanyadeva's 'Bharata Bhashyam'. The views of some reputed ancient and modern scholars are given below.

'Sangita Makaranda' is edited by Mangesh Ram Krishna Telang and published under the supervision of Baroda State Library and brought out under the Gaekwad Oriental Series. According to Telang, "If we take all the above circumstances into consideration, we are obliged to arrive at the conclusion that 'Sangita Makaranda' is an older work than 'Sangita Ratnakara'. But the mention of the name of Matrugupta, who is also mentioned by Sharngdeva in his 'Sangita Ratnakara' as one of the writers on music enables us to infer that the present work must have been written not earlier than seventh century A.D."[5]

Telang has mentioned the occurrence of the name of Matrugupta yet he is silent about the appearance of the name of Mahamaheshwara (Abhinava Gupta) or the Raga Turushka Todi in the text. The name of Narada is mentioned in almost all the works on music from Bharata, Dattila, Matanga to the authors of modern age.

It is an established fact that Narada is the Gandharva who brought down the Gandharvam (music) from the heaven and propagated on the earth. Datlila says—

"गान्धर्वं नारदादिभ्यः प्रत्तमादौ स्वयंभुवा
विधिवन्नारदेनाथ पृथिव्यामवतारितम्।।२।।"[6]

Dattila again refers to Narada while writing about Tanas as —"'agnistoma' etc., named by Narada and others." The names of the Tanas are neither mentioned in 'Naradiya Shiksha' nor any other available works of Narada. Some of them are mentioned in Vayu Purana. In 'Brihaddeshi' 84 Tanas with their descriptions and names are given.[7] Therefore, there should have been some other earlier works of Narada on music comprising the names of the Tanas.

In 'Brihaddeshi', Matanga refers to Narada about Gandhara

Grama. But Narada mentioned by Bharata, Dattila and Matanga is not the author of 'Sangita Makaranda' yet there is a probability that the work 'Sangita Makaranda' is based on, or contains some ideas and principles of some ancient work of earlier Narada.

Prof. Rama Krishna Kavi of 'Bharat Kosha' opines that 'Sangita Makaranda' is not a complete work. It is a brief compilation of Narada's views just to make it easy for the students of music to refer. According to him, it is written after 'Sangita Ratnakara'. About 'Sangita Makaranda' he writes thus :

"नारद प्रोक्तः एकः। अन्यो वेद प्रणीतः। आहत्य द्वौ ग्रन्थौ वर्त्तते। नारद प्रणीतः सप्तपरिच्छेदात्मकः संगीत रत्नाकरानन्तरं तज्जातीय एव लघु ग्रन्थो शिष्य सौकर्यार्थं प्रमाणभूतं नारद वाक्यात् लिखितः स्यात्। संगीत रत्नाकर मकरन्दर्यो बहवः श्लोकाः समानाः। मध्ये महामहेश्वर (अभिनवगुप्त) नाम गृहणात् अस्याति प्राचीनत्वं केश्चिकयुक्तं विहतमेव।"[8]

Rama Krishna Kavi is the only one who has placed 'Sangita Makaranda' after 'Sangita Ratnakara'. Again, according to him, by mentioning the name Maha Maheshwara (Abhinava Gupta) it has lost its claim to antiquity. This opinion does not seem proper. Because 'Sangita Makaranda' is a full fledged work complete in itself having a title which is explained by the author at the starting itself.

"गीतं वाद्यं च नृत्यं च त्रयं संगीतमुच्यते।
नारदेन कृतं शास्त्रं मकरन्दाख्यमुत्तमम्।।३।।[9]

For the other objection about the mention of Maha Maheshwara, it might be the interpolation of the copyist. This point is discussed later in this chapter. The Vaggeyakara Lakshanams, the merits and demerits of musicians are similar in both 'Sangita Ratnakara' and 'Sangita Makaranda' yet it does not prove anything solid. 'Sangita Makaranda' cannot be a compilation of the quotations of 'Sangita Ratnakara', as it has a totally different system of music without Vikrita notes and is based on Murchana system.

According to H.A. Popley, (author of 'The Music of India') 'Sangita Makaranda' is a work composed between the eighth and eleventh century. He believes that 'Sangita Makaranda' is prior to 'Sangita Ratnakara'. "He gives a similar account of Gandhara Grama of 'Sangita Makaranda'. Sharngdeva seems to have borrowed a good deal from this book."[10]

O.C. Ganguli, author of 'Ragas and Raginis' — an important work on Raga classification, feels very strongly and places 'Sangita Makaranda' as a work prior to 'Sangita Ratnakara'. According to him, 'Sangita Makaranda' comes next in order to 'Brihaddeshi' of Matanga.

He says—"The text of Sangita Makaranda, the next available record of the history of the Ragas, through bearing the considerable development that has taken place between the fifth and eleventh century ......".[11]

In the same work, he gives many details to establish the fact that 'Sangita Makaranda' is an ancient work belonging to eighth century. One of them is about the melodies mentioned in the work. Those melodies are identical to the melodies of Bengali songs collected under the name of 'Carya Viniscaya'. These songs are of the Buddhist mystic of Sahajiya sect by name Siddhacharya Luipa, who is placed by Binaytosh Bhattacharya in 669 A.D. while Harprasad Shastri has placed him in the tenth century which is incorrect.

Suresh Chandra Banerji, the author of 'A Companion to Sanskrit Literature,' opines that Narada is "an authoritative writer on 'Smriti' said to have flourished about 100 to 300 A.D. But this Narada is not the one connected with Gandharvam (music). "To a Narada is ascribed the works on music called 'Sangita Makaranda', 'Naradiyashiksha', 'Panchama Sara Samhita' and 'Raga Nirupanam".[12] His views on the work "Sangita Makaranda — attributed to Narada is in two parts, Sangita and Nritya of four chapters each may be assigned to the eleventh century....". "It mentions Mahamaheswara, i.e., Abhinava Gupta, its definition of Gandhara Grama is almost bodily repeated by Sarangdeva."[13]

Sri Krishnamachariyar, a well-known scholar and author of 'The History of Classical Sanskrit Literature' has assigned the work 'Sangita Makaranda' to eleventh century. "Sangita Makaranda of Narada is a later work ...... It mentions Mahamaheswara that is Abhinava Gupta in dealing with the faults of singers and its (Sangita Makaranda) definition of Gandhara Grama is almost repeated by Sarngdeva. It may therefore be assigned to 11th century A.D."[14]

Varadachari, the author of 'A History of Sanskrit Literature', opines — "The 'Sangita Makaranda' is attributed to the authorship of Narada". The text now available refers to the views of Abhinava Gupta. The critics place it between the seventh and eleventh century A.D."[15]

Dr. Arun Kumar Sen is of the view that 'Sangita Makaranda' is a work done between 'Natya Shastra' and 'Sangita Ratnakar'.

"प्रतीत होता है नाट्यशास्त्र व संगीतरत्नाकर के मध्य किसी समय संगीतमकरन्द की रचना हुई होगी।"(१)[16]

Prajanananda believes that the author of 'Sangita Makaranda' is the Narada-II in order after Matanga (vide 'Music its form, function and value').

Alain Danielou, the French author places 'Sangita Makaranda' and its author Narada after the Epic age. According to him, the 'Naradiya Shiksha' of Narada is the earliest work written on profane music". "He is quoted by all subsequent writers of the early period, who in turn are quoted by later Naradas—the authors of 'Sangita Makaranda' and the 'Chatvarimshachatta Raga Nirupanam'."[17]

In the bulletin of Sangita Natak Akademi (May 1956), under the heading 'Some names of early Sangita literature, following detail is given about 'Sangita Makaranda'. "Scholars opine that the Narada referred to as holding the ga - grama is the author of Sangita Makaranda which has that grama. This is to show the genuineness of Sangita Makaranda as a work of Narada .... The reference of Matru Gupta here definitely puts the date of the Sangita Makaranda after seventh century".[18]

The above excerpts are the views of reputed authors and scholars. The ideas provided by the various authors are put forward not in a chronological order or basis. Dr. S. V. Raghavan being a serious and thorough analytic minded person without any sort of prejudices, is quoted as the final and last word on the subject. It seems, he readily agrees that 'Sangita Makaranda', though not written before seventh century, it is not a later work than seventh or eighth century.

These are some of the views and statements regarding the time period of the concerned work, 'Sangita Makaranda'. Excluding Prof. Ram Krishna Kavi almost every author places 'Sangita Makaranda' before 'Sangita Ratnakara'.

Generally the date of a work is decided by these following factors. The internal evidences, language and style of the work, colophones, the names and personalities and places mentioned by the author, historical events described or referred to in the work. Generally, the author gives a self-introduction with his family background in his work.

To begin with, 'Sangita Makaranda' is written by an author under the eponymous name 'Narada' though frequently used by all the musicologists, the musicians; and the authors of musical work, it does not suggest anything about the period of our Narada of 'Sangita Makaranda'. Moreover, there are as many as four Naradas, having four different works on music ascribed to them. None of their works has been placed in a definite time period. Therefore, the name of the author does not help in deciding the time of 'Sangita Makaranda'.

The language of the work 'Sangita Makaranda' is very simple and archaic, without any polished figures of speech. All the subjects are described directly without using similies, metaphors, etc. The facts are explained in a very short way with simple words. The language is very simple which suggests an earlier period. The language is basically somewhat similar to that of 'Naradiya Shiksha' and 'Natya Shastra'. Whereas the language of 'Sangita Ratnakara' is highly polished and advanced. Dattilam as far as its language and style are concerned compares well with the language of 'Sangita Makaranda'. Therefore, the language used in 'Sangita Makaranda' denotes an earlier period (upto tenth century).

Yet, it is a probability and not a conclusion. The name of 'Sangita Makaranda' does not occur in any ancient or later works, though many verses and ideas are quoted from 'Sangita Makaranda'.

There is only one manuscript of 'Sangita Makaranda' available which is in the State Library of Baroda. It was written or copied by Krishnaji Dutta in 1677 A.D., that is 319 years ago. According to Telang, the manuscript was discovered by the wife of R. Ananta Krishna Shastri, the officer employed by the Baroda Central Library for tracing the manuscripts. It was discovered in Gadwal at a pundit's house in 1919. The concluding colophon is as follows :

"इति संगीत मकरन्दः समाप्तः।
शुभमस्तु।
शके शालिवाहने पिङ्गलनाम संवत्सरेः अश्विनमासे शुक्लपक्षे विजयदशम्यां विद्यापुर महानगरे श्रीमन्महागणपति दास कृष्णा जी दत्तेनेदं संगीत मकरन्दः
पुस्तकं लिखितम्। महागणपतिर्जयति।

This colophon throws light on that particular manuscript and its copyist. Now, the internal colophons mentions the names of the book and the author but nothing else.

"इति श्री नारदकृतौ संगीतमकरंदे वीणादेहनिरूपणं नाम द्वितीय पादः।"

The above colophon is produced here as an example. This type of colophon is given after every chapter that neither throws any light on the period of the author nor his work.

In 'Sangita Makaranda' Narada gives a list of names of deities and divine personalities related to music, musicians and scholars as was customary in those days at two places. In second chapter of 'Sangitadhyaya' as follows:

हरिर्ब्रह्माहरिश्चैव मतङ्गः कश्यपो मुनिः।
विश्वकर्मो हरिश्चन्द्रो भरतः कमलास्यकः।।
चण्डी व्यालश्च शार्दूलो नारदस्तुम्बुरुस्तथा।

वायुर्विश्वावसुः शौरिरांजनेयोऽंगदस्तथा।।१६।।
षण्मुखो भृङ्गिदेवेन्द्रः कुबेरः कुशिको मुनिः।
मात्रागुप्तो रावणश्च समुद्रश्च सरस्वती।।२०।।
बलिर्यक्षो किन्नरेशो विक्रमोऽपि यथाक्रमम्।
एभिः संगीतके प्रोक्ता माता द्वादश लक्षणाः।।२१।।[19]

wheras in the second chapter of 'Nrityadhyaya'.

सदाशिवहरिर्ब्रह्मा भरतः कश्यपो मुनिः।
मतङ्गो यश्च दुर्गा च शक्ति शार्दूल कोहला।।१।।
हनुमानस्तुंबुरुश्चैव अङ्गदश्चैव नारदः।
एते साहित्यसर्वज्ञो बुधास्तालान्प्रचक्रमु।।२।।[20]

The following are the names mentioned by Narada in the 'Sangitadhyaya' — Hari, Brahma, Matanga, Kashyapa, Vishwakarma, Harischandra, Bharata and Kamalasyaka, Chandi, Vyala, Shardula, Narada, Tumburu, Vayu, Vishwavasu, Showri, Devendra, Kubera, Kushika Muni, Matra Gupta (Matrugupta), Ravana, Samudra, Saraswati, Bali, Yaksha, Kinneresha and Vikrama. These names look like a jumble of divine personalities, gods, kings, scholars as well as names connected with music. It cannot be classified under a single order. Hari might be the name of Vishnu. Brahma is the creator who taught music to Saraswati. Matanga is the author of 'Brihaddeshi'. Here we miss the name of Dattila while Kohala is mentioned in the list of Nrityadhyaya. Some prominent names of the scholars mentioned by Narada in his 'Sangita Makaranda' are described in Appendix 2.

Among these names, Matrugupta is a name which is important as far as the time of 'Sangita Makaranda' is concerned. Therefore the details about Matrugupta is worth consideration. Krishnamacharyar says—"He (Matrugupta) was a very early writer . . . probably of about the beginning of the Christian era or even earlier Rajatarangini (iii 129-229) Kalhana gives a long account of the poet Matrugupta and his relations with King Vikramaditya Harsha Vardhana of Kashmir"[21]. Earlier in the same book on page 585 he has accounted of Harsha as—"Kalhana mentions King Harsha, Vikramaditya of Ujjain as the patron of Matru Gupta". "Harsha has written a commentary on Natya Shastra, which is quoted by Abhinava Gupta, Sharadatanaya and Bhoj as an authority." Dr. Raghavan mentions that "Matrugupta lived in King Shri Harsha's time during 607-647 A.D. He was a great poet and was later made the king of Kashmir."[22]

In the list of 'Sangita Makaranda', both Matrugupta and Vikrama as well as Samudra are mentioned. But the name Vikrama does not indicate the period or the particular Vikrama, the author meant. Because, Vikrama is an attribute given to many kings. The inclusion of Matrugupta with Vikrama probably suggests the name of Harsha of 607-647 A.D.

The names move like—Harishchandra, Kamalasyaka (Brahma), Chandi (either a poet or only Devi), Angada and Anjaneya, the same Anjaneya becomes Hanuman while mentioning in the second chapter of 'Nrityadhyaya'. In the later list, he teams Hanuman with Tumburu and Angada with Narada. He has mentioned the names of Kohala and Durga Shakti in the list of 'Nrityadhyaya' only. The names in the list do not lead us to any conclusion to settle the time though they suggest the lower limit of the time. Narada has not mentioned Rudrata, Nanya Bhupala, Paramardi, Somesa or Abhinava Gupta in the two lists of names he has given. All the other names mentioned by Narada are either myths — deities or Puranic personages. About the date of Matrugupta, Ramakrishna Telang furnishes the details. "But the names of Vikrama and Matrugupta are historical. As there have been several Vikramas, it is difficult to say which Vikrama is meant. Matrugupta who was a poet and writer on poetics is said to have lived in about the first half of the sixth century being a contemporary of Siladitya Pratapasila of Malwa (A.D. 550-600)".[23]

There is still one more view of Dr. S.V. Raghavan about Matrugupta and 'Sangita Makaranda' which emphasises the point. "The reference to Sangita Makaranda (p.13) to one Matragupta is evidently only to Matrugupta. Matrugupta lived in King Harsha's time 607-648 A.D."[24]

Thus from the list of authors and scholars mentioned in 'Sangita Makaranda' it may be decided that inclusion of the names of Matanga, Matrugupta, Kohala and Kashayapa and deletion of the names of Rudrata, Nanyadeva and Abhinava Gupta suggest that the period of the work might be between the seventh and tenth century. 'Bharata Bhashyam' is supposed to be a work of tenth century. Therefore 'Sangita Makaranda' might be after Matrugupta and before Nanya Bhupala.

As already stated the subject matter dealt in the work and its stage of development also play an important role in deciding the date of the work. Indian music has an antiquity of thousands of years. The stages of development may help to settle the time to some extent, but there are always exceptional cases.

The Raga-Ragini classification system of 'Sangita Makaranda' again creates controversy about its time. According to the stage of development of Indian classical music this Raga-Ragini system is said to be a later development, which comes after Grama Raga and Bhasha Ragas or to be more precise it comes after Sharngdeva's Raga classification. There is another school of thought about the Raga-Ragini system, that this system belongs exclusively to north Indian classical music and 'Sangita Ratnakara' and its system of music are applicable to both Carnatic and Hindustani system.

Broadly speaking, Indian music is divided into three stages of development based on its notes and melody construction. The treatises on music can roughly be divided into three periods according to the treatment of notes and scales.

The authors and treatises on music adopting the Grama Murchana system come under the first period. In this period, two Gramas — Shadja and Madhyama were the base of music. Murchanas were in prominance. These were formed by shifting the basic notes. Jatis and Grama Ragas were formed by using these Murchanas as basic scales. Vikrita notes were only two in number and they were termed as Sadharana. Antara Gandhara and Kakali Nishada were the notes which changed their positions. Shadja was not the basic or starting note for all purposes. Bharata, Dattila, Matanga, Narada of 'Sangita Makaranda' come under this category.

For the second period, those works and authors may be considered who accepted the Grama and Murchana system yet they placed their note on the Veena with twelve frets and their notes 'Ga', 'Ma', 'Pa', 'Ni' were not constant but 'Ri' and 'Dha' were constant and Shuddha. Their Vikrita notes were 'Ga', 'Ma', 'Pa', 'Ni'. Another trait of this period is the extinction of Jatis and prominence of Ragas. Murchanas were only used for name sake and the use of Vikrita notes indicated the prominence of a basic note 'Sa' though it was not declared openly. From 'Bharata Bhashyam' or more accurately from 'Sangita Ratnakara' onwards this second period occurs.

Again in the last period, the authors and scholars based their notes on twelve fretted Veena. The difference was in the Vikrita notes. They used only one Grama—Shadja Grama. 'Sa' became the basic note and Murchana disappeared. 'Sa' and 'Pa' became constant and other remaining five notes 'Ri', 'Ga', 'Ma' 'Dha', 'Ni' became changeable. The term Komal and Tivra for Vikrita notes were used by Lochana Kavi in his 'Raga Tarangini'. The scholars place him in the sixteenth or seventeenth century. This system is still followed.

The first period begins from the early Christian era, i.e., from-post Vedic or Epic period to ninth or tenth century. Nanya Bhupala also comes under this period. The term Vikrita is not used for the notes uptill Abhinava Gupta.

From the time of Sharngdeva, Vikrita notes appeared. Though only five Vikrita notes are used in actual practice, the later authors mention as many as 29 notes.

However, in 'Sangita Makaranda' Narada has described three Gramas with their arrangement of notes. Similar to Nanya Bhupala, Narada has based his Ragas on all three Gramas, but he has not confirmed or explained this fact anywhere. At the same time he has mentioned two Sadharana notes. The starting notes (Graha) of the Ragas are given by Narada, besides that there are Ragas which omit the note

Shadja, which confirms its belonging to the first period, from the second to tenth century.

He has mentioned two Sadharana notes as follows—

श्रुतिद्वयं चेत् षड्जस्य निषादः संश्रयेदसौ।
सा काकली मध्यमस्य गान्धारस्त्वन्तरः स्वरः।[25]

Narada does not mention about any other notes (Vikrita) except these two—Kakali and Antara, which ascertains that he is prior to 'Sangita Ratnakara' and probably after 'Brihaddeshi'. Therefore, the Svaras of 'Sangita Makaranda' denote the time of the work to be the seventh century onwards.

Raga classification also helps to determine the period of a work. The Raga-Ragini classification, (though 'Ragini' word is not used) is said to be of a later period than Grama Ragas and Bhasha Ragas and Ragas based on Geetis. The Ragas are classified under various categories by authors of different periods, starting from Matanga onwards. Every author has his own ideas about the classification of Ragas.

To arrive at the relationship of Raga classification to the time of a work; a short description of the evolution of Raga and its various stages might be helpful. Raga classification developed with the changing periods and music to meet the needs therein.

The Vedic music is adjudged as the earliest music by all the scholars, but does not mean that there was no music before the Vedic period. Two types of music were prevalent at that time, side by side. One was the Vedic with Vedic notes 'Krushta', 'Prathama', etc. This Vedic music had at first a single note called Archic and then developed two notes; Gathic followed by the Samic stage with three notes. The seven notes were evolved in later stages.

The second type was Loukika music. The term Loukika is used by Narada of 'Naradiya Shiksha' at the earliest in this sloka —

"ऋषीणां सप्तयास्त्विमालौकिकाः स्मृताः।"[26]

The Murchanas of Rishis are termed as Loukika. The commentator has used the word Loukika in two or three places. He has written as follows —

लौकिकानां गाने स्वराणां मध्यमादि....।

Even in Vedas there is mention of a music, i.e., Gatha, which was performed to entertain people. That sort of music had the description of king's qualities and valour, etc. It is a well-known fact that both Vedic and Loukika music were in practice side by side. The term Loukika stands for music related to the world; used only for entertainment and not for rituals or religious purposes. This might be the Gandharva which is propounded by Gandharvas like Narada,Tumburu and Vishvavasu.

In 'Naradiya Shiksha' it is ascertained that Gandharvas like Narada, Tumburu and Vishvavasu were not capable of singing Sama Gana because of its abstractness of notes.

तुम्बुरु नारद वशिष्ठ विश्वावस्वादयश्च गंधर्वाः।
सामसु निभृंत करणं स्वरसौक्षम्यात्तेऽपिहि न कुर्युः।[27]

The above sloka in 'Naradiya Shiksha' dealing with both the systems Gandharva and Sama Gana; establishes and strengthens the fact that Gandharva music was as old as the Vedic music.

In Harivansha Purana (second century A.D.) the stress has been laid on both the Gandharva and the Vedic music were practiced side by side.

गान प्रभाषं संचक्रे गन्धर्वाणामशेषतः।
अन्येषां चैव विप्राणां गानं ब्रह्मप्रभावितम्।"[28]

Then came the Margi and Deshi which are the two parts of Gandharvam. Margi had more restrictions regarding Tala, Pada, and Laya as it was used to propitiate God and deities.

Margi is the later development of Gandharva. Deshi also is a part of Gandharva but proved as most accommodating to suit the needs and tastes of different countries and the people. The name itself is suggestive of its origin.

The terms Margi and Deshi attained their importance in the period of Matanga. In 'Sangita Makaranda' the terms Deshi and Margi are mentioned but the term 'Gana' is not to be seen throughout the work even for once. The remarkable point is that the term 'Gana' is described by Abhinava Gupta and Sharngdeva in their works.

'Sangita Makaranda' seems to be a work on Deshi music, but it is peculiar. It is a work altogether different from other works. It has handled the Ragas in a different way giving much more importance to the time of singing and the emotive values of the Ragas.

The most controversial fact in deciding the time of 'Sangita Makaranda' is its classification of Ragas, Ragas and their Bharyas or Yoshitas. The above system is accepted as being in practice in the medieval period that is thirteenth century onwards. The Raga-Ragini system seems to have evolved from an entirely new conception probably based on Tantra. It is mostly time-originated and perhaps the Shat Grama Ragas are converted into six Ragas. This system of Raga and Bharyas might be another parallel stream of Indian music founded by Narada which is adopted in north India.

It is generally said and is a fact also that Bharata of 'Natya Shastra' has not dealt with Raga though he used the word 'Raga' in five different places. Therefore, the critics and scholars say that 'Raga' was a later development and it was not present at that time. But it is a well-known fact that in 'Naradiya Shiksha', 'Harivamsha Purana' and even in 'Natya Shastra' itself (though indirectly) Grama Ragas are mentioned.

"मुखे तु मध्यम ग्रामः षड्जः प्रतिमुखे स्मृतः।
साधारितं तथा गर्भे मर्शे कैशिकमध्यमः।
कैशिक च तथा कार्यं गानं निर्वहणे बुधैः।"[29] (३५३-५४)

Though the Shat Grama Ragas (five according to Bharata, seven according to Kudumiamalai inscriptions) were present in his time and were in practice, Bharata did not deal with them as his subject was dramaturgy and he was concerned with Jatis and Dhruva Gana based on them.

In his definition of Gandharva, Bharata explains that Gandharva is a combination of Tala, Svara and Pada. The music produced by stringed and all other instruments should be known as Gandharva.

"यत्तु तंत्री कृतं प्रोक्तं नानातोद्य समाश्रितम्
गांधर्वमिति तज्ज्ञेयं स्वर ताल पदात्मकम्।[30]

The above verse shows that Gandharvam covers the vocal music as its components are Svaras, Talas and Padas—Sahitya or literary wordings. Bharata is more interested in instrumental music as in dramaturgy instruments play comparatively more important role than vocal music.

There are two types of explanations for the above phrase, 'गांधर्वमिति तज्ज्ञेयं' one by Manmohan Ghosh and second by Dr. Janaki. According to Manmohan Ghosh,' the music played on the stringed instrument' is to be known as Gandharva '(गांधर्वमिति).' The latter explanation, according to Dr. Janaki, runs like this, "But I have rendered this expression as "included in the Gandharva" (Gandharvamiti as a single compound word) based on the 'Abhinava Bharati'.

गांधर्वो मितिर्मानं वर्त्तनम् अन्तर्भावोयस्य
गान्धर्वे तदन्तर्लीनमिति यावत् [31]

Now why is only the stringed music brought under the Gandharva? This is because the whole system of music is envisaged by Bharata as only a part of the drama presentation."[32]

If Bharata has not described about the Grama Ragas it does not mean that they had evolved after Bharata's 'Natya Shastra'. 'Grama Ragas' are mentioned in 'Naradiya Shiksha', 'Ramayana', 'Mahabharata' and 'Harivamsha Purana', 'Vayu Purana' and 'Markandeya Purana', besides in the 'Meghaduta' and 'Vikromorashiya' of Kalidasa. In 'Brihaddeshi' Matanga says :

"रागमार्गस्य यद्रूपं यन्नोक्तं भरतादिभिः
निरूप्यते तदस्माभिर्लक्ष्य (ल)क्षणसंयुतम्।।२७६।।"[33]

Matanga does not say that the Raga was not there at the time of Bharata etc. He mentions, "the description of Ragas which are not told by Bharata, etc.," means that Bharata did not describe about Ragas, because of his own free will as he has no use for them in this dramas.

A Raga is produced by the permutation and combination of notes and varnas (arrangements of notes), which leaves sweet soothing impressions on the mind. Matanga is the earliest authority on Raga who had used the term Raga and defined it in such terms in his 'Brihaddeshi'. He has mentioned ancient authors like Kashyapa, Durgashakti, Yashtika while describing the Ragas, but their works are not available at present.

"योऽसौ ध्वनिविशेषस्तु स्वरवर्णविभूषितः
रंजको जनचित्तानाम् स च राग उदाहृतः।"[34]

"रंजनाज्जायते रागः" gives the derivation of the word Raga.

This term 'Raga' is found in the form of 'Kaishika' in Ramayana (400 B.C.), Mahabharata (300 B.C.) and Harivamsha Purana (200 B.C.). Seven Grama Ragas accepted by the most are—Madhyam Grama, Shadja, Sadharita Pañchama, Kaishika, Shadva, and Kaishika Madhyama. There was another school which accepted only six Grama Ragas (Harivamsha Purana). Kaishika, one of the Grama Raga is mentioned in Ramayana in the following sloka—

"चरितं कैशिकाचार्यैडरैरावतनिषेविते"[35]

Therefore, it may be said that the concept of Grama Ragas was there in the beginning of classical period, i.e., 600-500 B.C.

In Harivamsha the use of Shad Grama Ragas prevailed. In the Vishnu Parva of Harivamsha, the term Shad Grama is used twice :

"जग्राह वीणामथ नारदस्तु षड्ग्रामरागादिसमाधियुक्ताम्"[36]
षड्ग्रामरागेषु च तत्र कार्यं तस्यैकादशवयवेन राजन्"[37]

Harivamsha Purana is placed in the second century B.C.

Therefore, Grama Ragas were existent in their own right from then onwards.

'Shiksha Granthas' are given the priority over Ramayana and Epic age. 'Naradiya Shiksha' belonging to this category and is placed in 800-500 B.C.[38]

In 'Naradiya Shiksha' seven Grama Ragas are described and named as Shadava, Panchama, Madhyama Grama, Shadja Grama, Sadharita, Kaishika Madhyama and Kaishika.[39] Five Grama Ragas are mentioned by Bharata, Shat or six Grama Ragas are enumerated in Harivamsha Purana. Starting from Narada of 'Naradiya Shiksha' Matanga and Kudumiamalai inscriptions give seven Grama Ragas. The same sloka of Bharata describing five Grama Ragas of Bharata मुखे तु मध्यम is quoted by Matanga and others. Their verse however, mentions seven Grama Ragas with a change of a line or two.

> "मुखे तु मध्यम ग्रामः षड्ज प्रतिमुखेभवेत्
> गर्भे साधारितश्चैवामर्शे तु पंचमः
> संहारे कैशिकः प्रोक्तः पूर्वरंगे तु षाडव।
> चित्रस्याष्टदशांगस्य त्वंते कैशिक मध्यमः"[40]

Bharata has left Panchama and Shadava in his 'Natya Shastra'. Matanga again quotes Bharata as—"जाति संभूतत्वाद् ग्रामरागाणमिति"[41] which ascertains the presence of Grama Raga during the period of Bharata. Grama Ragas get mentioned in the Buddha Jatakas and Jain granthas besides in the works of Kalidasa, Markandeya and Vayu Puranas.

These five, six or seven Grama Ragas serve as basis for the Raga classification system of Matanga, Sharngdeva, etc. Nanya Deva classifies his Ragas according to three Gramas including Gandhara Gramas. Therefore, the probability of six Grama Ragas (Harivamsha) serving as the origin of the concept of six male Ragas, with their five or six female Raginis to each is there. According to Harivamsha, Narada brought the music to the earth and trained the ladies of Bhima in music. Gandhara Grama also plays an important role in the music mentioned in Harivamsha and it is the special feature of 'Sangita Makaranda'.

Another possibility is the seven Geetis or Jatis(?) described by Matanga in his Brihaddeshi, especially Raga Geeti from which Bhasha and Vibhasha are derived. It is note worthy that the Ragas derived from Raga Geetis are eight in number and have male names while Bhasha and Vibhasha have female names and might be envisaged in the origin of Raga-Ragini classification.

The seven Geetis are accepted as root Ragas or parent Ragas, (the number may differ according to time, author, etc.) or male Ragas and new melodies are included as Bhasha, Vibhasha Geetis (female Ragas) Bhashanga, Kriyanga and so on. The Bhashà might have corrupted and changed into Bharya or vice versa. The relationship between the Raga-Geetis and Bhasha, Vibhasha seem to be similar to the concept of male-female Ragas. The male and female names of the Raga Geetis and Bhasha-Vibhasha Geetis are the pointers of the Raga-Ragini system or it might be possible that Matanga has merely indicated the already existing system of male-female Ragas based on Tantric practice.

It is a well-known fact that Matanga was a great follower of Tantra known as Agamas. According to him, the Gandharva Veda originated from the Lord Maheshwara.

"एवं स्वरान् विजानीयादुत्पन्नान् गीत सागरे
महादेवमुखोद्भूतान् देशी मार्गे च संस्थिताम्"[42]

He follows the Agama Grantha, while explaining the place and nucleus of Svaras.

'Brihaddeshi' as the name itself suggests is an extensive work on Deshi music but the available manuscript is incomplete. It's Vadyadhyaya, Taladhyaya and Deshi Ragadhyaya are not available till to date. The concluding sloka of the available manuscript seems to be the beginning of the chapter on Deshi Ragas. A contemplative verse which seems to be a 'Mangalacharana' verse for an elaborate chapter on Deshi Ragas is as follows.

बन्धुकाभां त्रिनेत्राममृतकरकलाशेखरां रक्तवस्त्रां
पीनोत्तुङ्गप्रवृत्तस्तनभरनमितां यौवनारंभरूढाम्।
सर्वालंकारभूषां सरसिजनिलयां बीजसंक्रांतमूर्तिः।
देवीं पाशांकुशाभ्यामभयवरकरां विश्वयोनिं नमामि।।
अतः परं प्रवक्ष्यामि देशीरागकदंबकम्।[43]

This contemplative verse resembles the dhyana slokas of Raga-Raginis of later authors. This sloka also suggests further contemplative and descriptive verses on Deshi Ragas. Since later part of the work is unavailable, nothing can be said about the missing portion. The frequent quotations of Deshi Ragas given by Nanyadeva and Rana Kumbha in his 'Sangita Raja' signify the fact that Matanga has described a large number of Deshi Ragas which are not present in the available text. Matanga might have elucidated the Deshi Ragas with descriptive slokas as deifying the Ragas might have been in practice at that time. The concluding sloka "बन्धुकाभां" has that type of description suggesting more descriptive slokas of Ragas.

'Brihaddeshi' does not have confirmed male-female Ragas; Raga and Yoshita Bharya system. Nevertheless, the names of the Grama Ragas are masculine, while the names of Bhasha and Vibhasha Geetis are feminine. As such, it is natural and most probable that this paves the way to male-female classification and the "Bhasha" became Bharya with the time.

Agamas or Tantras are called the fifth Vedas (पंचम वेद), Shankara has enumerated the titles of 64 Tantras out of which a few can be identified at present. Tantras are twofold —Agamas and Nigamas. It is in a dialogue form, between Lord Shiva and his consort Shakti. Where Devi does the questioning and Shiva provides the answers, it is called as Agama and Nigama is vice versa.

The term Tantra does not occur in the Vedas, Samhita or Smritis, but Agama stands for it. The reference of Agama either direct or indirect, can be seen in the Puranas, Samhitas and Smritis. However, Tantra Shastra does not refer to either Smriti or Purana, which proves its antiquity.

Tantric rituals used to be practiced throughout India, especially in north India — West Bengal, Assam, Rajasthan, etc., side by side with the Vedic rites and sometimes Tantric practices superceded the Vedic practice of yore.

According to Kalluka Bhatta, a well-known commentator, "Revelation (Sruti) is twofold — Vaidik and Tantric. In the popular knowledge and belief, they (Tantra) have practically superceded the Vedas over a large part of India."[44] The word Tantra "तन्त्र" is used in various meanings. Etymologically, the root 'तन' means to spread or 'Expand'.

"तन्यते विस्तार्यते ज्ञानं अनेन इति तन्त्रम्।"

This is the grammatical meaning. But in the work, variously called Agamas or Tantras, the word is said to refer to Shastra in which the knowledge concerning "तत्व" and "मन्त्र" is spread; this Shastra also saves the mankind from the circle of life and death. For example, the well-known Saiva Agama called "कामिक" says—

"तनोति विपुलानर्थान् तत्वमन्त्र समन्वितान्।
त्राणान् च कुरुते यस्मात् तन्त्रमित्यभिधीयते।"

Here "तन्त्र" is derived from its two constituent verbs —'तन' to spread and "त्रै" to protect. This is called "अक्षर निरुक्ति" (syllable etymology, not generally accepted by grammarians, being considered as fanciful).[45]

The Tantra itself is believed to have appeared from the fifth face of Parameshti (Siva). Though, the antiquity of Tantra is similar to the Vedas, the present available texts belong to sixth or seventh century. Therefore, it seems that the music was also twofold at that time—the Vedic and Tantric music. The treatises on Tantra like Yamalashtaka and others have some chapters devoted to music.

"In a way, it is appropriate to say that much of the old musical literature is preserved in these Tantras. Yamalashtaka Tantras is valuable for on account of its literary history. It is an elaborate index of contents of Sanskrit works on all the branches of knowledge"[46] says Krishnamachariyar.

There are 32 Yamalashtaka Tantras of which some treat the music and the concerned passage with music is worth quoting—

"गंधर्व वेदः षट्त्रिशंसहस्त्रग्रन्थ सम्मितः।
यत्र सप्तस्वरोत्पत्तिः कथनं परिकीर्त्यते
वीणातन्त्रकलातन्त्ररागतन्त्रम्
मिश्रतन्त्रं तालतन्त्रं गीतिका तन्त्रमेव च...
एवमादिनि गांधर्ववेदाः सन्ति सहस्त्रशः।"[47]

"Of the Yamalashtaka Tantra, the 9th Kalatantra treats of Rasa, Bhava, Natya and Kamasutra and the 19th Vina Tantra embraces the whole field of music".[48] Tantric worship has many rituals in which 'sound' plays an important role. The various kinds of sounds are applied to propitiate a particular deity and that particular letter is called 'Bijakshara'. Tantra is the scripture on the worship of male-female cosmic energies, i.e., Prakriti and Purusha.

The male-female Raga system reflects the Tantric elements in their composition. Music plays an important role in Tantric rituals. Tantra is mainly concerned with Shiva-Shakti and music and dance in general are accepted as the creation of Shiva-Parvati duo.

Though the 'Raga-Ragini' system might be a later invention, the idea of male-female Ragas might be as old as Tantras. Moreover, this classification belongs to north India, where Tantric practices were predominant.

There is a fable in 'Pancha Tantra' about a donkey and a jackal. The donkey describes about the music and enquires:

"तत् कथय कतमेन रागेण करोमिः"

Then explains the terms of musicology to prove his knowledge:

"रासभ आहाधिक्धिक् मूर्खः। किमहं न
जानामि गीतम् तद्यथा तस्य भेदान् श्रुणु-
सप्त्स्वरास्त्रयो ग्रामाः मूर्च्छनाश्चैकोनविंशतिः।
तानास्त्वेकोन पञ्चाशतिस्त्रो मात्रालयास्त्रयः (५५)

स्थानात्रयं यतीनञ्च षडास्यानि रसानवाः।
रागाषट्त्रिंशतिर्भावाचत्वारिंशत्ततः स्मृतम् (५६)[49]

The above details furnished by the donkey are applicable to the ancient music system of Grama-Murchana and the mention of 36 Ragas might be an indication to the Raga-Ragini system.

Pancha Tantra stories are as old as Buddha Jataka Kathas. But G.H. Ranade places them in the fifth century A.D.[50] This story confirms the 'Sangita Makaranda's' time period fixed by the scholars that is seventh to tenth century.

There is a story in 'Adbhuta Ramayana' about Narada Muni and his pride about his music. Once he was taken by Vishnu to a building, where numerous handsome men and women were weeping over their broken and disfigured limbs and to the query put forth by Narada for the reason of their weeping they answered that they were the Ragas and Raginis and that the broken limbs were caused by the wrongful singing of Narada.

"नारदं प्रोचुरपि ते त्वयाकृताङ्ककादयम्
वयं रागाश्च रागिण्यो गानेन भिन्न सन्धिना।।२६।।
भवता गीयते यर्हि-तर्हयवस्थेदृशं हि नः।"[51]

In the 'Adbhuta Ramayana' the term Raga-Ragini appears and Krishnamachariyar places it between the fifth to tenth century A.D.

There is yet another reliable religious work called Pancharatra with the rituals and ordinances to be followed in the Vaishnava tradition. There is much controversy about its time. Bhandarkar places it in tenth century A.D. There are other evidences about its being old and belonging to the Epic age.

In Agni Purana, the Pancharatra system is accepted and appreciated whereas in Padma, Varaha and Markandeya Puranas, Pancharatra is appreciated as a divine Agama and is recommended whenever the Vedic rituals are not practised.

आग्नये पाञ्चरात्रमतस्योपन्यासः क्वचिद् दृश्यते। नारद सात्वतं वैष्णवं तन्त्रं पञ्चरात्रोगम प्रोवाचेति भागवंते उक्तम्।
अग्निपुराणः (१/३/८)

It is also forbidden by Kurma Purana as it is counted in Moha Shastra.

"मोहशास्त्रेषु पाञ्चरात्र शास्त्रं गणितं कौर्मे"
(१/१६/१११-११६;२/२१/३२)"[52]

This Pancharatra may be placed in the range of fifth to seventh century. Now the concerned treatise 'Narada Pancharatra' is one of the oldest, if not the very first specimen of Vaishnava literature in Sanskrit. It is divided into five parts named as Ratras. In the 11th chapter of Prathama Ratra, the following verse supports the theory of antiquity of Raga-Ragini system.

"श्री व्यास उवाचः
अथः गन्धर्व राजस्तु भगवानाज्ञया विधेः
संगीतं च जगौ तत्र कृष्णरासमहोत्सवम्।।१।।
सुषमं तालमानञ्च सुतानं मधुरं श्रुतम्
वीणा मृदङ्गः मुरुजयुक्तं ध्वनिसमन्वितम्।।२।।
रागिणी युक्तं रागेण समयोक्तेन सुन्दरम्
माधुर्य्य मूर्च्छना युक्तं मनसो हर्षोकारणम्।।३।।"[53]

The above passage mentions about the Raga-Ragini system, time theory, Murchana system, etc. The data provides ample proof that Raga-Ragini or male-female classification of Ragas was in practice from the very beginning which, might have been based on Grama Ragas and most probably as a parallel system to Vedic music, to suit the needs of Tantric rituals. This male-female division is represented in all art forms, as in dance we have Tandava (male) and Lasya (female). Therefore, 'Sangita Makaranda' cannot be pushed forward to medieval period just because of its system of Raga classification.

There are still two more points of controversy to be

discussed before taking a final decision about the period of this work. The name of a Raga mentioned by Narada as Turushka Tundi (Turushka Todi) is the first anomaly. The following references may help to decide about the word 'Turushka' "That this word comes twice in the work suggests a contact with Mussalman music which is believed to have been prevalent in the time of Amir Khusro (1290-1360). Yet, Turushka need not have been an outcome of Moslem invasions of twelfth century. Because, 'Kalhana' in his 'Raja Tarangini' uses this word to refer Kusan kings, who were from Central Asia and staged a many attacks in seventh century". ('Bana's 'Harsa Charita', Cowell and Thomas, London, 1897, p. 290.)"[54]

The word "Turushka" which occurs in 'Vikramanka Deva Carita' of Bilhana in connection with the oil, i.e., Turushka Tailam, which is explained as equivalent to kerosene obtained from Persian oil field. This 'Turushka' word occurs in 'Aryamanjusrimula Kalpa' (Ed. Ganapati Shastri, Trivandrum Sanskrit Series, 1920, p. 83). P.K. Gode opines that Bilhana identifies 'Turushka' with Persian lands as per date of the work — 'Aryamanjusrimula Kalpa', supposed to be earlier than A.D. 900. Some rock oil was imported into north India between 500 and 1100 A.D., as per notes on the end pages of 'Vikramanka Carita' by Bilhana. It seems the word 'Turushka' was used for any alien country or person other than Indian. Therefore, 'Turushka' does not point out only the Mussalman invasion as such it does not push 'Sangita Makaranda' ahead in time.

The most important argument imposed by the scholars and critics in deciding the time of 'Sangita Makaranda' is the occurrence of the name 'Mahamaheshwara' with reference to the merits and demerits of the musician.

"गुणैः कतिपयैर्हीनो निर्दोषो मध्यमोत्तमः[55]
महामहेश्वरेणोक्तः सदोषो गायकाधमः।।"

Abhinava Gupta in his commentary on 'Natya Shastra' states:

उत्कृष्ट दोषयोगे तु तद्गानमेव न किंचित्[56]

The merits and demerits of a musician are dealt in chapter 33 of 'Natya Shastra'. Abhinava Gupta's commentary contains the above statement. He does not define the three categories of singer-uttama, madhyama and adhama. He argues that singing with major defects cannot be termed as music at all. Therefore, the quotation"सदोषो गायकाधम:" does not belong to Abhinava Gupta, since he simply condemned defective singing and does not categorise it.

'Mahamaheshwara' is an epithet applied to Lord Siva. Abhinava Gupta was an ardent follower of Agama traditions and used to be an authority on Tantra practices. That is why he preferred to be called as Mahamaheshwara, the supreme deity in Agama shastras. Therefore, Mahamaheshwara stands for Lord Siva and the adopted name of Abhinava Gupta as well. In 'Brihaddesi', Matanga mentions Maheswara which might be an addition to Kohala, i.e.,

"तथा चाह कोहलः महेश्वरः
षड्जवदति मयूर........"[57]

In 'Sangita Makaranda' the chapter which has this sloka with Mahamaheswara's name has many identical slokas appearing in 'Sangita Ratnakara' also. Either Sharngdeva copied them from 'Sangita Makaranda' or the copyist of Sangita Makaranda has sought the help of the text Sangita Ratnakara to rewrite the damaged portions of the original manuscript. Therefore, the 'Mahamaheshwara' might have come as an epithet, as Kohala Maheshwara or copied by mistake.

The reason of this decision is the non-inclusion of Abhinava Gupta's name amongst the scholars and musicians by Narada in each of the second chapter of Sangitadhyaya and Nrityadhyaya respectively. Sharngdeva enlists the name of Abhinava Gupta in his list. Furthermore Narada does not follow Abhinava Gupta regarding any of his musical concepts in his present work. He would have included Abhinava Gupta's name in his lists of scholars, if he has to mention the name afterwards. These facts generate a germ of doubt about the appearance of the name, in an unreasonable way. But this is the main reason given by all scholars for placing 'Sangita Makaranda' after tenth century. If these points are considered without prejudice, the name 'Mahamaheshwara' seems like a mistake by copyist rather coming from Narada. 'Sangita Makaranda', therefore can be placed before tenth century A.D.[58]

Considering all the controversial points about the period of 'Sangita Makaranda', it may be summed up like this. Almost all the authors and scholars of music place the 'Sangita Makaranda' in the period between seventh and eleventh century except Ramakrishna Kavi in his 'Bharata Kosha'. 'Sangita Makaranda' gets priority over 'Sangita Ratnakara' because of the language, subjects, the format and list of musicians besides the description of Gandhara Grama with its notes.

The occurrence of the names Matrugupta and Vikrama in the list of 'Sangita Makaranda' implies that it is not an earlier work than seventh century. There are many Vikramas in Indian history, yet this Vikrama seems to be the King Sriharsha (607 to 647 A.D.), who was the patron of Matrugupta.

The system of notes found in the 'Sangita Makaranda' indicates earlier to medieval period. No other Vikrita notes are mentioned except Kakali 'Ni' and Antara 'Ga'.

Though Raga-Ragini classification is believed to be the development of medieval period, it is discussed elaborately and has been decided that such classification might be a product of Agamas (Tantra). Shat Grama Ragas of Harivamsha and eight Geetis mentioned by Abhinava Gupta in his commentary[59] also supports the theory of six and eight Ragas respectively.

The feminine names allotted to Bhasha and Vibhasha Ragas by Matanga support the theory of antiquity of Raga-Ragini system. The 'Narada Pancharatra', the 'Adbhuta Ramayana', and the 'Pancha Tantra' stories also strengthen the above fact, by mentioning the term.

Narada does not use the term Ragini for his female Ragas but uses the term stree or Yoshita (wife). The male-female

Ragas which were in seed form during the period of Matanga might have developed into this Raga-Ragini system. Therefore, the 'Sangita Makaranda' should be placed in between 'Brihaddeshi' and 'Sangita Ratnakara' or earlier. For the word 'Turushka' the explanations have been furnished.

The occurrence of the name 'Mahamaheshwara' (Abhinava Gupta) on which every author critic or scholar has commented and decided the period of 'Sangita Makaranda' accordingly after tenth century has been fully discussed in favour of Narada's antiquity by adjudging it to be the mistake by chance of the copyist.

According to Dr. Raghavan, the earlier treatises are written in a dialogue form. This concept is applicable to 'Sangita Makaranda' also, as it is written in a dialogue form between Narada and Brahma. Thus the fact has been established that 'Sangita Makaranda' is an earlier complete work and may be placed between seventh and ninth century.

REFERENCES

1. *Sangita Makaranda* —Introduction, p. VIII.
2. *Ibid.*, p. 13.
3. *Ibid.*, p. 33.
4. *Ibid.*, vol. I, p. 46.
5. *Ibid.*,—Introduction, pp. VIII-IX.
6. *Dattilam*, p. 1.
7. See Appendix 1.
8. भरतकोष, पृष्ट ६६३
9. *Sangita Makaranda*, p. 1.
10. *The Music of India*, p. 14.
11. *Ragas and Raginis*, p. 17.
12. *Companion to Sanskrit Literature*, pp. 75 and 312.
13. *Ibid.*
14. *The History of Classical Sanskrit Literature*, p. 83.
15. *A History of Sanskrit Literature*, p. 214.

16. *Bhartiya Talon Ka Shastriya Vivechan*, p. 320.
17. *The Ragas of North Indian Music*, pp. 8-9.
18. *Some names of early Sangita Literature*, p. 23.
19. *Sangita Makaranda*, p. 13.
20. *Ibid.*
21. *The History of Classical Sanskrit Literature*, p. 817.
22. *Some names of early Sangita Literature*, p. 23.
23. *Sangita Makaranda*, Introduction, p. IX.
24. *Some names of early Sangita Literature.*
25. *Sangita Makaranda*, p. 7.
26. *Naradiya Shiksha*, Sl. 14, p. 18.
27. *Naradiya Shiksha*, p. 72.
28. हरिवंश, भविष्य पर्व, २०.६
29. *Natya Shastra*, Chapter 32.
30. *Natya Shastra*, vol. 4, Chapter 28, p. 5.
31. नाट्य शास्त्र, पृष्ठ ५
32. Role of Sanskrit in Indian Music, Dr. Janaki, *Journal of New Academy*, p.72.
33. Brihaddeshi, August, 1975, *Sangita*, p. 29.
34. *Ibid.*
35. *Ramayana*, Sundara Kanda (7-172).
36. *Harivansha Purana*, pp. 68-69.
37. *Ibid.*, pp. 82, 89.
38. *Bhartiya Sangita*, pp. 201-11.
39. *Naradiya Shiksha*, Slokas 5-12, pp. 25-27.
40. *Brihaddeshi*, August, 1975, p. 31.
41. *Ibid.*
42. *Brihaddeshi*, Sloka 88, p. 28.
43. *Ibid.*, sloka 367.
44. *Religion and Ethics*, p. 193.
45. This information is given by Dr. Janak.
46. *The History of Classical Sanskrit Literature*, p. 840.

47. *Ibid.* pp. 840-41.

48. *Ibid.*, p. 841.

49. पंचतंत्रम्. श्री विष्णु शर्मा. पृष्ठ ५५६–५७

50. *Hindustani Music: An Outline of its Physics and Aesthetics.*

51. *Adbhuta Ramayana,* 7th Sarg, p. 57.

52. अग्निपुराण. विषयानुक्रमनी. पृष्ठ ४८.

53. *Narada Pancharatra*, p. 76.

54. *Ragas and Raginis*, Footnote, p. 21.

55. *Sangita Makaranda*, p. 25.

56. *Natya Shastra*, Chapter 33, p. 397.

57. *Brihaddeshi*, p. 6.

58. *Ibid.*

59. *Natya Shastra* (गान्धर्वे गाने शुद्ध भिन्न गौड राग (बेसर) साधारण भाषा, विभाषा, अन्तर भाषा रूप गीत्यष्टको -----) Chapter 33, commentary, p. 395.

4

Nada, Shruti and Svara

The text

'Sangita Makaranda' is attributed to Narada. It is available as a single manuscript at the Baroda Central Library. It was found by the wife of R. Ananta Krishna Sastry in Gadhwal in 1919, while the couple were on an official tour in search of Sanskrit manuscripts. Shastry was an officer in the Baroda Central Library.[1]

The manuscript contains 32 folios written in Devanagari script. The size of a folio is 10¼ x 5½ inches and the texts is written on both sides and each side approximately contains 9 lines. The paper is coarse and white coloured yellowing a little bit with age. The whole work is written in black ink while the headings in the text are written in red ink and are fresh. The writing is legible and on the last three pages the copyist has painted geometrical designs in a circle with black and red ink.[2]

The condition of manuscript is good even after 319 years (copied in 1677 A.D.) but the writing has not faded. The work consists of 560 slokas in all.

The text and the contents of 'Sangita Makaranda' may be summed up as follows.

It contains two main Adhyayas or parts—namely 'Sangitadhyaya' and 'Nrityadhyaya' both divided into four 'padas' or divisions. The work introduces many novel features regarding Svaras, their origins, astrological particulars, unusual names of 22 Shrutis, five types of Nadas, the three Gramas with note arrangements, several types of Raga classifications time theory and so on. Yet, it is neither elaborate nor scientific nor explanatory like 'Sangita Ratnakara'. The language of 'Sangita Makaranda' is very simple. The copyist has created havoc at many places with corruption. Narada has not provided any list of topics dealt with the work of 'Sangita Makaranda'. The work is in a dialogue form between Narada and Brahma but in sotto voce. Only in a very few places the dialogue form of the work comes into light, i.e.

नारदस्य वचः श्रुत्वा ब्रह्मालोक-पितामहः।
साधु साधु महातेजा यत्वं मां परिपृच्छसि।[3]

The first pada starts with a prayer to Lord Shiva, who is supposed to be the founder of music and dance. The author begins his treatise on music with due salutations to Lord Shankara seeking His blessings. His dance is accompanied by various deities. In the starting sloka, Narada includes his name because, he mentions संगीतको नारदः which means that "Narada provides the music for the dance of Lord Shiva". At the very first instance, he establishes himself as a musician. In the third sloka, he defines the music and announces the name of the work and its author.

"गीतं वाद्यं च नृत्यं च त्रयं संगीतमुच्यते।
नारदेन कृतं शास्त्रं मकरन्दाख्यमुत्तमम्।।[4]

He proceeds ahead about the topics without giving any hints or lists of the subjects dealt with, as the work is very short compared to 'Sangita Ratnakara' or 'Bharata Bhashyam'. It is more similar in form to that of Dattilam or the available part of 'Brihaddeshi'.

The first pada of Sangitadhyaya deals with Nada, Svara, Grama, Murchana, Shruti, Svara Prakriti, Vikriti, etc. The

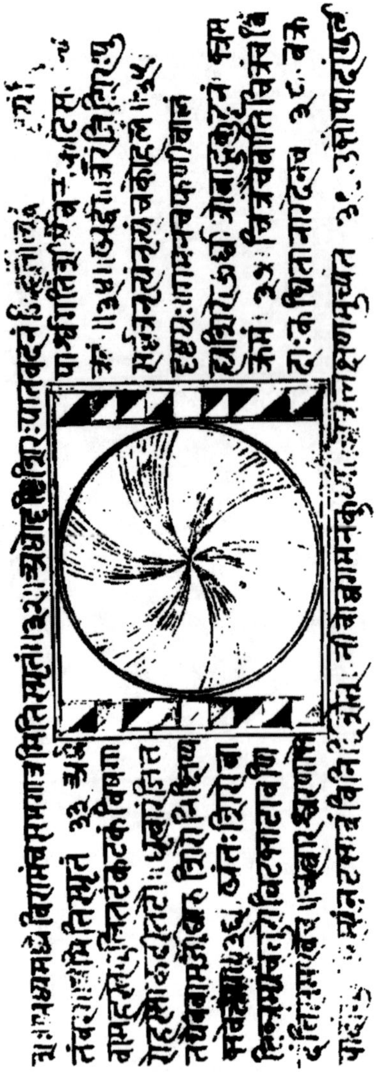

॥ संगीतमक
रंदाख्यपुस्तकं लिख्यतेमया कुर्वविघ्नंमहादेवलेखनायनमोस्तुते १ ३ ...गणे...शादे
वं...करंलोकशंकरम् संगीतशास्त्रंसं...दावक्ष्येलोकमनोहरम् १ ब्रह्मा...धरोह
रिश्चपटहीवीणाकरीभारतीवंशाढ्यौनाशीभास्करौश्रुतिधरा:सिद्धाप्सरा:किंनरा: नंदीभृ
ङ्गिरिटादिमर्दलधरा:संगीतकोनारद: शंभोर्नृत्यकरस्यमंगलतनोर्नंद्यात्सदापातुन: १
गीतंवाद्यंचनृत्यंच त्रयंसंगीतमुच्यते नारदेनकृतंशास्त्रंमकरंदाख्यमुत्तमम् २
अनाहतोहतश्चैवसनादोद्विविधोमत: यत्राश्रये...स्तयोर्मध्येनाहतो
पिनिरूप्यते ३ आकाशसंभवनादोय:सोनाहतसंज्ञित: तस्मिन्ननाहतेनादेविरामप्रा
प्यदेवता: ४ योगिनोपिमहात्मान:सदानाहतसंज्ञके मनोनिक्षिप्यसंयांतिमुक्तिंप्रयत

second pada is named as Sangitadehanirupanam. It compares music with Veena or presents the terms of music as parts of the Veena. The third pada of Sangitadhyaya deals with the most important and unique subject varieties of Raga classification and time theory. The fourth pada is akirnaka (miscellaneous) dealing with instruments, Gayaka lakshananam, Geeta dosha, Vaggeyakara lakshanam, etc., miscellaneous terms like Nada and Alapti are treated in short.

Now comes the second part — that is Nrityadhyaya. In Nrityadhyaya, dance gets least attention. Narada has enumerated and defined only 33 postures of dance in 33 slokas from 10 to 43 slokas of the concluding pada of the Nrityadhyaya. In the first pada of Nrityadhyaya, he deals with the properties of auditorium, audience, eminent courtiers and the scholastic personages patronised by the king. Narada defines poet, Bhata, musician, astrologer, physician, comedian, Sabhapati and participants, etc., and the seating arrangement of the court to witness a performance. Whereas in the second pada, 101 Tala names are given with their Matras and divisions. The Margi Talas and their origin are explained in the first pada itself after the subjects mentioned earlier.

The third pada explains about Tala, ten Tala Prabandhas. Dasha Pranas of Tala and the ten Pranas are described. Narada concludes this Pada by describing the signs of Druta, Laghu, Guru, Pluta, etc.

In the fourth and concluding Pada, Mridanga has been described in the starting nine slokas. The 33 postures of hands, waist and head are elucidated with names in short and that concludes the description of dancing. Therefore, it seems that the Tala played the most important role in dance and Tala Prabandhas are also meant for dancing with the change of Talas often. Though, the 101 Deshi Talas are mentioned alongwith five Margi Talas, they are hardly differentiated or distinguished properly.

So far as the general theme of the work is concerned, almost all the topics of music prevalent at that time are covered. But Narada does not go into details about any subject. Brevity and precision remain the keywords of his work. At times, it becomes very difficult to get the idea of the subject. For example, in describing the Raga, Narada gives only the starting note and the notes omitted in Shadva and Oudava Ragas.

According to critics and scholars the Raga-Ragini classification belongs solely to north India. Carnatic music of south has other classifications like Kriyanga, Bhashanga, Sankirna, Shuddha Ragas in past and at present the Carnatic system is based on Mela system.

Therefore, it may be said that 'Sangita Makaranda' of Narada belongs to the north Indian system of music with many peculiar traits. The classification of Ragas, which has diverse points of attraction and exceptional varieties are not found in any other contemporary or later works, which makes it a work of much importance.

Though the single manuscript of 'Sangita Makaranda' was discovered and published as early as 1920 A.D., it has not received its due credit and attention. As the work is very short and based on a single manuscript and it does not provide any substantial glimpse of the prevalent music of that period, it has been left untouched. Yet, the work 'Sangita Makaranda' is of much importance, because it serves as a link between 'Brihaddeshi' and 'Sangita Ratnakara', though the system of Ragas described in either works is different. Otherwise 'Sangita Makaranda' follows more or less the lines of 'Dattilam' or 'Brihaddeshi'.

The first chapter begins with a salutation to Lord Shankara as it is customary practice in India for successful completion of the work as well as a mark of an auspicious beginning of any type of literary work. It indicates that Narada (author) is a staunch devotee of Lord Shiva, who is incidentally the presiding deity of music and dance. It is said that Lord Shiva played the Dakka (a small hour glass shaped drum) 14 times and created the 14 Maheshwara Sutras.[5]

नृत्तावसाने नटराजराजो ननाद ढक्कां नवपंचवारम्
उद्धर्तुकामः सनकादि सिद्धानेतद्विमर्शे शिवसूत्र जालम्।

From these sutras, the language and the sound that have emanated. Shiva has the epithet of Nataraja — the King of Dance.

According to Tantra, the universe is created by Shiva and Shakti. The Nada or the primordial sound is the outcome of Shiva-Shakti combination. Thus originated Nada is used to compose the mantras based on impregnated letters called 'Bijakshara'. Music served as the purpose of a vehicle to recite these mantras and propitiate the deities concerned while performing Tantric rituals. According to Tantra, sound is all pervading and the most powerful element in the universe. Its proper use may create miracles or cause degeneration to the very existence of the universe.

The prayer or *mangalacharana* offered to Lord Shiva in 'Sangita Makaranda' supports the view that the work is more prone to Agama principles and the author basically is a follower of Tantric cult and a devotee of Shiva. Whereas the mythological Narada is supposed to be a staunch devotee of Vishnu and is a true Vaishnava. This Narada, the author of 'Sangita Makaranda', seems to be an entirely different person.

The arrangement of the subjects and topics in 'Sangita Makaranda' are neither systematic nor in continuation at one place or pada. They are scattered in between the assorted subject repeated by any number of times. For example, Nada has been discussed in the first chapter and then again in the fourth pada. The approach to the subject however is different. Therefore, for the convenience sake, the subjects are discussed under headings in order of priority as far as possible with some exceptions.

Nada

Nada is said to be the primordial sound generated from 'Akasha' which cannot be translated as sky. Space though a little better term from the sky, but it does not come very close to the real meaning of 'Akasha'. Akasha is one of the five elements (Akasha, Prithvi, Jala, Agni and Vayu) and it is the first and foremost of them. Its property is 'sound' or 'Shabda'.

Again the term Nada may generally be translated as sound, yet it is very subtle and abstract to be termed as sound. Nada means a living 'being', which is always felt and is omnipresent with manifest and unmanifest forms.

Unmanifest sound is causeless that emanates by itself without application of any outer force; friction, shock, etc. It is named as 'Anahata' which means "without striking". The sound that is produced without any type of striking. It is eternal, causeless and unmanifest. According to Tantras, this 'Anahata Nada' manifests itself in the 'Sunya' (void), which is named as 'Bindu'. In the materialistic language, it may be said that Anahata Nada is manifested, when Shiva and Shakti meet together. It is spontaneous. Anahata Nada can be heard by meditating with concentration on the special plexuse called Anahata Chakra, poised in the region of heart. This chakra contains twelve petals, each with the twelve first letters of the Devanagari alphabet. This chakra is considered to be the place where the Lord Shiva should be worshipped in the form of 'Pranava' or 'Om'.

हृदये अनाहतं चक्रं शिवस्य प्रणवाकृतेः।
पूजास्थानं तदिच्छन्ति दलैर्द्वादशभिर्युतम्।।[6]

Matanga gives importance to Dhvani

ध्वनिर्योनिः पराज्ञेया ध्वनिः सर्वस्य कारणं।
आक्रान्तं ध्वनिना सर्वं जगत् स्थावर जंगमम्।।[7]

After 'Dhvani' comes Nada, Matanga though describes the five general types of Nada, he does not describe or mention anything about Ahata or Anahata Nada.

Anahata Nada being unmanifest and causeless, the other type of Nada is Ahata—the manifest, caused by striking thing together or plucking, in short, caused by any artificial or natural vibration that can be explained. This Nada may be named as sound, yet as the music is based on this Nada, it should be refined to be used in music. This Nada is defined and described by many authors like Matanga and Sharngdeva, the later authors follow the suit. The importance of Nada, its etymology, origin and causes are given by all. 'Naradiya

Shiksha', 'Natya Shastra' and 'Dattilam' do not give any such explanation about Nada. In 'Sangita Makaranda' Narada also does not describe the etymology of the word Nada at the first instance in the first pada of Sangitadhyaya. The following sloka appears in the fourth pada—

"नकार प्राणभानदस्तकारमनलं विदुः
जातः प्राणाग्नि संयोगात् नादोऽभिधीयते।।१८।।"[8]

The same sloka with very little variation appears in 'Sangita Ratnakara'. Matanga also gives this sloka as follows—

"नकारः प्राण इत्याहुर्दकारश्चनलो मतः
नादस्य द्विपदार्थोऽयं समीचीनो मयोदितः।।२२।।"[9]

'Sangita Makaranda' does not present this etymology or the five divisions of Nada given by Matanga and 'Sangita Ratnakara' in the first pada at the beginning. Narada arrives at the Nada and its main divisions directly. Narada at the beginning says thus —

"आदौ नादोत्पत्ति निरूप्यते "[10]

and continues

अनाहतो हतश्चैव स नादो द्विविधो मतः।[11]

Matanga begins his work 'Brihaddeshi' with 'Dhvani', Bindu, Varna, Nada — its importance and five types of Nada based on the origin; various parts of the physical body in human beings.

'Sangita Ratnakara' is an elaborate and extensive work with systematic arrangement and scientific approach towards the subject. Sharngdeva commences his work with a prayer followed by narrating his family particulars and outline of work. Though, he too begins with Nada, he devotes much space to the formation of human body from the beginning which is the source of Nada.

Narada does not go into any unnecessary details either about himself or his work. After naming the two types of

Nada— Anahata and Ahata, he describes and defines the Anahata Nada in short.

आकाश संभवो नादो यः सोऽनाहतसंज्ञितः[11]

He explains that it is named as Anahata Nada, because it originates from the space by itself, then elaborates the use of unmanifest sound. This 'Anahata' Nada resides in the heart or Anahata Chakra, though it is not mentioned above. He says that yogis, sages and great souls attain the salvation through great mental concentration upon this Nada. Matanga does not mention about these two types of Nada. He begins with 'Dhvani' and Nada, and his work indicates his inclination towards the Tantra and Agamas. He elucidates the creation of Dhvani and Varna, according to the Tantra tradition.

Sharngdeva comes nearer to 'Sangita Makaranda'. He describes the Anahata Nada in the same way as Narada, yet with more elaborations of the same theme. In the second section, 'Pindotpatti Prakaram', the importance of Nada is discussed which is similar to that of 'Brihaddeshi' followed by manifest and unmanifest forms of Nada. As Nada is generated by the soul (आत्मा) residing in the physical body of human beings, the formation of the body from the very beginning is described at length:

आहतो अनाहतश्चेति द्विधा नादो निगद्यते।
सोऽयं प्रकाशते पिण्डे तस्मात् पिण्डोऽभिधीयते।[12]

The imaginary chakras are also described. After the description of such human embodiment, he refers to the two types of Nada, as Saguna — concrete and Nirguna — abstract, which are the means of worldly enjoyment and salvation respectively. The same attributes are allotted to the unmanifest or Anahata sound as by Narada in his 'Sangita Makaranda'. The single-minded meditation with deep concentration upon the 'Anahata' sound would result in salvation. According to Sharngdeva, this concentration is not possible for everybody. 'Nirguna' sound has neither pleasing nor unpleasing properties to the human ears and mind. It is very difficult to concentrate on something which has no form, foundation, cause or any property to meditate upon. Anahata Nada is a subtle, abstract sound residing within the body which can be heard by directing one's mind inward with full concentration. A condition practically met with highly spiritual people.

On the other hand, Ahata Nada with its concept of 'Saguna'—concrete sound is produced by the natural friction of things accessible to everyone. This Ahata or 'Saguna' sound is based on Shrutis and Svaras. Our ancestors, i.e., sages and seers have systematised the Ahata Nada and regulated it accordingly to be practiced and enjoyed by all the people. This music provides entertainment as well as spiritual upliftment and breaks the cycle of birth and death. According to Sharngdeva, either Anahata or Ahata Nada serves the purpose of spiritual upliftment and attainment of salvation. The result lies in the mental and spiritual standard of the candidate who practices it. Ahata Nada is easier to practice as it is this on which the concept of music is based.

Narada of 'Sangita Makaranda' means the same thing by mentioning Anahata as the Nada to be focussed upon by yogis, munis, etc. It is not concerned with music, but gods reside or take refuge in it. Narada as such does not have any specific definition or description of the Ahata Nada as the Nada in general indicates Ahata Nada only.

As regards to the Ahata Nada, Narada divides it into five different types in the first chapter. These five types of Nadas described by Narada in 'Sangita Makaranda' are entirely different from those of Matanga and Sharngdeva. Matanga and Sharngdeva differentiate those five types according to the physical regions of human body from where the Nada originate. Matanga names them as follows —

सूक्ष्मः अतिसूक्ष्मः व्यक्तः अव्यक्तः कृत्रिमः

They reside in the navel, heart, throat within the mouth and the face portion respectively.

सूक्ष्मो नादो गुहावासी हृदये चातिसूक्ष्मकः
कंठ मध्ये स्थितोव्यक्तः अव्यक्तस्तालुः
देशके कृत्रिमो मुखदेशे तु ज्ञेयाः पंचविधो बुधैः ।[13]

Sharngdeva differs a little from Matanga in the names and order of arrangement. He puts the 'Ati Sukshma' (अति सूक्ष्म) in the first position which is more correct according to order because it means very subtle and 'Sukshma' is subtle. These five types of Nada arise from the five points in the human body, starting from the lower portion of the body, i.e., starting from navel towards the head. Therefore, the Ati Sukshma should be the first which arises from navel, situated at the place and the sound produced from there should be the lowest or Ati Sukshma. According to the order of degree, Sukshma should come after Ati Sukshma. Therefore, Sharngdeva is correct in changing the order of the five types of Nada.

Narada of 'Sangita Makaranda' does not mention in the first chapter about these five types at the first instance. But he mentions in the fourth pada as follows—

नादोऽति सूक्ष्मः सूक्ष्मश्च पुष्टो अपुष्टोश्च कृत्रिमः।
इति पंचविधाधत्ते पंचस्थानस्थिताः क्रमात्।।१६।।

Narada gives importance to the order and classifies these five types of Nada under "Dehaja Nada." In the very beginning of 'Sangita Makaranda', he describes the five types of Nada, which are totally different from others as already mentioned. The fivefold Nada mentioned however, seems to be the different types of sounds produced by the four types of instruments and the fifth is naturally produced by physical body, i.e., human voice. They are:

1. **नख़ज** : Sound produced by nails that is from stringed instruments. It might be termed as plucking sound.
2. **वायुज** : Sound produced by wind or wind instruments.
3. **चर्मज** : Sound produced by leather pertaining to percussion instruments.
4. **लोहज** : Sound produced by metals pertaining to chimes of cymbals, etc.
5. **शारीरज** : Sound originating from the body.

This last type of manifest sound is again divided into five types according to their points of origin in the human body. These classification of sounds pertaining to the physical body is explained by all the ancient and later authors, but the five types mentioned by Narada, i.e., Nakhaj, Vayuj, Charmaj, etc., are unique, novel and not to be found anywhere else. The Dehaj Nada described by others also are mentioned by Narada. He calls Kritrima as 'Tara' (upper register) and says that is not used, as it is hard on ears and Ati Sukshma is also left behind, because it is too low to be heard by human ears. Therefore, three types of Nada — Mandra (heart), Madhya (throat) and Tara (head) are only found in practice. Narada handles the Nada in a very accurate manner without leaving any figment to imagination.

This later classification of Nada appears in the fourth Pada under the heading Swaradaya with topics like instruments, characteristics of the musician, Vaggeyakara Lakshanana, etc. which seems to be out of place. Narada could have described this classification in the first Pada itself directly after the classification based on the four types of instruments and the inherent human voice. This shows the disorderliness of the work. It is not only with Nada but the author does the same with other terms and subjects also.

Shruti

Narada proceeds ahead with notes instead of Shrutis. Narada of 'Naradiya Shiksha', Bharata and Nanya Bhupala also give priority to Svara. In 'Naradiya Shiksha' Shruti is totally omitted. 'Dattilam', 'Brihaddeshi' and later works follow the correct order, i.e., Nada, Shruti and then Svara. In 'Sangita Makaranda' though the Shruti comes after Svara, it is discussed in proper order in this chapter.

In 'Naradiya Shiksha', Narada does not mention the Shrutis while describing the terms of music as —

"सप्तस्वरास्त्रयो ग्रामा मूर्च्छनास्त्वेकविंशति।
ताना एकोनपञ्चाशदित्येतत् स्वरमण्डलम्।।[14]

He does not include the term 'Shruti' in the sloka. Neither

does he enumerate their number nor define the term elsewhere in a proper manner. He uses the term Shruti and its varieties Dipta, Ayata, Karuna, etc., in connection with Samagana. He uses only five types of Shrutis and their usage is only restricted to the particular order of Samik notes depending upon the compound words and vowels therein.[15] He also cognises the fact that Shrutis have no separate identity, though they are the ones which form Svara.

"यथाप्सु चरतां मार्गो मीनानां नोपलभ्यते
आकाशे व विहंगानाम् तद्वत् स्वरगताश्रुतिः।।"

According to him, Shruti's presence is concealed and not exposed to be seen or felt. He narrates them as the track by which fishes swim through the ocean water or the invisible air route of the birds. The Shrutis too cannot be seen, when enfolded by Svaras.

In 'Natya Shastra' the Shruti comes after Svara in the context of Grama arrangement and Bharata describes them in his famous 'Chatusarana'. By elaborating the four Saranas Bharata arrives at the twenty-two Shrutis. He never gives much importance to Shruti.

"श्रुतयो यतयश्चैव नित्यं स्वरगतात्मकाः"[16]

They are important only because of their being the cause of two Gramas — Madhyama and Shadja —

"अथ द्वौग्रामौ षड्जग्रामो मध्यमग्रामश्चेति।
अत्राश्रिता द्वाविंशति श्रुतयः.........।"[17]

Here अत्राश्रिता is described by Abhinava Gupta as :

ग्रामस्वरूपलाभ हेतवः इत्यर्थः[18]
नाट्य शास्त्र, पृष्ठ १६

Therefore, Shrutis are secondary and their importance ends with the formation of Svaras. They are exposed to human ears as Svaras only, whereas Dattilam defines them.

"श्रवणात् श्रुति इति संज्ञिताः[18]

Abhinava Gupta defends Bharata in dealing with the Shrutis after the Svaras. He quotes Matrugupta and Vishakhilacharya who opine—

"ग्रामविभागार्थमेव श्रुति कीर्तनं" and "ग्रामानंतरं श्रुतिरुद्दिशति स्म"[19] respectively.

Dattila though supposed to be the son and disciple of Bharata differs while dealing with the Shrutis. He places Shrutis prior to Svaras and Gramas, though he does not mention their 22 names. He defines the Shruti as "श्रवणात् श्रुति संज्ञिता" and is also of the opinion that Shrutis are 66 in all, 22 in each Sthana. Bharata also opines that in an octave, Sthana or Saptak, there are only 22 Shrutis. Dattila follows the same Shruti divisions in the formation of notes, i.e., four, three and two Shrutis accordingly while describing the two Gramas — Shadja and Madhyama. He explains about the seven notes of the two Gramas with their count of Shrutis as well—

ततः ऊर्ध्वं तृतीयः स्याद्वषभो नात्रसंशयः ।।१२।।
ततो द्वितीयो गान्धारश्चतुर्थो मध्यमस्तत।
मध्यमात् पंचमस्तद्वत् तृतीयो धैवतस्ततः।
निषादोऽतो (द्विती) यः (स्तः? स्यात्) ततः
षड्जश्चतुर्थकपंचमो मध्यमग्रामे मध्यमाद्यस्तृतीयकः।"[20]

Dattila does not describe about the 'Saranakriya' to get the Shrutis. In a single line he defines the Madhyama Grama. He does not explain or mention about the types of Shrutis, i.e., Dipta, Ayata, etc. Neither the types of relationship between Shrutis and Svaras nor the processes of Shrutis turning into Svaras are discussed in Dattilam as done by Matanga and later authors. These topics are not to be seen in 'Natya Shastra'.

Mataṅga in his 'Brihaddeshi' discusses in length about Shruti — the cause and relationship between Shrutis and Svaras.

He defines the Shrutis as follows —

"श्रूयते इति श्रुतयः"[21] and gives its etymology as —

"श्रवणे चास्य धातोक्तिः प्रत्ययसमुद्भवः ।।२६।।[22]

According to Matanga there is only a single basic Shruti (Nada) that arises out of the navel because of the friction caused by fire and wind. It passes upwards like smoke spreading up in ascension. This sound of Shruti takes the form of twenty-two Shrutis accordingly.

Quoting Vishwavasu, Matanga opines that there are two types of Shrutis — the one forming the note and the other present in between the notes.

श्रवणेन्द्रियग्राहयत्वाद् ध्वनिरेव श्रुतिर्भवेत्
सा चैकापि द्विविधाज्ञेया स्वरांतर विभागतः ।।[22]

Matanga explains the views of various scholars about the number of Shrutis, i.e., three types of Shrutis arise out of three points in the human body as per different properties of indriyas—सहजं, दोषजम् च अभिघातजं"[23]

Other scholars opine that there are four types of Shrutis depending on the four Dhatus of the body—Kafaj (कफज), Pittaj (पित्तज), Vataj (वातज), and Sannipataj (सन्निपातज), Some others found nine types of Shrutis. According to Matanga some scholars confirm only 22 Shrutis, while others are bent upon establishing the concept of 66 Shrutis. Another school of thought supports infinite Shrutis. The relationship between Shrutis and Svaras are discussed at length by Matanga in his 'Brihaddeshi' after the Saranakriya. The relationship between Shruti and Svara is discussed by Parshvadeva and later authors only. They are not discussed in this work and after 'Brihaddeshi', 'Bharat Bhashyam' comes in the order of time period, though it is not prior to 'Sangita Makaranda'.

Nanya Bhupala, the author of 'Bharata Bhashyam' gives the etymology and the definition of the word 'Shruti'. However, Shruti comes after Svara in 'Bharata Bhashyam'. He elucidates the types of Shrutis, their usage, emotions and the notes to which they belong. A full chapter is devoted therein to the Shrutis named Shrutyadhyaya.

The five types (जाति) of Shruti — Dipta, Ayata, Karuna, Mridu and Madhya are dealt in detail by 'Nanya Bhupala'. 'Natya Shastra', 'Dattilam' and 'Brihaddeshi' excluding 'Naradiya Shiksha' are silent about the five types of Shrutis. In 'Naradiya Shiksha', these types of Shrutis are related to the pronunciation of Vedic hymns. Narada deals with these in detail[24]. Yet, it does not compare favourably with the former arrangement of the Vedic and Gandharva notes explained by the author. Probably, the Samik Shrutis might have been different from the Shrutis of Gandharva music.

Nanya Bhupala is the earliest author, who describes about the five types of Shrutis in Shrutyadhyaya of 'Bharata Bhashyam'. This Shrutyadhyaya though named on 'Shrutis' starts from the Svaras with their deities, colour, origin, etc. Then the Grama and Shrutis are described in ascending order. Shruti is defined as :

"श्रुतिः श्रूयत इत्येवध्वनिरेषोऽभिधीयते।"[25]

Nanya Bhupala gives the same etymology as Matanga. The types of Shrutis are given by Nanya Bhupala after Narada of 'Naradiya Shiksha'. Nanya Bhupala has explained about them (Dipta, Ayata, etc.) in his 'Bharata Bhashyam' in the Shrutyadhyaya. He classifies the five types of Shrutis allotted to each of the seven notes.

The division is as follows :

1. Shadja has four Shrutis—Dipta, Ayata, Mridu and Madya.
2. Rishabha has three Shrutis — Karuna, Madhya and Mridu.
3. Gandhara has two Shrutis — Dipta and Ayata.
4. Madhyama has four Shrutis similar to those of Shadja, i.e., Dipta, Ayata, Mridu and Madhya.
5. Panchama has the same number of Shrutis, i.e., four like Shadja and Madhyama, yet different types of Shrutis. Panchama has Mridu, Madhya, Ayata and

Karuna. It is notable that Panchama does not take Dipta Shruti.

6. Dhaivata has Karuna, Ayata and Madhya Shrutis respectively.

7. Nishada has Dipta and Madhya Shrutis.

All the twenty-two Shrutis have been divided into these five types of Shrutis. The basis of such classification is neither explained by Nanya Bhupala nor Sharngdeva. Narada of 'Naradiya Shiksha' uses these varieties in the context of Samik notes, but he is unable to drive home the point. However, it seems that such classifications has something to do with the Rasas accorded to the notes by the ancient authors. This can be elucidated by giving the meaning of the names —

1. Dipta — illuminated and bright
2. Ayata — vast and wide
3. Mridu — delicate, soft and tender
4. Karuna — pathos
5. Madhya — medium and central.

These names indicate the emotions created by the particular Shruti thereby the Rasas or aesthetic colours related to notes containing the types of Shrutis, probably the timbre or sound quality of Shrutis.

The names given to twenty-two Shrutis are meaningful and suggest the nature of Shrutis. The names of the Shrutis are not given by Narada of 'Naradiya Shiksha', Bharata, Dattila, or Matanga. In 'Sangita Makaranda' which is proved to be the work prior to Nanya Bhupala's 'Bharata Bhashyam', the names of twenty-two Shrutis occur at the earliest. Nanya Bhupala gives the names of Shrutis which are followed by all the authors of the later period including Sharngdeva. They are given below :

तीव्रा, कुमुद्वती, मन्दा, छन्दोवती, दयावती, रंजनी,

रसिका, रौद्री, क्रोधा, वज्रिका, प्रसारिणी, प्रीति
मार्जनी, क्षितिः, रक्ता, संदीपनी, अलापिनी,
मदन्ती, रोहिणी, रम्या, उग्रा, क्षोभिणी।

But these names are not given by Narada of 'Sangita Makaranda'. His names of the twenty-two Shrutis are utterly different from others. They are the earliest and original names of Shruti.

'Sangita Ratnakara' comes after the 'Bharata Bhashyam'. In many places, 'Sharngdeva follows Nanya Bhupala and admits Nanya Bhupala's priority over him by including his name in the list of scholars. In 'Sangita Ratnakara' Shruti comes before Svaras and the definition is almost the same as the authors prior to him : "श्रवणात् श्रुतयो मतः". According to Sharngdeva, the twenty-two Shrutis are produced by twenty-two upward Nadis situated in the heart, throat and the head. Sharngdeva's Sarana Kriya is different from Matanga and Bharata. Neither Dattila nor Nanya Bhupala mentions the term 'Sarana', probably they take the Shrutis as an already existing factor. Sarana Kriya is meant to establish their existence in each note, i.e., 'Sa', 'Ma', 'Pa', = 4 Shrutis each, 'Ri', 'Dha', =3 Shrutis each and 'Ga', 'Ni' = 2 Shrutis each, etc. Sharngdeva's Sarana Kriya is different from that of Bharata and Matanga in the sense that he takes two Veenas of twenty-two strings for twenty-two Shrutis and performs the Sarana Kriya. To get the twenty-two Shrutis he advices to tune the first string to the lowest possible sound which can be heard easily and then to tune each further string a little bit higher from the first.[26] Sharngdeva does not explain the cause or relationship of Shruti and notes like Matanga, though Kallinatha devotes much time to the same. Sharngdeva says plainly that Svaras arise out of Shrutis. His twenty-two names of the Shrutis are similar to that of Nanya Bhupala. Sharngdeva neither defines the five types of Shrutis, i.e., Dipta, Ayata, Mandra, Madhya, Karuna, Mridu, nor explains their meaning. Moreover he does not describe their importance, or properties they attribute to the Shrutis. Sharngdeva only mentions the shruti names along with their Jatis—Dipta, Ayata, etc. and then the Shruti Jatis of the Svaras.

Parshwadeva in his 'Sangita Samayasara' enumerates 66 qualitative names of Shrutis, which are totally different from all the authors — ancient as well later. There are twenty-two Shrutis in each register thereby making a total of 66 in all. Parshwadeva follows Matanga's cause and relationship between the notes and Shruti.[27] Neither he describes nor names the five types of Shrutis.

With this background about Shrutis in ancient and contemporary or later works, the Shrutis dealt in 'Sangita Makaranda' may be studied. The first point to be remembered is the order of priority given to Svaras over Shrutis. Narada follows Bharata and unlike Dattila, Matanga, Sharangdeva and recent authors he gives priority to Svara, Grama and Murchanas over the Shrutis and their names.[28] Nanya Bhupala follows the same order. The second remarkable point his twenty-two names of Shrutis which are unique and totally different from other writers except Narayanadeva of 'Sangita Narayana'. In 'Sangita Narayana' the author has presented the same verses from 'Sangita Makaranda'; with the names and deities of Shrutis in each note.

सिद्धिः प्रभावती कान्ता सुभद्रा च मनोहरा
साधयन्ति स्वर षड्जे प्रजापति मुखोद्मतं[29]

Suprabha of 'Sangita Makaranda' appears as Subhadra and the rest is similar. Narayanadeva mentions 'Narada Samhita', while defining Geetam and quotes thus :

"नारद संहितायां धातुमातु समायुक्तं गीतमित्यभिधीयते।"[30]

The above verse mentioning the name of 'Narada Samhita' ascertains the presence of the work and its availability at the time of Narayanadeva. Krishnamachariyar also mentions, about 'Narada Samhita' on which this work of 'Sangita Makaranda' is based. Probably, Narada of 'Sangita Makaranda' gets twenty-two names of the Shrutis from 'Narada Samhita' which is not available at present. However, the names of the Shrutis are never mentioned by any author prior to Nanya Bhupala who comes after Narada of 'Sangita Makaranda'. Therefore, it is not justified to say that the names of Shrutis appearing in 'Sangita Makaranda', are purely imaginary or the later creation of Narada and not original. Nevertheless it could be proved that they are more authentic than the Shruti names of Sharngdeva and later authors copied from Nanya Bhupala as no earlier authors have given the names of Shrutis except Narada of 'Sangita Makaranda' and Nanya Bhupala. 'Sangita Makaranda' presents a different list of names of Shrutis which appears only in 'Sangita Narayana'. Therefore, it cannot be decided that which list of the names is original or gets priority over other. As 'Sangita Makaranda' gets the priority over 'Bharata Bhashyam', its names of Shrutis should be considered as the original or earliest one.

The names of all the twenty-two Shrutis of Narada are dissimilar to those in practice except 'Ugra' which appears in both lists.[31] Though this name 'ugra' occurs in both lists, it is assigned to the seventh Shruti by Narada, while others give it to the twenty-first Shruti.

Narada does not define the etymology of the term Shruti at the first instance. He only defines them in the chaturtha pada as: "**श्रवणात् श्रुतयो मताः**" He does not mention about the types (**जाति**) of Shrutis, and the 'Sarana Kriya' is completely left out in 'Sangita Makaranda'. Narada neither discusses about the cause nor the relationship between Shruti and Svara.

Narada does not give much importance to Shrutis similar to Narada of 'Naradiya Shiksha', Bharata and Dattila. According to him, the Shrutis are useful only in constructing and distinguishing the Gramas from one another. The number of Shrutis are important in making the seven notes. He assigns four Shrutis to Shadja, Madhyama and Panchama, three Shrutis to Rishabha and Dhaivata, two Shrutis each to Gandhara and Nishada, which is generally followed by the authors of past and present. Narada gives the names of the Shrutis with the note to which they belong and then gives the name of the deity from whom they have originated. For example:

सिद्धा प्रभावती कान्ता सुप्रभा च मनोहरा।
साधयन्ति श्रुतिः षड्जे प्रजापतिमुखोद्भूता।।[32]

And proceeds further with other six notes and their Shrutis and deities. The names of the deities causing the Shrutis and the subsequent note, are neither given by Nanya Bhupala nor Sharngdeva. This shows that Narada follow the tradition of Tantra in rendering almost every term and topic of music in his Sangita Makaranda. The deities named by Narada are all related to religious rituals either of Vedic or Tantric origin.

Chart 1

Sl.No.	*Name of the Shruti*	*Svara*	*Deity*
1.	Siddha, Prabhavati, Kanta, Suprabha	'Sa'	Prajapati
2.	Shikha, Diptimati, Ugra	'Re'	Agni
3.	Hladi, Nirviri	'Ga'	Vyahriti
4.	Dira, Sarpasaha, Kshanti, Vibhuti	'Ma'	Prithvi
5.	Malini, Chapala, Vama, Sarva Ratna	'Pa'	Soma
6.	Shanta, Vikalini, Hridayonmalini	'Dha'	Yaksha Raja
7.	Visarini, Prasuta	'Ni'	Yama Raja.

This shows the religious and devotional aspect of the author and of that period. Music was the medium to attain one's spiritual upliftment and it was a form of worship — 'Nadopasana' at that time. At present too, it has the same impact and purpose of propitiating the gods. But, it has lost that sole purpose and has become more or less a pure form of art. Narada emphasises that Svara forms the Grama with the help of Shruti and Jati. This Jati might constitute the five types of Shrutis—Dipta, Ayata, etc. but it is not clear.

जातिभिः श्रुतिभिश्चैव स्वराः ग्रामत्वमागताः।
तद्वत्तथैव वृत्यैव काव्यबन्ध प्रतिष्ठिता।।[33]

Narada is more concise in describing the Shrutis in 'Sangita Makaranda' as he devotes only nine slokas, i.e., 78-

86 in the first part of 'Sangita Makaranda'. He follows the earlier Narada of 'Naradiya Shiksha' and Bharata in giving the order of priority to Svara over Shrutis. Though the disciples of the latter do not follow him and Shruti gets the priority over Svara, e.g., Dattila and Matanga. At times, it seems that Narada follows the footsteps of Dattila regarding the types, relations between Svara and Shruti, Sarana Kriya, etc., by not mentioning them. At the same time he provides twenty-two original names of Shrutis. Narada gives the names of the deities of the notes and Shrutis which makes him to stand apart from others. As far as Shrutis are considered, 'Sangita Makaranda' is not very helpful in throwing light on the theoretical aspect of the Shrutis. Yet, it is an important work with special features and a way of approach to the subject.

Svara

Svaras are the most important and indispensable components of music; which is named as Gandharvam. The three components which make music are Svara, Pada and Tala — Notes, wording and the rhythm.

"गान्धर्वं त्रिविधंविद्यात् स्वरतालपदात्मकम्"[34]

Among the three, the first and foremost is Svara and Tala comes next.

Svara is defined by numerous authors. Yet, neither in Natya Shastra nor in Dattilam, Svaras are defined. Dattila says that those Shrutis used in singing however, get the position of notes.

"आद्रियन्ते च ये तेषु स्वरत्वमुपलभ्यते।।१०।।"[35]

Therefore, according to him the Svaras are the Shrutis which get the prominence and acknowledgement through exposure in singing. But he does not define the term Svara or goes in detail about its etymology. Dattila considers the Svara as a natural occurrence.

Matanga is the earliest author, who gives the etymology as well as the definition of Svara.

"राजृ दीप्ताविति धातोः स्वशब्दपूर्वकस्य च"

Definition - स्वयं राजते यस्मात् तस्मादेष स्वरः स्मृतः।"[36]

Nanya Deva also presents the general nirukti used by grammarians in shikshadhyaya—

स्वयमात्मानं रंजयति निपातनात्स्वर-निरुक्तिः ।।६६।।

He deals with the Svara elaborately giving their deities, caste, colour, astrological factors, etc.

In 'Sangita Ratnakara', Svara gets its scientific definition, which distinguishes it from Shruti. About the materialisation of Svara from Shruti, Sharngdeva observes that 'श्रुतिभ्यः स्युः स्वराः'[37] and leaves at that. His definition of note is as follows-

श्रुत्यनन्तरभावी यः स्निग्धोऽनुरणनात्मकः।
स्वतो रंजयति श्रोतृचित्तं स स्वर उच्यते।।२४।।

According to Sharngdeva, Shruti itself becomes Svara, but the difference lies in the quality of the sound, smoothness, continuity and resonance. It has a natural pleasing quality to the ears and the mind.

Parshwadeva in his 'Sangita Samayasara' presents a detailed study of Svara which serves as its definition. He quotes Kohala many times and gives his own opinion. First of all, he gives the same description and derivation of the term Svara as mentioned above quoting Kohala —

आत्मेच्छया नाभितलात् वायुरुधन्निधार्यते
नाडी भित्तौ तथाकाशे ध्वनिरक्तः स्वरः स्मृतः।।[38]

Parshwadeva says that Kohala believes the Svara to be indestructible (अविनाशी) and widespread (व्यापक) but disagrees with Kohala as Svara is neither eternal nor widespread, as it cannot be heard forever and from everywhere. However, this applies to a particular Svara played once.

The treatment of Svara in 'Sangita Makaranda' starts from the tenth sloka of Prathama Pada of Sangitadhyaya and continues upto the 48th sloka. In between, from 17th to 24th slokas, the author mentions about Ragalapti, Roopalapti (Roopakalapti) and describes about the importance and influence of Geeta (music). It makes no sense at that place and this portion should have appeared before the notes and after 'Nada' or even before 'Nada'.

At the first instance, Narada does not define the Svara as such, but definition appears in the third part of the Sangitadhyaya as follows—

> "श्रुत्यनन्तरभावी यः स्निग्धोऽनुरणनात्मकः
> स्वरो (स्वतो?) रञ्जयति श्रोतृचित्तं स स्वर उच्यते।"[39]

The same definition appears in 'Sangita Ratnakara' too. This definition of Svara appears in the beginning of the third part or pada, where the Ragas are described exclusively and this definition of Svara is glaringly out of place. However, Narada is not particular about the systematic approach to the subjects, as evident from the work of 'Sangita Makaranda'. There is lack of proper planning and it seems that Narada takes for granted many such descriptions and avoids them intentionally.

According to Narada, Brahma created the art of drama after much consideration and gifted it to the world. He Himself has ascribed the seven names (of Svaras) after drawing them from the Anahata Nada. This is the only fact he gives about the formation or appearance of the seven notes. Almost the whole of music depends upon and revolves around the gods, deities and heavenly bodies, as far as the author of 'Sangita Makaranda' is concerned.

> "आदौ बह्मा विचोयैर्व नाटयं लोके प्रपञ्चितम्
> अनाहतात्समाकृष्य सप्त नामानि योजितः।।१०।।"

The above sloka is the definition of notes, provided by Narada in the beginning. Therefore the notes materialised from the Anahata Nada with Brahma's help.

The ancient authors has linked the origin of notes to various parts of the physical body of human being, an old practice dating back to Vedic period. According to Vedas, there are two types of Veenas, "Shariri and Daravi Veena". The physical body is compared with a Veena in Aithareyaranyaka:

"अथ खल्वियं दैवी वीणा भवति, तदनुकृतिरसौ मानुषी वीणा भवति।"
(ऐतरेयारण्यक आ०-३ अ-२ स्व०-५, आनन्दाश्रम पुस्तक, पृष्ठ २३२)

The seven Svaras according to Narada of 'Sangita Makaranda' arise from navel, heart, throat, mouth, nose, teeth and lips in the respective order—Sa, Ri, Ga, Ma, Pa, Dha, Ni. However, this origin of notes is described by almost all the authors with slight differences.

In 'Naradiya Shiksha', the author leaves out the navel, mouth, teeth and lips. The Shadja arises out of throat, the Rishabha from the head, Gandhara from the nose, Madhyama from the head, heart and throat, Dhaivata from the forehead and Nishada from all the joints within the physical body.[40]

Moreover, Narada of 'Naradiya Shiksha' names the points from which the note is pronounced.

नासां कण्ठमुरस्तालु जिह्वा दंताश्च संश्रितः
षड्भिः संजायते यस्मात्तस्मात् षड्ज इति स्मृतः।[40]

In this sloka, Shadja is described as originating from the six places of the human body; as its name suggests. Shadja means born out of six. In the same way, Narada of 'Naradiya Shiksha' gives double description about the seven notes and their origin. He mentions navel (Rishabha), mouth, tongue, teeth, etc., subsequently as the origin.

Bharata of 'Natya Shastra' remains silent about these physical places from where the seven notes are supposed to arise, yet he approves the three octaves arising out of heart, throat and head. Bharata neither mentions about the Kula, Varna, deities and other things related to the religious and imaginary aspects of notes, Grama and Murchana. Dattila follows the footsteps of Bharata in this matter.

Matanga indicates his inclination towards Tantra tradition. However in the end of the vogue description of Svara,

Mataanga provides the same type of description regarding the seven notes arising out of seven places of human body.

कण्ठादुत्तिष्ठते षडजः ऋषभः शिरसः स्थितः
नासायश्चैव गांधारः उरसो मध्यमः स्वरः
उरसः शिरसः कंठादुत्थितः पंचमः स्वरः।[41]

Panchama arises out of head and heart. Dhaivata from the mouth and Nishada from all the points of physical body.

Matanga quotes Narada to establish the seven orders of note arrangements, i.e., Archic, Gathic, Samik, Svaranthara, Audava. Shadava and Sampurna. This following verse appears in 'Naradiya Shiksha' but only in parts (upto Svarantara only),[42] which again is an indication of a missing work of Narada on music.

आर्चिको गाडिकश्चैव सामिकश्च स्वरांतरः
औडवं षाडवश्चैव संपूर्णश्चेति सप्तमः।।
एकस्वरप्रयोगो (भि?हि) आर्चिकः सोऽभिधीयते।
गाडिको द्विस्वरो ज्ञेयस्त्रिस्वरश्चैव सामिकः।।
चतुःस्वरप्रयोगो हि कथितस्तु स्वरांतरः।।
औडवः पंचमेन धृतो[43]

Though, the last part of the sloka seems to be corrupt and incomplete as Shadava is not described, this particular sloka is not to be found in any other work.

Nanya Bhupala follows Narada of 'Naradiya Shiksha' in deciding the origins of the Svaras in the human body in the slokas from 24 to 31.[44]

Sharngdeva however, does not follow the suit in naming the organs from which the seven Svaras are produced by articulation. He names the three types of sounds (octaves): lower (मन्द्र), middle (मध्य), and upper (तार) produced by a single Nada in the ascending order from heart through throat to head. These places are the origins of the three registers: lower, middle and upper. As already explained, the single Nada generates from the navel and Sharngdeva leaves at that and does not mention any thing else about it.

Parshwadeva in his 'Sangita Samayasara' describes the specific number of places through which the sound produced in the navel (Nada) passes and forms the particular note or Svara, i.e.

> वायुः समुत्थितो नाभेरोष्ठ कण्ठशिरो ह्रदिः।
> पञ्चस्थान समुद्भूतः पञ्चमस्तेन कीत्तितः।।"[45]

However, Parshwadeva does not deal with the deities and other astrological factors related to the seven notes. He only mentions the castes of the Svaras, and divides them according to the number of Shrutis of the note, generally approved by the authors of his time.

All the other contemporary or little later works follow the same pattern in describing the Svaras with their caste, creed, colour, deities, native lands and other astrological factors as in 'Sangita Makaranda' excluding 'Natya Shastra' and 'Dattilam'. However, 'Sangita Makaranda' excells in furnishing more particulars of this type regarding the notes than any other work.

This concept owes its origin to Vedas. Neither it is an outcome of middle age nor mental creation to claim authenticity. Every sukta or Vedic hymns has a seer, metre and a deity. The same concept is followed in other arts in India, because every art, religion, philosophy are supposed to be originated from the Almighty. The art forms are known as a branch of Veda, i.e., Natya Veda, Gandharva Veda, etc.

The Svaras are classified under various categories in 'Sangita Makaranda'. Narada has illustrated the lineage, caste, colour, native lands, seers, deities, metres, Gotras, stars, Rashis and their governing deities. The emotional aspects of Svaras are also discussed at the end.[46]

Narada has initially narrated the physical organs from which the seven Svaras are produced, followed by the names of the birds and animals from the cries of which the idea of seven notes is conceived. Their sound variations are the cause of the pitch variations of the seven notes (Svaras). It is an established and well-recognized fact that music exists in the nature by itself. The cries of different animals and notes of birds are imitated by early man while trying to express his emotions through singing. In India, it is always accepted that nature is the mother of invention of all existing forms of art. Music too has its roots in nature. The nature sings, weeps or laughs with the human beings, and both cannot be separated at least in this context (art). Nature is reflected in all the works of art, whether it be dance, painting, architecture, literature and music.

Starting from 'Naradiya Shiksha' up to the concerned works at present, the origin of seven notes is accepted by one and all, as vividly pitched cries of birds and animals. Narada of 'Sangita Makaranda' is not an exception to the above statement. He has named peacock, chataka, goat, heron, cuckoo, horse and elephant as the producers of the seven varieties of sound pitch which are utilized as the basis for fixing of the seven notes respectively.[47]

Matanga and Sharngdeva differ from Narada of 'Sangita Makaranda' and name, 'Dardura' (frog) instead of 'Ashva' (horse) for the note Dhaivata. Narada of 'Naradiya Shiksha' names the cow as uttering the 'Rishabha' instead of 'Chataka'. Nanya Bhupala follows 'Sangita Makaranda' in accepting the horse as the producer of Dhaivata, but he discards 'Chataka' bird and names the bull (Rishabha) as producing the note 'Ri'. As a rule, later writers follow 'Sangita Ratnakara' and Sharngdeva.

This inter-relationship between the nature and music shows the attachment of human mind to nature. To him, the nature is a mother who provides everything from the gross materials of daily needs to the subtle and aesthetic necessities to satisfy his emotional urge and cravings.

Chataka is a mythological bird, which is said to have holes in its neck. It waits for the rain when it can drink water through the holes. Therefore, the waiting for anything or anybody with anguish or anxiety reminds one about the bird Chataka.

About the assumption of materialisation, imitation or production of sound notes from the cries of animals and birds, it cannot be said how far it is scientific or justified. However, this much can be accepted that the different cries mentioned by authors are definitely not of a similar pitch. They are certainly higher and may be lower according to different birds or animals even of the same species. Moreover no experiments have been attempted to record the cries of the said animals and birds and justify the facts.

A chart is attached to show the seven notes produced by seven birds and animals, according to 'Naradiya Shiksha', Matanga, 'Sangita Makaranda', 'Bharata Bhashyam' and 'Sangita Ratnakara'. 'Natya Shastra', 'Dattilam' and 'Sangita Samayasara', skip this description. From slokas 28 to 46 of the first part of Sangitadhyaya of 'Sangita Makaranda', the author proceeds with the mythological, religious and astrological factors of the seven notes. Their caste, colour, creed, native lands and other such details are furnished carefully, which is presented in a chart along with the details provided by other authors.[48]

Since it does not have any theoretical value at present, some of the points, which appear exclusively in 'Sangita Makaranda' are discussed here at par with those of 'Naradiya Shiksha', Matanga, Nanya Bhupala and Sharngdeva.

Bharata and Dattila are silent about the origin of the seven notes generated in the physical organism. Nevertheless, they admit the emanating of three octaves 'sthanas' from heart, throat and head, the cries of birds and animals related to the seven notes are left out by them. Those authors of later period, who have mentioned the points about the seven notes (which are mentioned above) are to be discussed. They can be named as Narada of 'Naradiya Shiksha', Matanga, Nanya Bhupala, and Sharngdeva. Parshwadeva is not included in the list, as he is silent about the astrological factors of the notes.

Generally, the deification and the forms, colour, caste, discovering seers, metres and other factors have the Vedic origin. In Vedas, the Vedic hymns are provided with these aspects, if not all, some aspects are attributed to the seven notes also by the ancient authors on music. Therefore, it seems peculiar that the approach of Bharata and Dattila to the Gandharva Veda is a little different than others. Parshwadeva too in his 'Sangita Samayasara' leaves out many points, yet he mentions about four Varnas or caste of the seven Svaras. Probably, he wants to remain secular as Veda are not his concern. The different aspects of seven notes are discussed in the following order in 'Sangita Makaranda'.[49]

The Vansha or lineage gets the priority over other factors in the present work. There are four types of Vanshas (lineage). They are — Deva, Pitru, Rishi, and Asura.

1. 'Sa', 'Ga' and 'Ma' belong to Deva,
2. 'Pa' belongs to Pitru (forefathers),
3. 'Ri' and 'Dha' are from Rishi (seers), and
4. 'Ni' has the Asura (demonic) ancestry.

Sharngdeva follows the same order, while Matanga leaves 'Ma'. Nanya Bhupala handles this point with a little difference. He believes that (lineage) particular note pleases the divinity and so on, i.e., Shadja pleases the deities and Rishabha pleases the sages, etc.[50]

This lineage may fall in tune with the moods, the seven notes are capable of creating or evoking the response of the so-called superior classes. Probably, the qualities and powers of the divinities, ancestors, seers and demons might be imbibed in the notes. The point to note is 'Sa', 'Ga', and 'Ma', get the superior lineage, i.e., Deva Vansha and the three Gramas are also in their name only.

The cast attributed to the seven notes are fourfold, as was and is still practiced in some places. They are Brahmin, said to be the high caste and capable of producing the priests and performing Vedic rituals.

Kshatriya — warriors by caste with ruling capability

Vaishya — business community

Shudra — serving community

In 'Sangita Makaranda', 'Sa' and 'Ma' are Brahmins

'Ri' and 'Dha' are Kshatriyas

'Ni' and 'Ga' belong to Vaishya and Panchama relates to Shudras.

Matanga does not furnish this caste system but he mentions only about 'Kakali' and Antara notes as being Shudra.

Narada of 'Naradiya Shiksha', Nanya Bhupala, Sharngdeva believe that—

1. 'Sa', 'Ma', 'Pa' are Brahmanas
2. 'Ri' and 'Dha' are Kshatriyas
3. 'Ni' and 'Ga' are Vaishya caste
4. 'Kakali' and 'Antara' notes belong to Shudra caste.

Parshwadeva presents the same classification with a slight difference. He does not name the particular note, but relates four Shrutik notes to Brahmins, three to Kshatriyas, two to Vaishya Jati while Kakali and Antara notes to Shudras, as they are not fundamental. Therefore, it seems that the caste system of the notes are mainly based upon their number of Shrutis which has justification.

Yet in 'Sangita Makaranda', 'Panchama', which has four Shrutis and is accepted as belonging to the Brahmin caste by all others, gets pushed down to the lowest caste, i.e., Shudra. Narada is very firm about this announcement of 'Panchama', caste and it is not at all a mistake. It might be, because in the older traditions, the term 'Panchama' was used as a synonym for casteless thing or individual.

These attributes however, provide some basic qualities and distinguished personality. Whether these are mere imagination or have some justification and significance is a fact worth analysis.

After Vansha and caste, the colour of the notes are

mentioned in 'Sangita Makaranda' it seems that seven is a very auspicious and important number in Hindu religion. There are seven notes, colours of radiation, main islands, sages, days in a week, seven seas and seven nadis. The seven notes under question too have their own colours.

They are :

1. 'Shadja' — Lotus or pink colour (पद्माभः)
2. 'Rishabha' — Light yellow colour (पिंजर)
3. 'Gandhara' — Golden colour (स्वर्णाभा)
4. 'Madhayama' — Bright (कुन्द) colour
5. 'Panchama' — White (सितः) or black
6. 'Dhaivata' — Yellow (पीत) colour
7. 'Nishada' — Mixed (कर्बुर) colour.

Narada left out green and blue colours. He has mentioned 'Sita' in two places, while giving the colour of 'Panchama'. In 'Sangita Ratnakara' it is written as 'Asita' which means—black exactly opposite to 'Sita' correlating to white. Black is more justifiable to Panchama; an outcaste according to Narada. Moreover, Narada of 'Naradiya Shiksha', Matanga, Nanya Bhupala and Sharngdeva declare in unison Panchama as of black colour. 'Naradiya Shiksha', 'Bharata Bhashyam' and 'Sangita Ratnakara' attribute the same colours to the seven notes excluding Panchama as 'Sangita Makaranda'. Matanga attributes green colour to 'Rishabha' instead of light yellow colour. Panchama remains black coloured as per Matanga.

The relationship between colour and sound is a subject of research at present. Each note has a particular colour, and can be identified from the colours it produces by certain technical gadgets.

It is said that the Anahata sound combines with colour at certain stage of meditation. India is famous for its yogic achievements and perceptions. Indian culture is the product of ancient and highly advanced seers. The facts and realities of distant future visualised by them earlier are taking a concrete shape today. Often many incidents of mythology (Hindu) were the laughing stock of every nation. Now the same nuclear weapons like missiles and related accessories have become a reality, which were supposed to be used during the battle of Ramayana. Therefore, the colours attributed to the seven notes might have specific scientific meaning. At present, the sound and colours are transmitted all over the world from a television centre.

Next comes the native lands or birth places of seven notes. According to Hindu mythology, which is more or less a part of eighteen Puranas, the world is divided into seven islands (Dwipas), separated by seven oceans. However, this concept may be compared with the seven continents and an equal number of oceans engulfing them. These seven Dwipas are :

1. Jambu
2. Shaka
3. Kusha
4. Krauncha
5. Shalmali
6. Shveta
7. Pushkara

"जम्बुशाककुशक्रौंचशाल्मलीश्वेतनामसु
द्वीपेषु पुष्करे चैव जाताः षड्जादयः स्वराः ।।३३।।[51]

India is situated in the Jambu Dwipa, according to the Vedas and Puranas. Narada elucidates the particular Svara and its native Dwipa. This aspect of Svara (native Dwipa) is mentioned by Sharngdeva and Narada of 'Sangita Makaranda' only and both are identical. The names of Dwipas and the corresponding Svaras related to them are :

1 Shadja — Jambu

2. Gandhara — Kusha

3. Madhyama — Krauncha
4. Panchama — Shalmali
5. Dhaivata — Shveta
6. Nishada — Pushkara

From these seven islands, the seven notes are collected and are placed in the Veena, as per Narada, but the name of the compiler is not mentioned.

The seven Rishis of the seven notes are mentioned after the native or birthplace of Svara. The seven names of Rishis mentioned in 'Sangita Makaranda' are very accurate and appropriate, as others have mixed the names of deities in the list. Narada of 'Naradiya Shiksha' names six Rishis for seven notes. He attributes 'Dha' and 'Ni' to Tumburu. Other five notes have Agni, Brahma, Soma, Vishnu and Narada respectively starting from Shadja to Panchama. Nanya Bhupala and Sharngdeva follow Narada of 'Naradiya Shiksha'.

The names of the Rishis mentioned in 'Sangita Makaranda' are totally different from others. They are :

1. Daksha — Shadja
2. Atri — Rishabha
3. Kapila — Gandhara
4. Vasishtha — Madhyama
5. Bhargava — Panchama
6. Narada — Dhaivata
7. Tumburu — Nishada

Other authors including 'Naradiya Shiksha' mix the name of Vishnu, Agni, Moon, Brahma, etc. Moreover, they repeat the same names Agni, Brahma, and Vishnu as the presiding deities of some of the seven notes as well. The deities governing the seven notes appear after the Rishis of the notes.

वह्निर्ब्रह्मा शारदा च शर्वश्रीनाथभास्कराः
गणेश्वरादयो देवाः षड्जादीनां तु देवताः ।[52]

1. Shadja — Agni
2. Rishabha — Brahma
3. Gandhara — Sharada
4. Madhyama — Shiva
5. Panchama — Vishnu
6. Dhaivata — Bhaskara
7. Nishada — Ganeshwara

The names of deities are given in 'Brihaddeshi', 'Bharata Bhashyam' and 'Sharngdeva'. Nanya Bhupala and Sharangdeva give similar names of deities, the only difference is that the deities of Dhaivata and Nishada interchange their places. Matanga's list of deities is not much different from the above list. His deities of Shadja and Rishabha exchange their respective places and Panchama is governed by Indra instead of Vishnu.

The next aspect related to Svaras, dealt by all the authors and similar to the last is the metre of the seven notes. This is something very peculiar as metre or 'chanda' can be applied to poetry, song, music or recitation only. One single note cannot possibly have a metre yet, seven metres are attributed to seven notes by all the authors. There is no controversy about the metre allocation to a particular note like.

1. 'Sa' — Anushtupa
2. 'Ri' — Gayatri
3. 'Ga' — Trishtupa
4. 'Ma' — Vrihati
5. 'Pa' — Pankti
6. 'Dha' — Ushnig
7. 'Ni' — Jagati

With the above mentioned description about the seven notes, other authors close the subject of mythological aspects of notes. But, Narada is not satisfied with this description of Svaras. He treats the seven notes as living beings by providing each note with not less than a horoscope except the time of birth, date and year parameters.

He names the Gotras of the seven notes, birth stars, Rashis (राशि) with their deities and divides the Seven Svaras into three Ganas—Rakshasa, Manusha, and Deva. These astrological descriptions are not found in any other work. These details make the work more ritualistic. If 'Natya Shastra' pays more attention to dramaturgy, and Gandharvam or music comes as a part used in drama, 'Sangita Makaranda' is more prone to ritualistic music with its exceptionally religious approach.

Now the practical aspects of notes dealt by Narada can be considered. After the calls of birds and animals, Narada of 'Sangita Makaranda' names four types of Svaras — notes as Sthayi, Sanchari, Arohi and Avarohi notes. He cites them as—

स्वराश्चतुर्विधा ज्ञेया रागोत्पादनगोचराः ।[52]

'Svaras' and not 'Varnas', as they are generally called. However, he does not define or describe them.

Having named the four types of Svara patterns to form the Ragas, the author describes about the four types of Svaras on the functional basis as Vadi, Samvadi, Anuvadi and Vivadi, i.e. Sonant, Consonant, Assonant and Dissonant respectively. The classification of Svaras, as such now are generally accepted by all.

Vadi is the main note and most used note in a Raga. *Samvadi* is the second important note and frequently used note after Vadi. This concept of Vadi and Samvadi rests on the interval of Shrutis. As Sonant (Vadi) is the fundamental and main note, it can be any among the seven notes, but the consonant note equally important as the sonant depends upon the Shrutis, and the interval from the sonant. Bharata,

Dattila and Matanga believe that the notes placed at the intervals of nine and thirteen Shrutis are mutually consonant.

Sharngdeva says :

"श्रुतयो द्वादशाष्टौ ययोरन्तरगोचराः।"[54]

The notes placed at the intervals of twelve and eight Shrutis are consonants. 'Ni' and 'Ga' though mutually consonant are termed as dissonants to 'Ri' and 'Dha' and to other notes as well.

This eight and twelve shrutis interval for the consonance of notes mentioned by Sharngdeva creates a little confusion. But the fact is Sharngdeva leaves the Shruti which a particular note occupies. He counts the Shrutis in between the notes and thus the idea remains the same.

Narada of 'Sangita Makaranda', though does not describe about the Shruti intervals and the Samvadi notes caused by the particular number of Shrutis lying in between two notes, while describing Shadja and Madhyama Gramas Narada agrees that Madhyama and Panchama are consonants of Shadja, i.e.,

"मध्यम पंचमः शुद्ध षड्जः संवादिरुच्यते।"[55]

In the same way, Panchama and Dhaivata are consonants of Rishabha in the Madhyam Grama which proves that Narada follows the same rule for Samvadi as followed by Bharata, Dattila, Matanga and of course Sharngdeva, i.e., nine and thirteen Shruti intervals.

'Sangita Makaranda' does not go into these details about the intervals of Shrutis. After mentioning the names of the four types of notes, the author illustrates the properties and inter-relationship of the notes — Vadi, Samvadi, Anuvadi and Vivadi with a simile. The four classes of notes are compared with the king (Vadi), minister (Samvadi), servants (Anuvadi), and enemy (Vivadi). This sort of comparison appears in 'Natya Shastra' and 'Sangita Ratnakara' too.

Vadi note is just like a king in a country and is the most important note in a Raga. Samvadi or consonant note represents the minister and in the absence of a king, shoulders the responsibilities of the State. Vivadi or dissonant notes are the enemies, who disturb the peace of the country and spoil the structure of a Raga.

The remaining notes Anuvadi or assonants are just like the servants who serve the king and minister strengthening the hands of the ruler. The Anuvadi notes, serve the same purpose in the Raga structure.

Thus Narada is not much helpful or inclined to theoretical aspects, because he is more interested in practical or ritualistic pattern of music. His lack of knowledge about the subject is not the cause for his brevity or silence about most topics. As already seen, though he does not discuss about the intervals of Shrutis, he however, approves the Samvadi (consonance) of Shadja, Panchama and Madhyama in Shadja Grama, etc. It might be said that his approach to the subject is different. Nanya Bhupala describes about the consonance and Vadi, Samvadi, etc. in fifth chapter—Alankaradhyaya where he deals about alankaras. He expresses similar views about them and devotes a full prakarana to the subject .

Another practical and down to the earth aspect of notes discussed by Narada of 'Sangita Makaranda' is the aspect of Rasas. These are supposed to be nine, but Bharata mentions about only eight Rasas. He leaves out the Shanta Rasa, somehow it can also be justified. Because, 'Natya Shastra' is a work on dramaturgy where various actions and feelings are accounted. Shanta Rasa is devoid of any actions, and get the feelings calmed which make it inapplicable in dramas.

Bharata employs Shadja, Rishabha in Vira; Adbhuta and Roudra Rasa. Vira Rasa can be termed as the heroic emotion and Roudra shows anger. These Rasas depict the particular mood of the actors and the situations of play. The third Rasa which is shown by Shadja and Rishabha is Adbhuta—wonder. Vira and Roudra Rasas are somewhat similar emotions with a little difference.

'Ma' and 'Pa' should be used in Shringara Rasa (erotic mood) and 'Hasya Rasa' according to Bharata. Therefore, 'Ma' and 'Pa' have both Shringara and Hasya (mirth) Rasa to their credit. But Karuna Rasa (pathos) gets more importance by having two notes 'Ga' and 'Ni' to get itself expressed. Vibhatsa (hatred) and Bhayanaka (terror) are expressed by a single note Dhaivata. However, in practice, a single note or two notes cannot make a song which requires other notes as well. Probably, these notes might have been given prominence over other notes in a particular song to produce the desired emotion. Another possibility is that the background music provided by instruments might have the above mentioned pair of notes to express the particular moods they possess just like chord system of the present day film music (background). Matanga and Sharngdeva follow Bharata in distributing the Rasas to the seven notes.

'Sangita Makaranda' has its own independent opinion about the nine Rasas, including Shanta Rasa, not mentioned by Bharata.

1. Shadja — Adbhuta and Vira (wonder and heroic)
2. Rishabha — Roudra (anger)
3. Gandhara — Shanta (peace)
4. Madhyama — Hasya (mirth)
5. Panchama — Shringara (erotic)
6. Dhaivata — Vibhatsa (disgust)
7. Nishada — Karuna (pathos)

Narada does leave Bhayanaka or terror. It seems that Bhayanaka is a mood which does not deserve to get expression through music. Music is a divine art form to attain the spiritual upliftment, where terror has no place. He should have left Vibhatsa (disgust) also, which too is not a refined feeling to be expressed through music. The Rasa remains the concluding topic about the notes.

The astrological factors like — Gotra, Stars, Rashi and other similar things are described by Narada of 'Sangita Makaranda' only. Nowhere else these particulars have appear. Charts are attached forthwith to present those particulars given by Narada.

However, the astrological details pertaining to the seven notes deserve some explanations. Why should he furnish so much information which seems to have no relevance to practical music and what must be the purpose?

In India from the very beginning, every single action has been linked with some or other religious or social ceremony. Astrology was one of the outstanding achievement of India. At present too, the horoscopes play a major part in marriages and fixing auspicious day and dates for performing or starting of any work. In India, the laymen also have at least a working knowledge of astrology and planetary positions of his horoscope. Every malefic planet is propitiated and appeased by certain rituals accompanied by mantras. In Carnatic music Muthuswamy Dikshitar; one of the musical trinity of Carnatic music and an ardent worshipper of Shakti has composed nine navavarna kritis and nine navagraha kirtanas for the common people who are not capable of performing Navavarna pooja, and to please the nine planets by singing their praise respectively.

During the invasion and rule by foreigners, the Indians and their culture got suppressed and ridiculed by them. Not only they but our own people have dismissed our culture calling it as superstitious. Music as such was a kind of ritual to attain the specific result by singing the specific songs containing the notes which pleased the planets or deities. Here the stars and other factors of astrology really help to decide the music suitable for both—the singer and the concerned deities which rule over that particular period.

The gods are worshipped to fulfill the wishes of men, cure diseases, to get boons and to achieve salvation too.

"धर्मार्थ काम मोक्षाय इदमेवैकसाधनम्"

Obviously, Narada furnishes the details like Rishis, Rashis, stars, deities, and Ganas related to the seven notes, to make the rituals, performed with the musical chants based upon notes more fruitful. By knowing the astrological details of the notes, one could select the suitable notes to perform the rituals to propitiate the desired deities and appease the malefic deities.

A properly performed Vedic sacrifice is supposed to grant Adrishta (unforeseen) results, including the materialistic attainments. The same belief exists about 'Gandharva'. The Tanas named Agnistoma, etc., are believed to fetch the result of the similarly named Yajnas. The miseries caused by planets, their movements and placings in the horoscopes is believed to be cured by performing 'Homa' (Havans) and by wearing particular coloured clothes and gems or donating to Brahmins. In the same way, the use of particular notes belonging to the unfavourable stars and planets may influence the malefic planets and their transitional periods and also invoke the favourable attitude of the planets and stars.

These factors and adrista motives show that ancient music was through and through formed with a transcendental ritualistic purpose. This applies to the ancient music of all the eastern and western countries — China, Mesopotamia, Egypt and so on. Music in the past was not a mere form of entertainment.

In 'Sangita Makaranda', Nada appears in the very beginning of the work. Nada is twofold — Ahata and Anahata. The common definition of Nada appears in the fourth pada of Sangitadhyaya. The outstanding feature of Nada in 'Sangita Makaranda' is its five types, which is very novel and unique. They are — Nakhaj, Vayuj, Charmaj, Dehaj and Shariraj. The general five types of Nada — Sukshma, Atisukshma, etc., also appear later as the types of Dehaja Nada.

Shruti comes after Svara in the same way as in 'Natya Shastra'. For the sake of convenience it is discussed after Nada and before Svara. Shrutis are also not defined at the first instance. The twenty-two names of Shrutis given by Narada differ from those of others. In 'Raga-Kalpadruma', and 'Sangita Narayana', however, similar names of Shrutis are given. 'Bharata Bhashyam' which is the earliest work giving the names of Shrutis after 'Sangita Makaranda' is followed by other authors.

The topic Svara in 'Sangita Makaranda' is dealt in detail and each Svara is treated like a human being. Narada mentions their place of birth, colour, caste, governing deity, etc. According to Narada, Brahma drew the seven Svaras from Anahata Nada and placed them in the Veena thereby making them (Svaras) available to all. Narada means to say that the seven notes belonging to Ahata Nada also have appeared from Anahata Nada.

The minor descriptions of Svara being similar to other authors Narada has given additional details as such—Gotra, planets, Rashis, star, Ganas and the deities governing the Rashis of the notes. Another special feature is the inclusion of 'Shanta Rasa' which is left out by Bharata and other authors. His names of Dwipas, Rishis and deities are much accurate and acceptable. In short, Nada, Shruti and Svara of 'Sangita Makaranda' have their own individuality as dealt by Narada in a different but interesting way, not less than a living being.

REFERENCES

1. *Sangita Makaranda,* Introduction, p. 10.
2. Copies of designs and a page of text is attached.
3. *Sangita Makaranda,* p. 14.
4. *Ibid.,* p. 1.
5. *Bharatiya Sangita Ka Itihas,* p. 232.
6. *Sangita Ratnakara,* Part I, p. 90.
7. *Brihaddeshi,* p. 1.
8. *Sangita Makaranda,* p. 23.
9. *Brihaddeshi,* p. 2.
10. *Sangita Makaranda,* p. 1.
11. *Ibid.,* p. 2.
12. संगीत रत्नाकर, प्रथम ग्रन्थ, पृष्ठ ३२

13. *Brihaddeshi*, Sl. 25, p. 2.
14. *Naradiya Shiksha*, p. 15.
15. According to B.C. Desai, *Bharata Bhashyam*, p. 976.
16. *Natya Shastra*, vol.4, p. 8.
17. *Ibid.*, vol.12, p. 15.
18. *Dattilam*, Sl.9, p.1.
19. *Natya Shastra*, p. 12.
20. *Dattilam*, Sl. 12-14, p. 1.
21. *Brihaddeshi*, p. 2.
22. *Ibid.*
23. *Ibid.*
24. *Naradiya Shiksha*, Sl. 9-18, 7th Kandika, pp. 40-43.
25. *Bharata Bhashyam*, p. 86.
26. *Sangita Ratnakara*, vol. I, Sl. 10-16, pp. 69-73.
27. *Sangita Samayasara*, pp. 7-8.
28. *Sangita Makaranda*, p. 8.
29. From the manuscript, 3rd folio.
30. Manuscript-*Sangita Narayana*, 2nd folio.
31. See Appendix 3 for the names of Shrutis.
32. *Sangita Makaranda*, Sl. 78-84. p. 8.
33. *Ibid.*, Sl. 86, p. 9.
34. *Natya Shastra*, vol. IV, Sl. 11, p. 7.
35. *Dattilam*, Sl. 10, p. 1.
36. *Brihaddeshi*, p. 25.
37. *Sangita Ratnakara*, vol. 1, p. 79.
38. *Sangita Samayasara*, p. 10.
39. *Sangita Makaranda*, p. 14.
40. *Naradiya Shiksha*, pp. 28-29.
41. *Ibid.*, p. 10.
42. *Ibid.*, Sl. 2-3.
43. Brihaddeshi, Sl. 64-69, p. 28, *Sangita*, May 1975.
44. *Bharata Bhashyam*, part I, p. 66.
45. *Sangita Samayasara*, p. 14
46. See Appendix 4.
47. *Sangita Makaranda*, p. 2.

48. See Appendix 3.
49. See Chart 2.
50. See Chart 3.
51. *Sangita Makaranda*, p. 3.
52. *Ibid.*
53. *Ibid.*
54. *Sangita Ratnakara*, Vol. I, p. 92.
55. *Sangita Makaranda*, p. 15.

5

Grama Murchana and Tanas

Grama — The concept of Grama is difficult for us to visualize and understand, because the system of Grama became extinct with time and now only a single, Grama, i.e., Shadja Grama is in practice, which does not serve the purpose as in the past. The Grama and Murchana belong to a period when fretted instruments were not present and stringed instruments, i.e., harp typed instruments were used to perform or accompany the songs. The different notes were played on separate strings which were tuned accordingly. As there were no Vikrita (flat or sharp) notes, Murchanas were used to form different melodies.

At present, Shadja has become the *tonic*, fundamental or basic note, Murchanas have been discarded and five Vikrita notes have appeared in an octave. Santoor, Svaramandals are the only the multiple stringed instruments now used and other ancient harp type of instruments have in course of time gradually disappeared.

Therefore, Gramas and Murchanas have lost their importance. Yet, they were the basis of our ancient music, and as such they are important and worth studying.

Grama stands for a village in Sanskrit. A village in the past is used to be a close knit, well planned and self-dependent unit. The four classes of people are well accommodated in their assorted places.

In the same way, the notes are arranged in such a systematic manner in a Grama that Murchanas can be formed by transposing the notes one by one.

"ग्रामः स्वर समूहः स्यान्मूर्च्छना तु स्वराश्रया।"[1]

Gramas are the collection of Svaras, Murchanas depend upon the notes of Grama.

As far as 'Sangita Makaranda' is concerned, Grama is a very important topic. Gandhara Grama is a very controversial topic and the first author to describe the Gandhara Grama is supposed to be Narada of 'Sangita Makaranda'. Narada has described the arrangement of notes of Gandhara Grama and the names of its seven Murchanas.

In 'Naradiya Shiksha' three Gramas are described with their seven Murchanas. He names the three Gramas — Shadja, Madhyama and Gandhara and the three sets of seven Murchanas belonging to each Grama. The three sets of Murchanas are supposed to please the Devas, Pitrus and Rishis, but they are not named as belonging to a particular Grama. From the names of the Murchanas it seems that the Murchanas of Gandhara Grama belong to the Devas. The forty-nine 'Tanas' arising out of three Gramas are also mentioned in 'Naradiya Shiksha' — 20 from Madhyama Grama, 14 from Shadja Grama and 15 Tanas arise from Gandhara Grama.[2]

'Sangita Makaranda' does not attach much importance to the definition. Its definition of Grama is also very short —

"ग्रामः स्वर समूहः स्यान्मूर्च्छना तु स्वराश्रया।"

Naradiya Shiksha only names the Gramas but does not define them.

In 'Natya Shastra' Bharata does not define the Gramas. He mentions that there are two Gramas — Shadja and Madhyama which the twenty-two Shrutis forming the notes depend upon—

"अथ द्वौ ग्रामौ षड्जग्रामो मध्यमग्रामश्चेति
अत्राश्रिता द्वाविंशतिश्रुतयः स्वरमण्डल साधिता।"[3]

Dattila in his turn follows the 'Natya Shastra' and just names the Gramas without any definition.

It is Matanga who furnishes the definition and meaning of the term Grama. He first asks the question about Grama and provides the answer himself.

"अथः किमुच्यते ग्राम शब्देन। ननु कति ग्रामा भवति।"
"कस्मादुत्पद्यते ग्रामः किं वा तस्य प्रयोजनम्।"[4]

"What is called as a Grama? How many Gramas are there? From where does the Grama evolve and what is its use?"

Then Matanga answers in a very systematic order. Grama is a collective noun possessing Svaras and Shrutis. Matanga compares the Grama with a village (in Sanskrit, Grama stands for a village). Matanga mentions that as the families live in a village together in their respective places according to their positions, the Svaras and Shrutis also stay in a Grama according to their positions and order. In India, however the village is very much attached to its customs and systems, which applies to the musical Gramas too.

Matanga again says —

सामवेदात् स्वरा:जाताः स्वरेभ्यो ग्रामसम्भवः।[5]

The Svaras originated from the Sama Veda and with the Svaras Gramas are formed. Matanga mentions three Gramas, i.e., Gandhara Grama too. But he cites that Gandhara Grama is mentioned by Narada, which is not used by human beings.

Nanya Bhupala in his 'Bharata Bhashyam' defines Grama in detail and discusses the three Gramas with their notes in detail. He says that different Gramas are formed according to the distribution of Shrutis to particular notes, i.e., in

Shadja Grama the Shruti divisions are normal, in Madhyama Grama, Panchama loses one of its Shrutis and Dhaivata gets one more Shruti. In Gandhara Grama, 'Ga' gets two more Shrutis. Therefore, Shrutis are the main deciding factor of a Grama.

"ग्राम-त्रय-विभागं च श्रुति भेद कृतं तथा
द्वाविंशति तथा श्रुति यथा ग्रामेष्वपि त्रिषु।"[6]

Nanya Bhupala has elaborated the Gandhara Grama and named the Ragas based on Gandhara Grama.

Sharngdeva gives the same definition of Narada of 'Sangita Makaranda'.

"ग्रामः स्वर समूहः स्यान्मूर्च्छनाऽऽदे समाश्रयः।"[7]

Sharngdeva describes only two Gramas and quotes Narada while describing Gandhara Grama, its notes and the names of Murchanas of Gandhara Grama.

'Natya Shastra' does not even mention the name of Gandhara Grama anywhere. Bharata names only two Gramas Shadja and Madhyama, Dattila mentions the name of Gandhara Grama and Matanga also follows Dattila. Both quote Narada and say that it is not practised on the earth. Nanya Bhupala says that Bharata does not speak about the Gandhara Grama as it is unearthly.

"गान्धार ग्रामश्च भरतेनालौकिकत्वान्नोपदेशितः।"[8]

Therefore, Narada of 'Naradiya Shiksha', Narada of 'Sangita Makaranda', Nanya Bhupala are the authors who describe Gandhara Grama. Sharngdeva does not add anything original to the description of Gandhara Grama provided by Narada.

In 'Sangita Makaranda' Narada describes about Gandhara Grama, its tonal arrangements and the names of Murchanas in eight slokas from 49-56. He also comments that it is supposed to be used in the heaven (स्वर्गलोक) only:

"षड्ज मध्यम गान्धार ग्राम त्रयमुदाहृतम्।।४६।।

षड्ज मध्यमश्चैव चैतो भूमौ प्रकल्पितौ।
स्वर्ग लोकेऽपि गान्धारः प्रसिद्धो न महीतले।।५०।।"[9]

In the description of Shadja Grama and Madhyama Grama, Narada follows the general order accepted by all, i.e., 'Sa' Grama —4, 3, 2, 4, 4, 3, 2 and 'Ma' Grama—4, 3, 2, 4, 3, 4, 2 Shrutis. Narada also confirms that in Shadja Grama, Shadja is in consonance with both Madhyama and Panchama. In the same way, in Madhyama Grama, Panchama is the consonant to Dhaivata and Rishabha. Narada again mentions that Panchama has only three Shrutis, while Dhaivata of Madhyama Grama gains a Shruti and has four Shrutis.

"सोपान्ते पञ्चमस्तिस्त्रो धैवतस्य चतुःश्रुतिः।"[10]

Thus Madhyama Grama is described in a systematic manner.

Gandhara Grama, which is the special feature of 'Sangita Makaranda', is not defined in very clear terms though the arrangement of notes of Gandhara Grama is given and the same is reproduced by Sharngdeva in his 'Sangita Ratnakara'.

The description of Gandhara Grama appears incomplete and confused, though the order of Shruti distribution in the former part of the scale is clear. The latter part seems to be rather confused and incomplete. In 'Sangita Ratnakara', the same description of Gandhara Grama is presented in a correct language.

यद्रा धस्त्रिश्रुतिः षड्जे मध्यमे तु चतुःश्रुतिः।।३।।
रिमयो श्रुतिरेकैका गांधारश्चेत् समाश्रितः
प श्रुति धो निषादस्तु ध श्रुति स श्रुतिं श्रितः।।४।।
गांधार ग्राममाचष्ट तदा तं नारदो मुनिः।।"[11]

Narada says that though the aforesaid (Gandhara) Grama is not prevalent on the earth and resides in the heaven, it is defined theoretically.

"अप्रसिद्धोऽपि भूलोके क्रमाद्लक्ष्येऽपि नारदः।
तत्सु (स्व?) रूपं देवलोके ज्ञातव्यं शास्त्रलक्षणैः।"[12]

The description of Gandhara Grama runs like this —

"यदा धस्त्रिश्रुति षड्जे मध्यमे तु चतुश्रुतिः।"[13]

This is the general order of the notes 'Sa' and 'Ma' with four Shrutis and 'Dha' three Shrutis.

"रिमयोः श्रुतिरेकैका गान्धारस्य समाश्रया।।५४।।[13]

Here the author takes one Shruti from 'Ri' and 'Ma' each and allocates them to Gandhara which normally has two Shrutis only. Thus 'Ri' loses one Shruti and has two Shrutis in Gandhara Grama and 'Ma' has three Shrutis instead of its normal four Shrutis. Gandhara in its own Grama has four Shrutis.

पंचमश्रुतिरेका च निषाद श्रुतिसंश्रया।
गान्धारग्राममाचष्टे तदा तं नारदोऽप्रवीत् ।।५५।।[14]

Narada says that Nishada takes one Shruti from 'Panchama' which has four Shrutis. In the above sloka, nothing has been explained about Shadja of Gandhara Grama, which has only three Shrutis in the 'Ga' Grama. The last part of the last line of the above sloka seems to be incomplete. It does not say anything about Shadja. Either a line or a word between निषादश्रुति and संश्रया is missing. Sharngdeva presents the same line with a difference and clears the ambiguity —

"प श्रुति धो निषादस्तु ध श्रुतिं सश्रुतिं श्रितः।"

Sharngdeva says that 'Dha' takes a Shruti from 'Pa' and passes it to Nishada and the latter gets two Shrutis one each from 'Dha' and 'Sa'. Therefore, 'Sa' of Gandhara Grama has only three Shrutis.

Nanya Bhupala gives an elaborate description of Gandhara Grama, but an important line describing the 'Ga' Grama is missing in the published work of 'Bharata Bhashyam'. Nanya Bhupala's Gandhara Grama is identical to the 'Ga' Grama of 'Sangita Makaranda' though words are missing at places and the Shrutis allotted to Nishada are not clear. But the Svaramandala Prastara of all the three Gramas of Bharata Bhashyam presents a clear picture of Gandhara Grama and its Shruti divisions. His Gandhara Grama description is given below:

> **"चतुश्रुतिश्चगान्धारः प धौ त्रिश्रुतिको यदि**
> **गान्धार ग्राममित्येवं राजनारायणोऽभ्यधात्।"**[15]

Probably, the correct original manuscript of 'Sangita Makaranda' was available to Nanya Bhupala and Sharngdeva. The missing or incorrect verse of 'Sangita Makaranda' regarding Gandhara Grama might be the copyist's mistake.

Now the three Gramas — Shadja, Madhyama and Gandhara, can be explained with their prospective Shrutis and consonants.

Shadja Grama —

Place of Shrutis	—	4,	7,	9,	13,	17,	20,	22
Notes	—	Sa,	Ri,	Ga,	Ma,	Pa,	Dha,	Ni.
Shrutis	—	4	3	2	4	4	3	2

Consonants — Sa-Ma and Pa, Ri-Dha, Ga-Ni, Ma-Ni.

Madhyama Grama —

Place of Shrutis	—	13,	16,	20,	22,	4,	7,	9
Svara	—	Ma,	Pa,	Dha,	Ni,	Sa,	Ri,	Ga
Shrutis	—	4	3	4	2	4	3	2

Consonants — Sa-Ma, Ri-Pa and Dha, Ga-Ni.

Gandhara Grama —

Shrutis	—	9,	12,	15,	18,	22,	3,	5
Svara	—	Ga,	Ma,	Pa,	Dha,	Ni,	Sa,	Ri
	—	4	3	3	3	4	3	2

Consonants — Ri-Dha, Sa-Ma, Ga-Dha and Ni.

But 'Ri' and 'Dha', or 'Ga' and 'Dha' have no similar number of Shrutis.

Now about the Gramas, the other authors except Narada of 'Naradiya Shiksha' and 'Bharata Bhashyam' are of the opinion that there are only two Gramas, viz., Shadja and Madhyama Grama and Gandhara Grama is not practiced in the world. Sharngdeva names the Gandhara Grama and presents the description of the same with its Murchanas mentioning the name of Narada as the authority of the Grama but does not make any addition of his own. 'Natya Shastra' names only two Gramas and there is no hint about Gandhara Grama. Dattila says —

"ग्रामौ द्वौ षड्जमध्यमौ
केचिद् गान्धारमप्याह स (तु) नेहोपलभ्यते।"[16]

Matanga opines that there are two Gramas, Gandhara Grama is mentioned by Narada, but it is not used by human beings.

"षड्जमध्यम संज्ञौ तु द्वौ ग्रामौ विश्रुतौ किल
गांधारं नारदो ब्रूते स तु मर्त्यैर्नगीयते।"[17]

Shadja and Madhyama Grama with their order of notes and tonal qualities are similar in all the works without any controversy. From 'Sangita Makaranda' onwards, the description of Gandhara Grama is included.

'Naradiya Shiksha' is the earliest to mention Gandhara Grama with its seven Murchanas, but the arrangement of the notes is not given in that work.

Nanya Bhupala accepts three Gramas and gives the Murchanas and Tanas of Gandhara Grama and names the Ragas based on Gandhara Grama. His 'Ga' Grama is identical to the Gandhara Grama of 'Sangita Makaranda', though words are missing at places and the Shrutis allotted to Nishada are not mentioned at the first instance. His Svaramandala Prakarana of Gandhara Grama is given below which shows the similarity of 'Ga' Grama of Nanya Bhupala and Narada of 'Sangita Makaranda'.

ऊर्ध्वायतादि-रेखायां गान्धारं विन्यसेत्तथा ।
ऊर्ध्वा रेखा चतुर्थी या लिखित्तस्यां च मध्यमम् ।।६७।।
पतितायां द्वितीयायां पञ्चम्यां चैव दक्षिणे।
धैवतं पञ्चमं चेति क्रमेण विनिवेशयेत्।।६८।।
गान्धार-मध्यमाविद्ध-रेखा-पुच्छ-द्वये पुनः।
षड्जं चैव निषादं विन्यसेत्क्रमशो क्रमशो बुधः।।६९।।

This Svaramandala is copied out from 'Bharata Bhashyam' (page 86). Nanya Bhupala says that though the Gandhara Grama is used by Gandharvas residing in the heaven and its formation is known to the divine beings only, its Svaramandala Prastara is given above. He says that it is not used on the earth, because of its exceptional high and extreme low pitch as well.

अतितार अति मन्द्रत्वान्नात्र गायन्ति मानवाः ।।५६।।[18]

Nanya Bhupala defines the Grama in a very different and practical way. He opines that Gramas are formed, because of the displacements of Svaras by either gaining or losing their Shrutis.

"एषां मध्ये श्रुत्युत्कर्षापकर्षवान् स्वरविशेष
प्रधानभूतस्वरोपचितो ग्रामः इत्युच्यते।।३५।।"[19]

He explains the three Gramas and links them with main Vedic notes — Svarita, Udatta and Anudatta which again confirms the presence of Gandhara Grama during Vedic period. He mentions them as :

षड्जग्राम प्रसन्नादिरनुदात्त प्रधानकः।
मध्यमः स्वरितादिश्च स्यादुदात्त अनुदात्तवान्।।३७।।
उदात्ताविस्तु गान्धार ग्रामः सप्ति (?) रिहोच्यते।
एवं स्वरं त्रयकृता ग्राम त्रंय भेदा भवेयुः।।३८।।[20]

This is a very peculiar and special idea provided by Nanya Bhupala only. He links—

Shadja Grama with Anudatta

Madhyama Grama with Svarita

Gandhara Grama with Udatta.

Now about the deities of the three Gramas, Matanga quotes Narada, as : —

देवकुल समुत्पन्ना षड्जगांधारमध्यमाः।
एतेषां देवता ज्ञेया ब्रह्मा विष्णु महेश्वराः।।

Nanya Bhupala does not mention the names of the deities of Grama or the singing time and season in the first part. But, in Ragadhyaya he gives the same time and season. Sharngdeva mentions the names of gods presiding over the three Gramas, their singing time and seasons which is similar to that of 'Sangita Makaranda'.

The question arises as to why the three notes get the position to form Gramas on their name — Shadja, Madhyama and Gandhara, while other notes are left out as if they are less important. If it is because of the Shruti numbers that counts, then Panchama also is a four Shruti note. 'Pa' also might possess a Grama to its name, but it is not the case while 'Ga' which has only two Shrutis is credited with a Grama.

Matanga explains that 'Sa', 'Ga' and 'Ma' are born in 'Deva Kula', they belong to divine lineage so they are capable of forming the Gramas.

"देव कुल समुत्पन्नाः षड्ज गान्धार मध्यमा।"

Nanya Bhupala says that Grama positions are given to the notes having four Shrutis. Panchama loses one of its Shrutis in Madhyama Grama, thus forfeits its right of having a Grama to itself. But 'Ga' owning a Grama is again questionable as it has two Shrutis. The remarkable point is Narada— the authority on 'Ga' Grama does not discuss about Gandhara's right of owning a Grama. But Nanya Bhupala certainly defends Gandhara forming a Grama of its own. He says in Gandhara Grama 'Ga' has four Shrutis.

"तर्हि गान्धारस्य द्विश्रुते कथं ग्रामत्वम्? सत्यम्।
गान्धारः षड्ज ग्रामे मध्यम ग्रामे च द्विश्रुतिः।
स्वग्रामे तु चतुःश्रुतिरेव।।५।।"[21]

Narada of 'Sangita Makaranda' does not discuss about these controversies. He simply justifies the cause of Grama position given to Shadja and Madhyama Grama.

"षड्ज प्राधान्यमाद्यत्वादमात्यादिगतस्तथा (?)
ग्रामः स्यादथ लोपत्वान्मध्यमस्तु पुरः सरः।"[22]

Shadja is the first important note holding more ministers, (Samvadi notes) hence it gets a Grama on its name. Madhyama is a note which cannot be omitted in any Grama, so it also holds a Grama. About 'Ga' Grama, Narada says nothing which seems to suggest that it is indisputable, because it is born in the heaven and used by divine beings.

'Naradiya Shiksha', 'Natya Shastra' and the 'Dattilam' do not consider this question as worthy of discussion. Sharngdeva accepts the ideas of 'Sangita Makaranda' about 'Sa' and 'Ma' Gramas and justifies that 'Ga' gets importance, because of its high birth.[25] He follows 'Naradiya Shiksha' and 'Brihaddeshi' in giving the importance to Gandhara.

'Sangita Makaranda' names Brahma, Vishnu and Maheshwara as the deities of Shadja, Madhyama and Gandhara Grama. Gandhara Grama is governed by Maheshwara, which stresses the point that it is used in Tantra practices. These deities are accepted by Matanga, Nanya Bhupala and Sharngdeva as well.

The seasons allotted to the three Gramas are winter, summer and rainy season, i.e., Hemanta, Grishma and Varsha. Forenoon, midday and afternoon are the respective time to use 'Sa', 'Ma' and 'Ga' Gramas.

The arrangement of notes in each Grama presented by Narada of 'Sangita Makaranda' is as follows:

Shadja Grama —

Svara —	Sa	Ri	Ga	Ma	Pa	Dha	Ni
Shrutis —	4	3	2	4	4	3	2

Madhyama Grama —

Svara —	Ma	Ga	Ri	Sa	Ni	Dha	Pa
Shrutis—	4	2	3	4	2	4	3

Gandhara Grama —

Svara —	Ga	Ma	Pa	Dha	Ni	Sa	Ri
Shrutis—	4	3	3	3	4	3	2

While the 'Sa' and 'Ga' Gramas are in ascending order,

'Ma' Grama is in descending order, presents the illusion of Vedic scale. Nanya Bhupala gives the Madhyama Grama notes as—Ma - Pa - Dha - Ni - Sa - Ri - Ga, which is more appropriate.

This descending order given by Narada of 'Sangita Makaranda' for Madhyama Grama is thought provoking. Three Gramas are mentioned in Puranas, e.g., Vayu, Markandeya, and Agni. Except Bharata, several authors say that Gandhara Grama became extinct or unused on the earth following its unusually high pitch and tunelessness. Nanya Bhupala names Gandhara Grama as — "गान्धार पूर्वकः" twice.

"गन्धर्वैं गीयते स्वर्गे ग्रामो गान्धारपूवर्कः
अतितार अतिमन्द्रत्वान्नात्र गायन्ति मानवाः ।।५६।।[24]

Therefore it seems that Gandhara Grama was the earliest one that disappeared with time and lost its importance thereby. Then Madhyama Grama might have flourished and practised during Vedic period, for the Vedic scale was supposed to start with the note 'Ma' in descending order. Probably, the Shadja Grama was used in post-Vedic period and in Loukika music and Gandharva music as well. Though Shadja Grama is as old as other Gramas, its usage might have been different. The above idea is just a suggestion and without any concrete evidence about the time, the conclusion is impossible. Matanga in his 'Brihaddeshi' asserts that Shadja Grama is more important than Madhyama Grama.

Murchana

In 'Sangita Makaranda', Murchana is the topic presented with much negligence and incorrect names of the Murchanas. There is much repetition of the names of Murchanas and their starting notes but with mistakes. The seven Murchanas of each Grama are given — twice without paying any attention to correct the names, which suggest the precarious and damaged condition of the original manuscript. This part of the 'Sangita Makaranda' is the worst affected and most confusing.

Murchanas can be compared with scales producing different kinds of melodies. These Murchanas arise out of Gramas starting from a different note each time and pronouncing the seven notes in a systematic ascending and descending order. Seven Murchanas can be produced by a Grama. Shifting the basic note makes the seven varieties of Murchanas.

Indian music of the past was based on these scales. Murchana is defined by some authors only. The position is as follows: Narada of 'Naradiya Shiksha' does not define a Murchana. According to Bharata —

"क्रम युक्ताः स्वराः सप्त मूर्च्छनेत्याभिसंज्ञिताः"[25]

Seven notes in their respective order are called as Murchana. Dattila does not define the Murchana. Matanga as usual gives the meaning, etymology and definition of Murchana.

Derivation "मूर्छा मोहसमुच्छ्राययो"

मूर्छते येन रागो हि मूर्छनेत्यभि संज्ञिता
आरोहण अवरोहण क्रमेण स्वर सप्तकम्।।६४।।[26]

Murchana indicates the stunned state of senses or deception of mind. When a Raga is formed by sudden state of stunned deception due to the materialisation, it is called Murchana. Ascending and descending order (systematic) of seven notes are termed as Murchana. Nanya Bhupala opines—

स्वराणां मूर्च्छना मूर्च्छा-धातुर्मोहे समुच्छ्रये।
स्वरेभ्य उत्थितो नादः स्वरेष्वेवहि मूर्च्छति।।२।।[27]

According to Nanya Bhupala, when the notes get affected (Moha) Murchana is born.

Sharngdeva furnishes a very simple definition like Bharata. Narada of 'Sangita Makaranda' also gives the same plain definition of Murchana like Bharata and says —

"क्रमात् स्वराणां सप्तनामारोहश्च अवरोहणम् मूर्च्छनेत्युच्यते"[28]

Here the author has written that the Aroha and Avaroha of seven notes in their respective orders are called Murchana. Parshvadeva in his 'Sangita Samayasara' defines Murchana more elaborately.

"मूर्च्छना शब्दनिष्पत्ति मूर्छाः मोहे समुच्छ्रये
मूर्छयते येन रागो हि मूर्च्छनेत्यभिसंज्ञिता।
आरोहण अवरोहण क्रमेण स्वर सप्तकम्
मूर्च्छना शब्दवाच्य हि विज्ञेय तद्वविचक्षण।"[20]

According to K.C. Brihaspati, Parshvadeva takes the meaning of Murchana as 'arising' or rising, i.e., (उभार). Therefore, the place from which Raga arises is called Murchana.

The definition and description of Murchanas are almost similar according to all the authors. Every Grama can produce seven Murchanas. Bharata, Dattila, Matanga and Sharngdeva accept only fourteen Murchanas from the two Gramas — Shadja and Madhyama, Sharngdeva, though quotes Narada; his Gandhara Grama with seven Murchanas, does not accept it.

After defining the word Murchana, the names of seven Murchanas belonging to each Grama are given with its starting notes.

Narada of 'Naradiya Shiksha' gives seven Murchanas with their names but without mentioning the names of the Gramas to which they belong. He gives the names as seven Murchanas of Deva, seven Murchanas of Pitru and seven Murchanas of Rishis.

His seven Murchanas of Rishis are similar to those of Shadja Grama. Narada says that these seven Murchanas of Rishis belong to Loukika music. They are — Uttara Mandra, Abhirudgata, Ashvakranta, Souvira, Hrishyaka, Uttarayata, Rajani. They are starting with the notes 'Sa', 'Ri', 'Ga', 'Ma', 'Pa', 'Dha', 'Ni', respectively.

Bharata's seven names of the Murchanas of Shadja Grama are as follows:

Uttaramandra, Abhirudgata, Ashvakranta, Matsarikrita, Shuddha Shadja, Uttarayata and Rajani.

In 'Naradiya Shiksha' the names Matsarikrita and Shuddhashadja are replaced by Souvira and Hrishyaka which belong to Madhyama Grama according to Bharata and the other authors including Narada of 'Sangita Makaranda'.

Narada of 'Naradiya Shiksha' then enumerats the seven names of Murchanas belonging to ancestral forefathers (Pitrus). These should belong to Madhyama Grama but their names are totally different. They are—Apyayani, Vishwabhrita, Chandra, Hema, Kapardini, Maitri and Varhati. Narada of 'Naradiya Shiksha' is of the opinion that these seven 'Pitru' Murchanas are used by Yakshas—a tribe just like Gandharvas, well versed in music. The music was threefold excluding the Vedic and Loukika Gana, i.e., Gandharva Gana, Yaksha Gana and Deva Gana. They are used in colloquial language even today in south India. Nanya Bhupala gives the same names and quotes Narada as the author of these names of seven Murchanas belonging to Madhyama Grama. He says—

"नारदेनापि मुनिना प्रोक्ता नामान्तरे तु याः
मूर्च्छना ग्राम भेदेन तासां नामाभिधीयते।।३४।।"[30]

Nanya Bhupala at the same time gives the general names of seven Murchanas of Madhyama Grama accepted by other authors, i.e., Souvira, Harinashva, etc. In 'Naradiya Shiksha' seventh Murchana of the supposed Madhyama Grama Murchana is named as 'Varhati', while Nanya Bhupala names it as Chandramasi which seems more correct.

Bharata, Dattila, Matanga, Nanya Bhupala, Narada of 'Sangita Makaranda' and Sharngdeva are of the same opinion and the names of seven Murchanas belonging to Madhyama Grama are basically similar. The slight differences are incorrect versions due to copyist's mistakes, because of the illegible condition of the original manuscripts.

Narada of 'Naradiya Shiksha' does not give the names of the three Gramas to which the sets of Murchanas belong, instead he names as—Deva Murchana (Gandhara Grama),

Pitru Murchana (Madhyama Grama) and Rishi Murchana (Shadja Grama). His names of Pitru Murchanas are not to be found anywhere else except reproduced as quoted by Narada in 'Bharata Bhashyam'. Another remarkable point is Narada of 'Naradiya Shiksha' gives importance to Gandhara Grama by giving priority over other two Gramas, while naming its seven Murchanas. He names them as the seven Murchanas of Deva.

The names of the Murchanas of Gandhara Grama according to 'Naradiya Shiksha' are as follows : Nandi, Vishala, Sumukhi, Chitra, Chitravati, Sukha, and Vala.

As Gandhara Grama is not mentioned by Bharata, and other authors (Dattila, Matanga, etc.) have not described it or its Murchanas, only Nanya Bhupala and Sharngdeva need to be considered. Sharngdeva too quotes Narada as the authority on Gandhara Grama. He is indifferent to its usage and does not discuss or gives any support to establish the Grama on his own accord. Therefore, only Nanya Bhupala remains to be considered besides Narada of 'Sangita Makaranda'.

As mentioned earlier, Nanya Bhupala is a strong supporter of Gandhara Grama's existence on the earth with the other two Gramas and its supposed extinction and emigration to the heaven afterwards. He has based many Ragas on Gandhara Grama.

His seven names of Murchanas of Gandhara Grama are lifted from 'Naradiya Shiksha', only difference being the seventh name 'Vala' replaced by Alapa. Narada of 'Sangita Makaranda' also uses Alapa instead of 'Vala' which seems to be the correct name. Again Nanyadeva mentions that though Gandhara Grama is not described by Bharata and others but described by *us* according to Agamas, which again indicates the Tantra element in the practice of Gandhara Grama.

"अस्माभिश्चागमानुसारेण प्रदर्शितः।"[31]

Narada of 'Sangita Makaranda' gives the following seven names of Gandhara Murchanas —

Nanda, Vishala, Sumukhi, Chitta, Chitravati, Shubha

and Alapa. The sixth Murchana 'Shubha' is named as 'Sukha' by Narada and Nanya Bhupala. These seven names are given twice in 'Sangita Makaranda' on pages 6 and 9. On page 6 the first Murchana appears as Sara (सरा), which is corrected on page 9 as 'Nanda'.

Bharata, Dattila, Matanga and Sharngdeva accept 14 Murchanas; all evolving out of two Gramas. Parshvadeva is also of the same opinion, but he accounts that there are two types of Murchanas, according to their number of notes.

Murchanas with seven notes = 14

Murchanas with twelve notes = 14

Therefore, there are 28 Murchanas according to Parshvadeva. Narada of 'Naradiya Shiksha', Nanya Bhupala and Narada of 'Sangita Makaranda' accept twenty-one Murchanas from three Gramas.

Now we shall consider the number of notes in a Murchana. Every author has accepted the seven notes in the respective proper descending and ascending order. The remarkable point is they have not mentioned as either ascending or descending order.

Therefore, a Murchana is meant to be starting from a note, going upwards upto the seventh note, returning the same way and ending on the starting note. Though, this type of order is meant by all authors, they explain, only one way that is ascending order, i.e., Uttara Mandra Murchana is explained thus — Sa — Ri — Ga — Ma — Pa — Dha — Ni. But the reverse order of the Murchana is not given, it is only understood. From this type of Murchana, one gets access upto Nishada or the last note on which the Murchana ends.

Therefore, Matanga proposes Murchanas of twelve notes to get access over the tara saptaka to expand the Raga. Matanga explains thus —

"यद्वाप्याचार्यैः सप्तस्वरमूर्च्छनाः प्रतिपादिताः स्थान
त्रितयप्राप्यर्थं द्वादशस्वरैरेव मूर्च्छनाः प्रयुक्ता इति।"[32]

He quotes Nandikeshwara —

"द्वादशस्वरसंपन्ना ज्ञातव्या मूर्च्छना बुधैः।
जाति भाषादि सिद्धयर्थं तारमन्द्रादि सिद्धये।"[32]

Then Matanga says that with seven notes one cannot produce an effective and perfect picture of Raga, its form in the lower or upper register and then he gives the order of twelve noted Murchanas—

Uttara Mandra —

Dha - Ni - Sa - Ri - Ga - Ma - Pa - Dha - Ni - Sa - Ri - Ga.

Rajani —

Ni - Sa - Ri - Ga - Ma - Pa - Dha - Ni - Sa - Ri - Ga - Ma and so on.

This twelve noted Murchana is not accepted by later authors or Bharata and Dattila, though it has its advantages, probably evolved by Nandikeshwara for practical purposes. Abhinava Gupta rejects and condemns the idea of twelve noted Murchanas. Parshvadeva, a much later author accepts this and counts them in his Murchanas making their number as twenty-eight. Narada of 'Sangita Makaranda' does not interfere in these controversies. According to him, there are only twenty-one Murchanas. Moreover, Matanga is not against the Murchanas with seven notes and the twelve noted Murchana was already existing before the time of Matanga.

Now in 'Sangita Makaranda' the names of the seven Murchanas of each Grama are mentioned twice. At first on page 6 this sloka appears.

षड्ज ग्राम स्वराः
स रि ग म प ध नि
षड्जे तूत्तरमन्द्रादौ रञ्जनी चोत्तरायता।
शुद्ध षड्जा मत्सरीकृदश्वक्रान्ताभिरुद्गता।
ताः शुद्ध मध्य मार्गेण पारं च हृष्यकाः(?)

Madhyama Grama —

मध्यम ग्राम स्वराः

म ग रि स नि ध प
संवीरा हरिणाश्वा च स्यात्कल्लोपनता यता (?)
शुद्ध मध्या तथा चैव मादली पौरकी तथा
क्रमात् सप्तस्वरा ह्येते मध्यम ग्राम संश्रिताः
हृष्यकान्तेति विज्ञेया मध्यम ग्राम सुस्वराः।।६१।।

Gandhara Grama —

गान्धार ग्राम सुस्वराः
सरां विशाला सुमुरवी चिता चित्रावती शुभा
आलापा चेति गान्धारग्रामे स्युः सप्त मूर्च्छनाः।।६२।।
ग म प ध नि स री

The same names are repeated on page 7, except the Murchanas of Gandhara Grama with many mistakes. Again on page 9, the names of 21 Murchanas are given with little or no mistakes.

The slokas 66 to 77 elucidate the Gramas and Murchanas in a summative way. Narada defines the Murchanas as :

'क्रमात् स्वराणां सप्तानामारोहणश्चावरोहणम्।

Yet, it should not be understood that a Murchana is an Aroha and Avaroha of notes. Simha Bhupala in his commentary says that Murchana is based on the systematic order of seven notes only. It is not based on Aroha and Avaroha order.

"स्वराणामेव मूर्च्छनत्वं न तु आरोहण
अवरोहणरूपायाः क्रियाया इत्यप्युक्तं।"[33]

Murchana is the name of placing the Svaras in their proper order. Matanga opines that Murchana should be in ascending order.

"मूर्च्छना आरोहक्रमेण तानोऽवरोहक्रमेण भवेदिति भेदः"[34]

All the authors accept the principle of forming Murchanas in descending order, but what they mean is shifting of the starting note of each Murchana in descending order. But the Murchana order of notes should be ascending, i.e.,

Sa - Ri - Ga - Ma - Pa - Dha - Ni — Uttaramandra

Ni - Sa - Ri - Ga - Ma - Pa - Dha — Rajani

Dha- Ni - Sa - Ri - Ga - Ma - Pa — Uttarayata

Pa - Dha- Ni - Sa - Ri - Ga - Ma — Shuddha Shadja

Ma - Pa - Dha- Ni - Sa - Ri - Ga — Matsarikrita

Ga - Ma - Pa - Dha- Ni - Sa - Ri — Ashvakranta

Ri - Ga - Ma - Pa - Dha- Ni - Sa — Abhirudgata.

Abhinava Gupta explains as :

"अक्रमत्वे मूर्च्छनात्वं मा भूदिति
तथा हि षड्जादारोहणं निषादान्तं, धैवतात्
पञ्चमान्तं, पञ्चमान्मध्यमान्त, मध्यमाद्गान्धारन्तं
गान्धारादृषभान्तमृषभात् षड्जान्तं षड्जश्च
द्वितीयसप्तकान्तर तार स्पृष्टो भवति।"[35]

The seven Murchanas with their notes arrangement given above belong to Shadja Grama. The explanation given by Abhinava Gupta clearly shows that the seven Murchanas should be in this order of arrangement. It is approved by all authors except Nanya Bhupala.

Matanga in his Mandala of Murchanas gives both Shadja Grama and Madhyama Grama Murchanas. His Shadja Grama is same as given above. Madhyama Grama Murchanas are given below which again are similar and accepted by all authors again except Nanya Bhupala. Nanya Bhupala is of the view that a Murchana should begin and conclude on the same note. Now Madhyama Grama Murchanas are as follows:

1. Ma - Pa - Dha - Ni - Sa - Ri - Ga — Souviri
2. Ga - Ma - Pa - Dha- Ni - Sa - Ri — Harinashva
3. Ri - Ga - Ma - Pa - Dha- Ni - Sa — Kalopanata
4. Sa - Ri - Ga - Ma - Pa - Dha- Ni — Suddha Madhya

5. Ni - Sa - Ri - Ga - Ma - Pa - Dha — Margi
6. Dha- Ni - Sa - Ri - Ga - Ma - Pa — Pouravi
7. Pa - Dha- Ni - Sa - Ri - Ga - Ma — Hrishyaka

This type of Murchanas belonging to both Shadja and Madhyama Gramas are standardised by all authors including Narada of 'Sangita Makaranda'.

Nanya Bhupala favours the Murchanas of eight notes. He opines that the Murchanas should end on the starting notes only.

"तत्र येनैव स्वरेण तूच्छ्रायो गीतानामुद्ग्राह प्रवर्त्तते
तेनैव स्वरेण यदाऽपोहः समाप्तिरपि भवति, तदा
'स रि ग म प ध नि स' इति स्वर सन्निवेशे सति।"[36]

According to Nanya Bhupala, the Murchana should be like this—

Shadja Grama —

1. Sa - Ri - Ga - Ma - Pa - Dha - Ni - Sa — Uttara Mandra
2. Ni - Sa - Ri - Ga - Ma - Pa - Dha- Ni — Rajani
3. Dha- Ni - Sa - Ri - Ga - Ma - Pa - Dha — Uttarayata
4. Pa - Dha- Ni - Sa - Ri - Ga - Ma - Pa — Hrishyaka
5. Ma - Pa - Dha- Ni - Sa - Ri - Ga - Ma — Souviri
6. Ga - Ma - Pa - Dha- Ni - Sa - Ri - Ga — Ashva Kranta
7. Ri - Ga - Ma - Pa - Dha- Ni - Sa - Ri — Abhirudgata

The basic principle of Murchana is same, but Nanya Bhupala prefers eight noted Murchanas. Now comes Gandhara Grama Murchana, though not clearly presented by Narada or Nanya Bhupala. The probable arrangement of notes in the seven Murchanas of Gandhara Grama is given below —

1. Nanda — Ga - Ma - Pa - Dha - Ni - Sa - Ri
2. Vishala — Ri - Ga - Ma - Pa - Dha- Ni - Sa

3. Sumukhi — Sa - Ri - Ga - Ma - Pa - Dha - Ni

4. Chitta — Ni - Sa - Ri - Ga - Ma - Pa - Dha

5. Chitravati — Dha - Ni - Sa - Ri - Ga - Ma - Pa

6. Shubha — Pa - Dha - Ni - Sa - Ri - Ga - Ma

7. Alapa — Ma - Pa - Dha- Ni - Sa - Ri - Ga

Narada of 'Sangita Makaranda' does not elaborate or mention the Murchanas with their notes. He only explains it as :

"मध्यमस्थान षड्जेन मूर्च्छनारभ्यते क्रमात्।
अधः स्थानैर्निषादाद्यै षड्जः स्यान्मूर्च्छनाक्रमात्।
मध्यमध्यममारभ्यसंवीरी मूर्च्छना भवेत्।
षड्जस्थानपदोधस्थस्वरादारभ्यते क्रमात्।"[37]

Thus he explains that the first Murchana of Shadja Grama starts with the Shadja of middle octave, and after that the lower note from the Shadja, i.e., 'Ni' should be taken for the next Murchana and so on. In the same way, first Murchana of Madhyama Grama should start with the Madhyama of middle octave and should be followed by the Murchana of a lower note — 'Ga', though the sloka does not explain it properly.

Sharngdeva is also of the same opinion and the above sloka of 'Sangita Makaranda' appears in 'Sangita Ratnakara' in its correct form.

"मध्यस्थानस्थ षड्जेन मूर्च्छनाऽऽरभ्यतेऽग्रिमा
अधस्तनैनिषादाद्यैः षडन्या मूर्च्छनाः क्रमात्।"[38]

Even if the copyist has copied from 'Sangita Ratnakara' the above and many other similar slokas, the question naturally arises as to why the slokas are copied with too many avoidable mistakes. The probable answer might be that 'Sangita Makaranda', being an original work, 'Sangita Ratnakara' has lifted many slokas from the original manuscript, which decayed with the time. The copyist might not be having a good knowledge of Sanskrit or was unable to decipher the damaged portions of the original manuscript. He tried his best to restore it without consulting 'Sangita Ratnakara'. But at certain places, the copyist has lost his patience and has copied from 'Sangita Ratnakara'. However, this chapter containing Murchana is the worst hit part of the work so far retrieved.

'Sangita Ratnakara' comes to the rescue of 'Sangita Makaranda' with the correct form of slokas in many places, i.e.,

"षड्जस्थानस्थितैराद्यैस्थान्याद्याः परे विदुः।"

The correct form of the above sloka appears in 'Sangita Ratnakara' as follows —

"षड्जस्थानस्थितैर्न्याद्यै रजन्याद्या परे विदुः"।

'स्थान्याद्यौ' does not make any sense. This is where 'Sangita Ratnakara' is of great help in solving the confusion as both the slokas are similar except the name 'Rajani' is misspelt. There are many such instances; all of which cannot be discussed here.

The Types of Murchanas

All the authors agree on one point about the types of Murchanas — that is their number. There are four types of Murchanas. The controversy arises in naming the type. Starting from Bharata to Nanya Bhupala, the four types of Murchanas are as follows —

संपूर्णा, षाडवा, औडवा एवं साधारणकृता

Sampurana, Shadava, Oudava and Sadharanakrita.

Sampurana — Seven noted Murchanas

Shadava — The Murchanas consisting of six notes

Oudava — Five noted Murchanas

Sadharana Krita — The Murchanas having Sadharana notes.

These are the four types mentioned by Bharata also in the first instance. Matanga, Dattila and Nanya Bhupala follow Bharata. But the idea of Bharata about these four types of Murchana is not very clear. Another hitch in the four types of Murchana is the basic principle of Murchanas which confirms that the ascending and descending order of *seven* notes, called as Murchana. Shadava and Oudava types of Murchanas have only six and five notes respectively. They might be named as Tanas. Bharata clearly says that —(एवमेता: स्वरक्रम)

अपि च—

> **क्रमयुक्ताः स्वराः सप्त मूर्छनेत्यभिसंज्ञिताः।**
> **षट्पंचस्वरकास्तानाः षाडवौडुविताश्रयाः।।३२।।**
> **साधारणकृताश्चैव काकलीसमलंकृताः।**
> **अंतरस्वरसंयुक्ता मूर्छना ग्रामयोर्द्वयोः ।।३३।।**[39]

Bharata confirms the statement that seven notes are necessary for forming a Murchana. Then how can the Shadava and Oudava note formations be termed as Murchana? Moreover, he names the other four types also—Shuddha or Sampurana, Santara, Sakakali and Sadharana Krita.

Santara — having the note Antara 'Ga'.

Sakakali — Kakali Nishada is included in the seven notes.

Sadharana Krita—Both Antara 'Ga' and Kakali Nishada are included instead of Shuddha 'Ga' and 'Ni'. Dattila, Matanga, Nanya Bhupala support the former types of Murchanas, i.e., Sampurana, Shadavita, Oudava and Sadharanakrita. Narada of 'Sangita Makaranda' and Sharngdeva support Bharata, Narada mentions—

> **'चतुर्धा ताः पृथक् शुद्धा काकली कलितास्तथा।**
> **सान्तराः सद्वयोचेताः षट्पंचाशदुदीरिता।।७२।।"**[40]

Sharngdeva also has no doubt about the above types of Murchanas. Bharata after giving the names Sampurana, Shadava, Oudava, and Sadharanakrita, counts only 14 Murchanas. Therefore, he does not recognize Shadava and Oudava as Murchanas. Dattila and Matanga do not accept these four types of Murchanas mentioned by Bharata himself, i.e., Sampurana. Sadharanakrita, Kakali, Samalankrita, Antara, Svarasamyukta. They do not give any explanation for not accepting these four types and ignore the presence of these four types entirely. They might have taken the two later types — *Kakali Samalankrita* and *Antara Svarasamyukta* as parts of Sadharanakrita.

Matanga explains that Tanas are different from Murchanas, because Murchanas are in ascending order while Tanas are in descending order. He quotes Vishakhila to support his idea.

"मूर्छनारोहक्रमेण तानोऽवरोहक्रमेण भवतीति भेदः।"

Matanga provides examples for Shadavita and Oudavita Murchanas.

Sharngdeva says that Murchanas are supposed to be of seven notes and Tanas have six or five notes. Therefore, Shadava and Oudava types of scales cannot attain the position of Murchanas. Bharata also seems to be of the same opinion.

After describing the Kakali and Antara Svara, Narada of 'Sangita Makaranda' mentions —

यस्यां यावन्ति यौ मध्ये तस्येमौ ग्रामयोः क्रमात्।
मूर्च्छनास्तावदित्येवं भरतेन च चर्चिता।"[41]

These notes, Kakali and Antara, when included in a particular Grama, the Murchanas arising out of that Grama are called after that particular note, i.e., Kakali or Antara, and belong to that Grama. If Kakali note is included in Shadja Grama, the Murchanas arising out of that Grama are called as Sakakali Murchana of Shadja Grama. Narada names Bharata as the supporter of this theory. Bharata is also of the opinion that Murchanas either with Antara 'Ga' only or Kakali 'Ni' only are two separate types and Sadharana Krita has both 'Antara', 'Ga' and Kakali 'Ni' in its scale. However, Narada of 'Sangita Makaranda' has no doubt about his four type of Murchanas, i.e., Shuddha or Sampurna or Purna in his first type of Murchana followed by Kakali Kalita, Santara, Sadvayopeta.

About Murchanas, the other special feature mentioned by Narada of 'Sangita Makaranda' is their birthday falling on the fortnights which is called 'Paksha' (पक्ष) in Sanskrit. There are two Pakshas according to the 'cycle of moons' waning and waxing period. First fifteen days after the new moon day is named as Shukla Paksha, and after the fullmoon till the new moon day; the intermediary 15 days are called as Krishna Paksha. There are two Pakshas in a lunar month.

The seven Murchanas of Shadja Grama are born in the seven days of the Pratipada. For these seven Murchanas the particular name of the fortnight (Paksha) is not mentioned by Narada. It seems that he means Shukla Paksha Pratipada for Shadja Grama. Madhyama Grama and Gandhara Grama Murchanas are said to be born on Krishna Paksha Pratipadas; Madhyama Grama Murchana in first seven days of Krishna Paksha and Gandhara Grama Murchanas on the second half of the fortnight of Krishna Paksha. Narada names the Ashtami Tithi of Krishna Paksha for Gandhara Grama. The significant point is Narada does not mention the names of the deities of the Murchanas as is his usual custom. Nanya Bhupala gives the names of the deities of all Murchanas. Murchanas are said to be twenty-eight in each Grama, a total of fifty-six in Shadja and Madhyama Gramas. After including the Murchanas of Gandhara Grama, the number of Murchanas becomes eighty-four. Incidentally, Tanas are also said to be eighty-four.

Some musical terms -- Tanas, Alankara, Varna, Vritti and *Jatis.* : 'Tana' is a topic of importance dealt by all the ancient authors. At present the term 'Tana' has lost its past meaning and application. Tana is a group of notes in serial order but less than seven notes. It may consist of six or five notes. Tana's etymology is given by Kallinatha like this:

तन्यते विस्तार्यते इति तनोतिर्धातोः

Narada of 'Sangita Makaranda' says that —

रागास्तन्नन ताना द्य.......... ।

which means that Tanas are used to establish a Raga. Matanga says that Shadavita and Oudavita are Murchanas and there are Tanas also which have six and five notes. The difference between Tanas and Murchanas are the descending and ascending order of notes respectively. Dattila and Nanya Bhupala are of the opinion that Shadavita and Oudavita. Murchanas are termed as Tana also.

"पंचस्वरा षट् स्वराश्चमूर्छना या प्रकीर्तिता:।
(तनना? ताना) श्चतुरशीतीस्तु ता एवाप्तैरुदाहृता।"[42]

Sharngdeva says that —

"तानाः स्युर्मूर्च्छनाः शुद्धाः षाडवौडुवितिकृताः।।"[43]

The definition of Sharngdeva is more clear. Tanas are Murchanas of six and five notes belonging to the Shuddha types of Murchanas.

There are different opinions about the number of Tanas. Tanas are mentioned by Narada of 'Naradiya Shiksha'. He is of the opinion that Tanas are forty-nine in all together, belonging to the three Gramas.

"विंशति मध्यमग्रामे षड्जग्रामे चतुर्दश।
तानान् पञ्चदशेच्छन्ति गांधार ग्राममाश्रितान्।।"[44]

According to Bharata there are eighty-four Tanas based on Murchanas. Bharata mentions it as :

"षटपञ्चस्वरकास्तानाः षाडवौडुविताश्रयाः।"
तत्र मूर्च्छनाश्रितास्तानाश्चतुरशीतिः। तत्रैकोनपञ्चाशत् षटस्वराः
पञ्चत्रिंशत् पञ्चस्वराः।"[45]

As per the above sloka, forty-nine of them are Shadava (six noted) and thirty-five of them are Oudava (five noted).

Matanga observes it as follows —

षाडवा औडुविताश्च मिलित्वा
चोभय ग्रामिकस्तानचतुरशीतिर्भवन्ति।"[46]

Nanya Bhupala defines Tana like this. Kallinatha has followed him.

"परस्परेण तन्यन्त इति तान संज्ञा लभन्ते।।६५।।
तनु विस्तार इत्यस्माद् धातोः कर्मणि तत्र तान सिद्धिः।[47]

Nanya Bhupala gives a vast description and varieties of Tanas. He quotes Narada of 'Naradiya Shiksha' and Bharata as accepting 49 and 84 Tanas. But he believes that by Prastara Kriya there might be thousands of Tanas. Nanya Bhupala again expounds a new idea—

सम्पूर्ण-स्वर-ताना ग्रामाः राग-मूल-रागाः,
षट् स्वर-ताना भाषा-विभाषाः। पञ्चस्वर-ताना
अन्तर भाषा-श्चतुःस्वर तानाः क्रियाङ्ग-रागानुत्पादयंति, इति
स्थितम् (६७)"[48]

He justifies the above fact as an already existing theory, i.e., Grama Raga and Root Ragas have seven noted Tana. Six noted Tana produces Bhasha and Vibhasha Raga. Antara Bhasha Ragas are evolved from five noted Tana. Tanas with four notes produce Kriyanga Ragas.

Again Nanya Bhupala explains that Narada of Naradiya Shiksha has given the number of Tanas (49) which are used in Yajnas, whereas Bharata's 84 Tanas are used in music.

"सामगाने प्रयुज्यन्ते तानाः यज्ञोपयोगिनः।
गीतोपयोगिनस्ताना भरतेनोपदर्शिताः।।३८।।"[49]

Nanya Bhupala enumerates more than 19,000 Tanas in all. The names of the eighty-four Tanas are given as Agnistoma, etc., are the names of Yajnas. Dattila mentions that these Tanas are called as Agnistoma, etc., by Narada. By singing them, one may attain the same result as from performing the Yajna itself.

Mukund Lath, the author of "Dattilam—A Study", states, "The names Agnistoma, etc., given to Tanas are not to be found in the extant 'Naradiya Shiksha' (ascribed to Narada) but that they were known through an ancient and unbroken tradition, is testified by the fact that roughly the same list of names is obtained in the Vayu Purana, the Brihaddeshi, 'Sangita Ratnakara', the 'Sangita Raja' and other texts."

Matanga names the eighty-four Tanas in his 'Brihaddeshi'. These names are basically the names of various Yajnas (forms of offerings to various gods) to get the desires fulfilled. It is accepted by one and all that the Tanas bestow the same boons as performing the particular Yajṇa.

Now Nanya Bhupala enumerates some five thousand and forty Tanas adopting Shadava, Oudava and Poorna note patterns. He has described elaborately the Tanas with their names, deities, etc. His counting ends like this in the concluding sloka-

"इति सप्ततियुक्ता स्यादष्टशती तैस्यधिका।
ऊनविंशतिः साहस्त्री तानाः स्युः समुदायतः।।"[50]

Sharngdeva mentions the eighty-four names of Tanas and classifies them according to the notes — (five and six) they have and to the Gramas to which they belong. He also provides the information about the permutations and combinations of Oudava and Shadava Tanas. He predicts the result of singing those Tanas in a single line thus —

"यद्यत्नामा यस्तानस्तस्य तत्फलमिष्यते।"[51]

Narada of 'Sangita Makaranda' gives a very short account of Tanas. He introduces the Tanas like this —

तानाश्चतुरशीतिस्तु ता एतस्मिन्निरूपिता।
अग्निष्टोमादि नामानि तैरुक्ता नारदादिभिः।।"[52]

and the next line fails to make any clear impact —

"देवनारदयोगेन तत्पुण्योत्पादनाय ते।"

Narada neither gives the names of the Tanas nor describes them. Bharata gives eighty-four Tanas evolving from two Gramas and Narada of 'Naradiya Shiksha' mentions forty-nine Tanas out of three Gramas. But Narada of 'Sangita Makaranda' does not mention the number of Gramas involved in producing eighty-four Tanas. He has devoted only two slokas for the Tana and then Kuta Tanas are mentioned in another sloka. The first two lines about Tanas are as follows —

सप्तस्वरास्तथा सप्तमूर्च्छना याः प्रकीर्तिताः
तानाः चतुरशीतिस्तु ता एवास्मिन्निरूपिताः।"[53]

According to Narada, Tanas, evolve from the seven Murchanas based on seven notes and eighty-four in number are named after the Yajnas. The Tanas are supposed to fulfil the wishes of the singer as the performance of Yajnas.

Kuta Tanas

Kuta Tanas are also a group of notes consisting of seven, six or five notes, but, not in the usual order of descending or ascending sequence of a scale. Narada of 'Sangita Makaranda' defines Kuta Tana thus —

"क्रममुत्सृज्य तन्त्रीणां तानान्ये मूर्च्छनासु याः
अपूर्णाश्चैव पूर्णाश्च कूटतानास्तु ते स्मृताः
पूर्णाः पञ्चसहस्त्राणि त्रयस्त्रिंशश्च सोभयाः।
कथयन्ति प्रतिग्राममुपयोगेन धेनुना।।१००।।"[54]

He gives the number of Purna and Apurna Kuta Tanas as five hundred and thirty-three in all. Narada does not describe the Kuta Tanas with their scale as is done by Sharngdeva, Nanya Bhupala, Matanga and others. He remarks that Kuta Tanas are derived by using each one of the Gramas.

Bharata does not give much importance to Kuta Tanas. Dattila defines Kuta Tanas with their number as Narada of 'Sangita Makaranda'.

"क्रममुत्सृज्यतन्त्रीणां तननै मूर्च्छनास्तु याः
पूर्णाश्चैवाप्यपूर्णाश्च कूटतानास्तु ते स्मृता।"

Playing the strings by breaking the existing sequencial order makes Kuta Tanas. The order of a Murchana is disturbed by playing and leaving the notes at random is called Kuta Tana, i.e., Sa- Ga - Ri - Pa - Ma - Dha - Ni is a Kuta Tana (Purna), while a Apurna Tana is Sa, Ga, Ma, Dha, Pa, Ni (six noted — Shadava).

In short, the Tanas help to establish a Raga and to find the notes in all the registers. At that time, Tanas and Kuta Tanas were mathematically derived from the seven notes. There were some notes which could never be omitted, i.e., Madhyama, some notes were not omitted in one Grama while others were not omitted in another Grama. The more strict rules and regulations pertaining to the practical side of music required these pre-planning and calculations of Tanas and other such factors. As music was used for ritualistic purposes, incorrect music was capable of creating harm by displeasing the deities instead of pleasing them.

Vritti

The term Vritti is used in many ways and has various meanings also. But here, it is related with the importance of instruments and vocal music in a particular programme or more accurately in a song number. They are threefold: Dakshina, Vritti and Chitra. At that time, vocal music was given priority over instruments as it had Svara, Tala and Pada as well. But it is also an established fact that the scholars and authors of those days had a through knowledge of instruments. They understood the drawbacks of human voice with its instability and shortcomings as well to exhibit any microscopic differences of Shrutis etc.

Now, the vocal music was and is always accompanied by instruments. But the portions played by instruments and sung by the vocalists are planned according to these three Vrittis.

"दक्षिणा वृत्ति चित्रा च वृत्तिस्तानास्वयं विधिः
प्रधानं गीतंमुभयं वाद्यं चेति तथा क्रमम्।"[55]

The same sloka is found in 'Dattilam' also.

Dakshina

When vocal music is prominent and the part played by instrument is less, it is named as Dakshina Vritti.

Vritti

In this type both Vocal and Instrumental music are equally applied and none is more important than the other.

Chitra

This again is the reverse of Dakshina. Instrumental music dominates the song (vocal) in Chitra Vritti. Vocal part is less than instrument.

There is another type called Shuska when only instruments are used to create a special effect without any vocal part. This is more used in dramaturgy. In 'Natya Shastra' the same types of description regarding Vrittis are given—

"तिस्रस्तु वृत्तयः चित्रा दक्षिणा वृत्ति संज्ञिताः।
वाद्य गीतोभय गुणा निर्दिष्टास्ता यथाक्रमम्।"[56]

Bharata describes these Vrittis giving more attributes about them, i.e., *Chitra Vritti* has instrumental music, fast Laya, equal Yati, and starts before the beat — 'Anagata Graha'. Abhinava Gupta explains that when Chitra Vritti is devoid of vocal accompaniment it is called Shuska. As for the name of 'Vritti' he says that the term Vritti means the part played by instruments and vocal music, so it is named as 'Vritti', because it has the natural property of the term Vritti—equal importance to vocal and instrumental music.

"यत्र सममेव द्वयोर्व्यवहारस्तत्र साम्येन वर्तनाद् वृत्तिर्नाम।"[57]

Jati

This is the most discussed and important topic of music of the past. These Jatis are called the 'Raga Mata's'. Bharata has remarked that whatever is sung in the world, comes under Jatis and nothing is beyond Jatis. But, Narada of 'Sangita Makaranda' does not pay much attention to Jatis except naming them. He mentions at first two types of Sadharana — Svara Sadharana and Jati Sadharana. Those Jatis having Sadharana notes, i.e., Kakali, etc. are known as Sadharana Jati.

Narada of Sangita Makaranda's is silence about Jatis

confirms that his system of music is entirely different from the then prevalent system, though he affirms that eighteen Jatis are named by Brahma.

"जातयोऽष्टादश ह्येव ब्रह्मणागदिताः पुरा।
तद्विदित्वा नारदेन गीत रूपाणि वर्णयन्।"[58]

Narada gives the names of eighteen Jatis — seven from Shadja Grama and eleven from Madhyama Grama. Others, including Bharata have divided them as Shuddha and Vikrita Jatis. The copyist has played his part in giving the incorrect and incomplete names which do not make any sense, but correct version of slokas are found in 'Natya Shastra'. The names of Jatis are given in slokas 105 to 109 of 'Sangita Makaranda'.

"षड्जश्च ऋषभश्चैव धैवते च निषादके
षड्जादिश्चैपरा चैव ततो वै षड्जकैशिकी।
षड्जमध्या तथा चैव षड्ज ग्राम समाश्रिता।
अथ रागान् प्रवक्ष्यामि मध्यम ग्राम संश्रयान्।
शुद्ध मध्यस्तथा शुद्ध तारादि शुद्धका
गान्धार मध्यमा चैव गान्धारादि व्यवस्थिता।
पंचमोदीच्यवा चैव सन्धयन्ति तथैव च
कूर्मारवा च विज्ञेया तथानी कैशिकी तथा"

These names are given below in correct form.

Shadja Grama

1. Shadji — षाड्जी
2. Arshabhi — आर्षभी
3. Dhaivati — धैवती
4. Nishadini — निषादिनी
5. Shadjodichyavati — षड्जोदीच्यवती
6. Shadja Kaishiki — षड्ज कैशिकी
7. Shadja Madhyama — षड्जमध्यमा

Madhyama Grama

1. Gandhari — गान्धारी
2. Madhyama — मध्यमा
3. Gandharodichyava — गान्धारोदीच्यवा
4. Panchami — पंचमी
5. Rakta Gandhari — रक्ता गान्धारी
6. Gandhara Panchama — गान्धार पंचमा
7. Madhyamodichyava — मध्यमोदीच्यवा
8. Nandayanti — नंदयंति
9. Kurma Ravi — कूर्मारवी
10. Andhri — आंध्री
11. Kaishiki — कैशिकी

Narada of 'Sangita Makaranda' does not categorise the Jatis as Shuddha Vikrita. He gives the names according to their Gramas but does not mention anything about them.

This shows that his work is entirely based on a different concept which respects Murchanas, yet it is not based upon Jatis.

Alankaras and Varnas are dealt in the next chapter— second pada of Sangitadhyaya. They are mentioned as the parts of the Veena which represents the music as a whole. Narada mentions only 14 Alankaras and not 19 as accounted by himself. They are —

1. Prasannadi
2. Prasannanta
3. Prasanna-adhyanta
4. Prasanna madhya
5. Kramaduchita (Krama Rechita)

6. Bindu
7. Nirvrita (The alankaras no. 7 and 8 are mentioned as one in 'Dattilam'.)
8. Pravrita
9. Prekho (Prenkha)
10. Vihvala
11. Kampita
12. Kupita
13. Vijrumbhita
14. Vivardhana.

Perhaps, he has counted the Varnas also as Alankara, because Sharngdeva divides his Alankaras into four types of Varnas, that is, Sthayi Gata Alankara, etc., (based on Sthayi Varnas).

Dattila names only thirteen Alankaras by counting Nivrita and Pravrita as one. Bharata, Matanga and Nanya Bhupala mention about thirty-three Alankaras—Sharngdeva exceeds all by giving sixty-three Alankaras, and the later authors follow him. According to Sharngdeva —

विशिष्ट वर्ण संदर्भः अलंकारं प्रचक्षते।

Alankara is the embellishment made up of specific Varnas. Bharata says —

"शशिना रहितेव निशा विजलेव नदी लता विपुष्पेव
अविभूषितेव च स्त्री गीतिरलङ्कारहीना स्यात्।।"[59]

Alankara is an important topic which deserves to be discussed in detail. But as Narada of 'Sangita Makaranda' does not pay much attention to the Alankaras they are not discussed in detail.

Gramas and Murchanas are treated elaborately by Narada of 'Sangita Makaranda'. Though there are too many errors committed by the copyist, it is not incomprehensible. Because, the subject is well known and dealt by authors of the past and the present. Both the Gramas and Murchana systems may be said to have become extinct in the sense that the meaning and application have changed.

'Sangita Makaranda' is the earliest work which speaks about the three Gramas and on the note arrangement of 'Ga' Grama, which is quoted by Sharngdeva.

The seven Murchanas of Gandhara Grama are given and their names correspond with the names mentioned by 'Naradiya Shiksha'. In 'Naradiya Shiksha' the governing bodies of Murchanas are given but 'Sangita Makaranda' does not follow the suit. Probably, the Gandhara Grama is the most ancient Grama belonging to Vedic or pre-Vedic period. The Shadja Grama and Madhyama Grama are similar to the Gramas of the other authors. He gives the scale of Madhyama Grama in descending order corresponding to Vedic scale, i.e., Ma - Ga - Ri - Sa - Ni - Dha - Pa. His three Gramas have Brahma, Vishnu and Maheshwara as their presiding deities.

Narada attributes importance to the note Shadja, which has more consonants and Madhyama's importance depends upon its indispensability. 'Ma' had that feature in the past which 'Sa' has now. The Svaramandala of Gandhara Grama, reproduced in this work is not from the 'Sangita Makaranda'. In 'Sangita Makaranda', though the names of Murchanas of Ga Grama appear their starting notes are not given. But the Grama portion of 'Sangita Makaranda' is complete in itself, though the order of arrangement of the topic is interrupted by other topics like names of Shruti and Svara, etc.

In 'Sangita Makaranda', the definition of Murchana is given in a very simple manner without derivation. Narada gives the seven names of Murchanas of all the three Gramas. He gives the Shadja of Shadja Grama and Madhyama of Madhyama Grama as the starting note of the first Murchana of each respective Grama. The subsequent Murchanas start from the lower note next to the starting note of the first Murchana. His definition of Murchana appears in the middle after naming the twenty-one Murchanas. According to Narada of 'Sangita Makaranda' Murchanas can be started either using the lower and middle octave, or middle and upper octave as the occasion demands. Rajani which starts on the note 'Ni' can be placed on the note 'Sa' while 'Harinashva' which starts from 'Ga' can be started from 'Ma'; the starting notes of Shadja and Madhyama Grama. The author wants to say that the starting notes of all Murchanas can be replaced by the initial note of the two Gramas, to make the starting of all Murchanas on one basic note, yet without changing the Shruti intervals.This relaxation of the system is provided to stabilise the starting notes of the Shadja Grama and Madhyama Grama; 'Sa' and 'Ma' yet maintaining the interval of Svara and Shruti of each Murchana intact. Narada for the first time has left out the names of deities of Murchanas whereas Narada of 'Naradiya Shiksha', and Nanya Bhupala have given the names of deities. His four types of Murchanas — Shuddha, Santara, Kakali Kalita and Sadvayopeta—are very practical and justified as they are original.

The only drawback in the work is its disarrangement and disorderly handling of the topics. All the terms and topics are there, but scattered everywhere and one has to search for the points and collect them. Sometimes, the definition comes in the end or middle and some explanations get mixed up with other topics. The names of the Murchanas appear thrice, but one cannot make out the names of the Murchanas without previous knowledge or consulting of other works. However, Murchanas, their definition, names, starting notes and types are given and explained properly. The Tanas are treated briefly but the purpose is served. Mostly the works of that period are similar except 'Bharata Bhashyam' or 'Sangita Ratnakara'. Moreover, 'Sangita Makaranda' is not an extensive work. It needs rearrangement and text correction.

REFERENCES

1. *Sangita Makaranda*, p. 5.
2. *Naradiya Shiksha*, p. 16.
3. *Natya Shastra*, vol. 2, p. 15.
4. *Brihaddeshi*, p. 17.

5. *Ibid.*
6. *Bharata Bhashyam,* vol. 1. p. 72,
7. *Sangita Ratnakara,* vol. I, p. 99.
8. *Bharata Bhashyam,* Part I, p. 113.
9. *Sangita Makaranda,* p. 5.
10. *Ibid.*
11. *Sangita Ratnakara,* vol. I, p. 100.
12. *Sangita Makaranda,* p. 5.
13. *Ibid.*
14. *Ibid.*
15. *Bharata Bhashyam,* Part I.
16. *Dattilam,* Sl. 11, p.1.
17. *Brihaddeshi,* Sl. 91, p. 17.
18. *Bharata Bhashyam,* vol. I, p. 76.
19. *Ibid.,* p. 72.
20. *Ibid.*
21. *Ibid.,* p. 75.
22. *Sangita Makaranda,* p. 7.
23. *Sangita Ratnakara,* vol. I, p. 102.
24. *Bharata Bhashyam,* part I, p. 76.
25. *Natya Shastra,* vol. IV, ch. 28, p. 25.
26. *Brihaddeshi,* p. 17.
27. *Bharata Bhashyam,* part I, p. 111.
28. *Sangita Makaranda,* p. 7
29. *Sangita Samayasaram,* p. 16.
30. *Bharata Bhashya,* part I, p. 114.
31. *Ibid.,* p. 113.
32. Brihaddeshi, *Sangita,* May, 1975.
33. *Sangita Ratnakara,* vol. I, p. 105.
34. *Brihaddeshi,* p. 20.
35. *Natya Shastra,* Chapter 28, p. 25.
36. *Bharata Bhashyam,* part I, p. 115.
37. *Sangita Makaranda,* p. 7.
38. *Sangita Ratnakara,* Vol. I, p. 105.
39. *Natya Shastra,* p. 27.
40. *Sangita Makaranda,* p. 7.
41. *Ibid.,* p. 8.

42. *Dattilam*, p. 10.
43. *Sangita Ratnakara*, Vol. I, p. 115.
44. *Naradiya Shiksha*, p. 16
45. *Natya Shastra*, chapter 28, p. 27.
46. Brihaddeshi, p. 20. *Sangita*, May, 1975.
47. *Bharata Bhashyam* p. 125
48. *Bharata Bhashyam*, part I, p. 128.
49. *Ibid.*, p. 130.
50. *Ibid.*, p. 134.
51. *Sangita Ratnakara*, Vol. I, p. 227.
52. *Sangita Makaranda*, p. 10.
53. *Ibid.*
54. *Ibid.*, क्रममुत्सृज्य *appears as* क्रममुद्गन्थ्य in the manuscript.
55. *Ibid.*
56. *Natya Shastra*, Chapter 29, p. 100.
57. *Ibid.*, p.101
58. *Sangita Makaranda*, p. 10
59. *Natya Shastra*, Chapter 29, p. 92.

6

The Physical Body of Music

This chapter appears in the second pada of Sangitadhyaya and the topic might have appeared as the introductory. While the first pada of Sangitadhyaya is considerably longer one comprising 114 slokas, this one has only twenty-four slokas. It cannot be justified as the gist of 'Sangita Makaranda.' It is very unique in the sense that no contemporary or ancient authors have a similar description of music like Sangita Deha Nirupanam. After delineating Nada, Shruti, Svara, Grama, Murchana, Tanas and other miscellaneous terms, Narada of 'Sangita Makaranda' presents this picturesque comparison of Veena and music. As the topic indicates, the 24 slokas are dedicated to the imaginary body of music. The Vedic comparison of Daravi Veena and Daivi Veena seems to be the basic principle of this description. Here the music with its parts, terms and subjects are represented and portrayed as a Veena. This is not a type of Uddeshadhyaya of 'Sangita Makaranda'. Because it does not cover all the subjects dealt in 'Sangita Makaranda'.

This unusual description of music again denotes the imaginary as well as idolising tendency of the author. The Veena has many parts and music too is made up of many small parts like notes, Murchanas, Grama and ideas like Vadi, Samvadi, etc. Therefore, the parts which make a whole

Veena are compared with the theoretical parts of the music. Iconography was and is the tradition with India. Every being of the world is the reflection of cosmic power and everything has a life within its lifeless frame.

In the beginning, he visualises the music as *Nada Brahma*, the underlying consciousness of every being that should be evoked and worshipped by all. This forthcoming description of music, according to Narada, would entertain the kings and enrich the knowledge of the scholar. Music which lives in the Alapa, notes and songs, however, is a natural gift to human beings from Brahma and is just like a Veena. Though, the music is abstract without any visible form, yet is compared with a Veena that is given by Brahma to Narada.

"वीणादेहं प्रवक्ष्यामि तदङ्गानि यथा क्रमम्।"

Now the body or form of the Veena is compared with music. The following description of the Veena depicting the music is presented by Narada.

Three Gramas form the three heads of Veena with three faces called Mandra, Madhya and Tara Sthana. The musical Veena has four tongues—Vadi, Samvadi, Anuvadi and Vivadi. The four types of instruments form the playing technique of the Veena. The mridanga, Deshi music, etc., are the side techniques (Upanga). This Veena (music) has seven eyes made from seven notes and twenty-two Shrutis are its ears. The Veena has two hands formed by Ragalapti and Roopakalapti.

The Veena has generally four materials — two types of wood, (Sandal and Daru) Alabu and Tantri or strings. As the Svaras have four classes according to their Shruti divisions, the four materials represent four types of caste system.

Sandalwood	—	Brahmins
Daru (wood)	—	Kshatriyas
Alabu Gourd	—	Vaishyas
Tantri Strings	—	Shudras.

The deities presiding the types of Ragas of this Veena are:

Brahma—Shadava, Rudra—Oudava and Vishnu—Sampurana. There are endless Ragas emanating from this Sangita Veena.

Narada gives the four Varnas and 14 or 13 Alankaras which are already discussed. Gamakas are 19, according to Narada of 'Sangita Makaranda', and serve as the feet of the music. Narada observes that this Veena is neither male nor female, as such it is only a personification of music, which is Brahma Veena. He infers that whoever will listen to this pious description of Veena representing the music will certainly be relieved from his sins. He will beget sons and grandsons, acquire wealth and reap good harvest. His enemies will be uprooted and his kingdom will expand and most of all, he will attain salvation.

The most important aspect of the chapter is the names of the scholars and musical personalities given by Narada, which provide some clues to the time period of the author, which is already discussed in the third chapter.

This chapter, as such has no theoretical value, as the terms appearing are not defined or explained, but occur only as the various parts of the musical Veena.

7

Classification of Ragas

Ragas are the main part of Indian music. Raga is something very different in nature from the melody of western music. At present the melody-based music survives only in India. The prominent feature of Indian music is Raga, which has no counter-part in any music of the more progressive countries. The term Raga is first named and defined by Matanga.

"योऽसौ ध्वनि विशेषस्तु स्वरवर्ण विभूषितः।
रंजको जन चित्तानां स च राग उदाहृतः ।।

This definition of Raga is applicable even today. The main property of Raga is "रंजको जन चित्तानां" the pleasing quality i.e., to please the minds of the people. Ragas are formed with notes and varnas (four types of patterns of notes).

Narada of 'Sangita Makaranda' gives much importance to Ragas in general and the various kinds of classifications prevalent at that time. The Ragas are discussed in the third part of Sangitadhyaya consisting of 92 slokas.

Raga is not defined by Narada of 'Sangita Makaranda'. Narada of 'Naradiya Shiksha' mentions about Grama Ragas and has enumerated the seven Grama Ragas with their names. Bharata does not mention about Ragas in the real sense, though the word Raga occurs five times in 'Natya

Shastra'. Yet, there is a sloka naming five Grama Ragas with their use in the drama. Matanga, Nanya Bhupala and Sharngdeva describe about the Ragas. Matanga's work 'Brihaddeshi' is incomplete as far as the available text is concerned. Two parts of the 'Bharata Bhashyam' are only published, the second part contains Ragadhyaya, which has only Ragas based on Shadja Grama and some Ragas of Madhyama Grama. All the Ragas appearing in 'Sangita Makaranda' cannot be described in full because Narada does not provide any practical hints about the Ragas, i.e., types of notes, etc. Furthermore 'Sangita Makaranda' gives the singing time of certain Ragas, starting notes of Sampurana and other two types Ragas, omitting notes of Shadava and Oudava Ragas and various types of classification of Ragas—Masculine, Feminine and Neuter Ragas, Ragas and their Bharyas etc. Obviously, these descriptions are of no help in reconstructing the Ragas mentioned in 'Sangita Makaranda'. However, the reconstruction of the Ragas of past is not possible, even of Sharngdeva, as the notes of the Ragas can not be compared with the present notes. Murchana system, it seems, was out of practice during the time of Sharngdeva. It is not possible to comprehend the practical side of the Ragas of 'Sangita Makaranda' or of any other work upto 'Sangita Ratnakara'. Therefore, the Ragas of 'Sangita Makaranda' are described as they appears in the text and are compared with the Ragas of 'Brihaddeshi', 'Bharata Bhashyam' and 'Sangita Ratnakara', wherever possible, i.e., subject to the presence of the particular Ragas in these works.

In the work of 'Sangita Makaranda' Narada stresses on his first hand information from Brahma about all the subjects concerned. Here in this chapter too Narada asks Brahma with folded hands to enlighten him about the singing time of Ragas --

कति रागा प्रगातव्या प्रभाते सप्त सुस्वराः
तथैव कति रागाश्च केनात्र प्रतिपादिताः ।[1]

And it is Brahma Himself who appreciates the question and replies :

"तत्सर्वं प्रवक्ष्यामि रागवेला निर्णयम्

यत्सुरैस्तन्न विज्ञातं नर किन्नरनायकैः
देशी राग रहस्यं च साम्प्रतं श्रुणु यत्नतः।"[2]

Here the important point to note is the term "Deshi Raga" which indicates the type of Ragas described in this work. 'Sangita Makaranda' describes about Deshi Ragas of seventh and eighth century.

'Sangita Makaranda' explains about many types of Raga classification. Ragas are classified according to their time of singing, the number of notes they take; their gender and the general classification followed at that time, i.e., Raga having three, five or six wives each.

With above mentioned dialogue between Narada and Brahma, the classification of Ragas according to the time of their singing begins, but the term Raga is neither defined nor described.

In 'Naradiya Shiksha', Harivamsha and Kudumiamalai inscriptions, Grama Ragas are described. In Harivamsha, six Grama Ragas (**षट् ग्राम रागा**) are mentioned. 'Naradiya Shiksha' and 'Kudumiamalai' inscriptions mention seven Grama Ragas, whereas Bharata has named only five Grama Ragas.

Matanga has described seven Geetis and based his Ragas on these seven Geetis. They are—Shuddha, Bhinna, Goudi, Raga (vesari) Sadharani, Bhasha and Vibhasha Geetis. Matanga says that basically there are only five Geetis—Shuddha, Bhinna, Goudi, Vesara, and Sadharana, but Yashtika added three more—Bhasha, Vibhasha and Antarabhasha. Shardula preferred only one more Geeti, i.e., Bhasha Geeti. Durgashakti accepts only five basical Geetis. However, the Geetis of Bharata are totally different, he speaks about Padashrita Geetis only. They are Magadhi, Ardha Magadhi, Prathula and Sambhavita. But Narada does not describe any Geetis or Grama Ragas as the basis of his Ragas. His approach to the subject of Raga is peculiar. He commences with the time of singing of the Ragas. He categorises them into two classes—Suryamsha and Chandramansha, i.e., Ragas related to the sun and affiliated to the moon respectively.

'Sangita Makaranda' is the earliest work where the times of Ragas are discussed. The time theory which is still practised in Hindustani classical music has lost its importance in Carnatic music. However, the time theory belongs to the Vedic period and is not a recent development. It has its nucleus in the Soma Yajna and its three Savanas—Pratah (morning), Madhyanha (noon) and Aparahna (afternoon).

The different kinds of Sama hymns are assigned to various seasons.

"रथान्तर साम त्रिवृत्स्तोमो वसन्त ऋतुः।
वृहत्साम दशस्तोमा ग्रीष्म ऋतुः।
वैरूप पंचसाम सप्तदशस्तोमो वर्षा ऋतुः।
शाक्वररैवते सामनी......हेमन्त ऋतु।"[3]

Some particular 'Samas' dedicated to certain gods namely—Vasava, Rudra, Vishvedeva, etc., are to be sung in the morning, noon and afternoon Savanas according to Chandogya Upanishad.[4]

Therefore the time theory of the music prevailed there from the Vedic period.

Bharata has mentioned the time for using the Dhruvas—Praveshiki, Naiskramiki and Akshepaki, but he is not very particular about the singing side. He is of the opinion that the particular Dhruva should be used to indicate the time—

"प्रावेशिक्याश्रया यास्तु पूर्वाह्मार्धे तु ताः स्मृताः।
नक्तन्दिव समुत्थास्तु नैष्कामिकयाः स्वकालजाः
सौभ्याः पूर्वाह्मकाले तु मध्याह्ने दीप्तिसंश्रयाः।
अपराह्ने तथा मध्याः (सशोकाश्च) संध्यायां करुणाश्रयाः।"[5]

But Bharata is more concerned with the emotions and incidents that take place on a particular time and is not much interested in the time theory of music. Bharata believes that indication of time should be given by a particular Dhruva. Forenoon should be indicated by Praveshiki Dhruva and so on.

Matanga is the first and earliest author to mention the term Raga, but his available text (incomplete) does not indicate anything about the time of Ragas. Bharata and Dattila do not mention about the time theory of Jatis. Bharata deals in Gandharva as a part of dramaturgy only and not as an independent subject. The actual time theory of Ragas cannot be managed within the short limit of time used in dramaturgy.

After 'Sangita Makaranda', 'Bharata Bhashyam' discusses, about the time theory. Nanya Bhupala accords morning, noon and afternoon time to the three Gramas—Shadja, Madhyama and Gandhara respectively. He mentions time and seasons, during which the Gramas, Geetis are to be used. In the fifth Adhyaya of 'Bharata Bhashyam' (Part I) the time and seasons of Gramas along with time and seasons of Ragas are also given, e.g., Takka and Kakubha.

"शुद्धा भिन्ना च या गीतिरायामे प्रथमे मता।
मध्य-प्रहर-युग्मे च गौड़ी गीति प्रशस्यते।
गीतिर्या वेसरा नाम सर्व गृहण कारिणी (हारिणी)
दिनस्य प्रथमे भागे सा गेया गीत वेदिभिः।
"मध्य-प्रहर युग्मे च गौड़ी गीतिः प्रशस्यते।"[6]

Nanya Bhupala allocates times to the five Geetis Shuddha, Bhinna, Goudi and Vesara and Sadharani and states that Ragas belonging to the Geetis should be sung in the time of that particular Geetis.

"यस्य यस्य तु रागस्य या या भाषा प्रकीर्त्तिता
तस्य तस्यैव च काले सा तासामपि कीर्त्तिताः।"[7]

Moreover, he is not much serious in following the time concept. According to Nanya Bhupala, the time of the Raga should be followed only to get boons, name and fame, but Ragas can be sung at any time to get one's daily needs.

"अपां श्रेयो-विशेषाय कालस्य नियमः स्मृतः
गीयो सर्व काले तु सर्वा नित्यार्थ सिद्धये।"[8]

From 'Sangita Makaranda' onwards, the time concept of

Ragas is dealt by all the authors, alloting the time to the Ragas.

Sharngdeva has given the singing time for Grama Ragas only. Besides the time and season for twenty Ragas. He does not furnish the time for singing Bhasha Ragas, Upanga or Kriyanga or any other Ragas. But as his Ragas are based on Grama Ragas only, perhaps the time of the Grama Raga might be applicable to their Bhashas and other Ragas derived from that particular Grama Raga. He says—

"भिन्न कैशिकः—
गेयोऽह्नः प्रथमे यामे शिशिरे शिववल्लभे।[9]

In 'Sangita Makaranda', Narada at first mentions the names of Ragas according to their time of singing. His third pada of Sangitadhyaya starts with the heading "अथ राग नामान्युच्यन्ते" and it literally suits the chapter. Because, Narada of 'Sangita Makaranda' gives the names of the different classes of Ragas with a little or no description, confining only to Suryansha and Chandransha Ragas. In between, he names Pratahkala (morning) and Madhyanha (noon time) Ragas, apportioning them with the appropriate Praharas. 'Praharas' or 'Yamas' are eight in a day of twenty-four hours. Each is of three hours duration and are divided in day and night—four praharas each. The Ragas coming under 'Suryansha Ragas', supposed to be sung in the morning are 19 in number and are named below—

1. Gandhara
2. Deva Gandhara
3. Dhannasi
4. Saindhavi
5. Narayani
6. Gurjari
7. Bangala
8. Pala (ta) Manjari
9. Lalita
10. Andola Srika
11. Sourashtreya
12. Jaya Sakshika
13. Mahlara
14. Samavedi

15. Vasanta
16. Shuddha Bhairava
17. Velavali
18. Bhupala
19. Soma Raga.

Now the Ragas of noon time are mentioned below and they are 14 in all.

1. Shankarabharana
2. Poorva
3. Balahamsa
4. Deshi
5. Manohari
6. Saveri
7. Dombuli
8. Kambhoji
9. Gopi Kambhoji
10. Kaishiki
11. Madhu Madhavi
12. Bahuli (2 types)
13. Mukhari
14. Mangala Koushika

Narada of 'Sangita Makaranda' remarks —

"एते रागविशेषास्तु प्रातःकाले तु देवताः।"

that these Ragas have morning deities.

After this list of daytime Ragas, 17 names of Chandramansha Ragas are given which include Goudi, unanimously accepted as a noon Raga by all the authors including Narada of 'Sangita Makaranda'.

1. Shuddha Nata
2. Salag Nata
3. Shuddha Varatika
4. Goula
5. Malava Gouda
6. Shri Raga
7. Ahari
8. Ramakriti
9. Ranji
10. Chaya
11. Sarva Vartika
12. Varatika
13. Dravatika
14. Deshi
15. Naga Varatika
16. Karnata
17. Goudi

In accordance to the author by singing these Ragas in the evening, one may get wealth in abundance.

Narada has not written these comments systematically after the particular list of Ragas. One has to search for every explanation, comments, topics and then arrange them properly to make sense.

The names are mostly incorrect, repeated twice or thrice and every time they appear with a slight change in the spelling, which is misleading and confusing as well. For example, Malhara appears as Malhara, Malahari, Malvari, etc. Dhanashri appears as Dhannasi, Dhanyasi, Dhannashi and Dhannashri. There are many such misspellings and sometimes the name totally changes, i.e., Ramakriti as Ramakriya or Ramakri. Patamanjari as Palamanjari, Padamanji and Phadavanji.

From these lists, one can only know that Ragas are distributed among the eight praharas of the day as is emulated at present. But the principles of the dividing factor remain inaccessible which is but natural. Because, Narada does not provide any clear instructions regarding the principles.

Thereafter Narada of 'Sangita Makaranda' explains further that the Ragas belonging to daytime or night should be allotted a similar times in a Prahara before sunrise (night) or a Prahara after sunrise (daytime).

"प्रहरैकोदयादर्वाक् प्रहरैकोदयोपरि।
देशाक्षी भैरवा शुद्धा नादं यत्प्रहरोंद्भवम्।"

Thus Narada mentions that these Ragas—Deshakshi and Shuddha Bhairava have been allotted the time—three hours from the sunrise, In the same way, Chandramansha Ragas Varatika; Dravatika should be sung in the same time, i.e., three hours from the sunset.

Malhari, Mahuri and Andoli get the morning time—three hours after sunrise, while Chandramansha Ragas—Ramakriti; Chayanata and Ranji should be sung during the three hours after sunset.

The Gouda Ragas belongs to the noon time. Shuddha, Salanga Nataka should be sung after three Praharas of the sunset. With these Ragas, Narada of 'Sangita Makaranda' concludes his allocation of time to the Ragas.

"एवं कालविधि ज्ञात्वा गायेद्यः स सुखी भवेत्।"

Morning Ragas	*Time*
1. Deshakshi 2. Bhairava Shuddha	First Prahara of sunrise
3. Malhari 4. Mahuri 5. Andoli	A prahara after sunrise
Night Ragas	*Time*
1. Varatika 2. Shuddha Dravati	During the Prahara before sunrise
3. Ramakriti 4. Chaya Nata 5. Rangaka	A Prahara before sunrise
6. Gouda Ragas	Noon time
7. & 8. Shuddha, Salanga Natika	After three Praharas (of sunset)

After giving the time of five morning and five evening Ragas, Narada mentions Gouda Ragas and two night Ragas. The morning and Chandramansha Ragas are balanced accurately. Bhairava and Deshakshi correspond with the evening Ragas of Shuddha Varatika and Dravatika. Both sets have the identical time, one belonging to the morning and the other belonging to the evening but to the same first Prahara before and after sunrise. In the same way, Gouda Ragas and Shuddha Salanga Natas belong to the fourth Prahara of morning and evening.

Narada of 'Sangita Makaranda', proceeds after concluding the time concept with a few examples enlist the consequences of not following the time concept of Ragas. He observes that neglect of the rules regarding the time factor might hurt the Ragas and the listener would suffer from poverty with a short life span.

But there are occasions, when this time concept may be ignored. They are as follows—Singing for spiritual purposes, to praise God, benefactor, on auspicious occasions, i.e. marriage etc. Listening to Raga Bhairavi is an atonement for untimely singing.

The time theory of 'Sangita Makaranda' concludes on this note. Thereafter a list of Ragas is given without introduction or conclusive information about the given list. Though the list appears after the list of the Ragas of Suryansha and Chandramansha, it has nothing to do with the time theory. It cannot be an exhaustive list of Ragas appearing in the 'Sangita Makaranda' because many Ragas are missing in the list which appear afterwards and there are such Ragas also which appear in the list only. They are given below :

1. Shree Raga
2. Malava
3. Malava Kaishika
4. Saveri
5. Megh Ranji
6. Hendola
7. Kaishiki
8. Tundi
9. Turushka Tundi
10. Bangali
11. Mahuri
12. Deva Kriya
13. Raga Hansi
14. Deshakshi
15. Bhairavi
16. Salang Bhairavi
17. Kambhari
18. Karnata Bangala
19. Shuddha Hindolika
20. Punnata
21. Shuddha Nata
22. Sarang Natika

23.	Velavali	39.	Madhu Madhavi
24.	Chaya Nati	40.	Malvari
25.	Raga Rang	41.	Gurjari
26.	Varati	42.	Sourashtri
27.	Dravati	43.	Lalita
28.	Naga Varatika	44.	Naga Dhvani
29.	Karnata Mishra Nati	45.	Kambhoji
30.	Shuddha Varatika	46.	Dhanashri
31.	Kaumodaki	47.	Kolahara
32.	Malhari	48.	Chaya Gouda
33.	Saranga	49.	Rama
34-35.	Two Bahulis	50.	Dombulika
36.	Troti	51.	Vasanta Bhairavi
37.	Pahatika	52.	Saveri
38.	Mukhari	53.	Saindhavi

Repetition of the Ragas are always there as can be seen. These Ragas appear on page 16, slokas 26 to 34.

Saveri is repeated twice and a number of Ragas not included in the list, but mentioned elsewhere are—Ahari, Devagandhari, Ramakriya, Gundakri, Patmanjari, Nilambari etc. The point to note about the list is the absence of Grama Ragas which indicates a totally new concept of Ragas. However there are names of Ragas which appear in 'Brihaddeshi', 'Bharata Bhashyam' and 'Sangita Ratnakara' which will be discussed later.

Raga Classification of other Authors

Many Ragas of 'Sangita Makaranda' are described in 'Brihaddeshi' of Matanga under the heading 'Bhasha Lakshanam', where the Ragas born out of Bhasha Geeti are discussed.

Matanga explains the Bhasha Ragas thus by quoting Yashtika—

"पूर्वं ग्रामद्वयं प्रोक्तं ग्रामरागास्तदुद्भवा।।
ग्राम रागोद्भवा भाषा भाषाभ्यश्च विभाषिकाः।
विभाषाभ्यश्च संजातास्तथा चांतरभाषिका।।
भाषा विभाषा कथितास्त्रयाधिका सप्तर्तिबुधैः।"[10]

There are two Gramas and from them Grama Ragas are born. From these Grama Ragas, Bhasha Geetis are derived, in the similar manner Vibhasha from Bhasha and Vibhasha Ragas produce Antara Bhasha Ragas. This is Yashtika's classification of Raga. The names of Grama Ragas mentioned later by Yashtika are not the seven original Grama Ragas but the Ragas derived from the seven Ragas by adopting five or seven Geetis accordingly, which is not explained clearly.

As Matanga has already stated that his Raga system is based on seven Geetis including Bhasha and Vibhasha he leaves out Antara Bhasha. He mentions 15 Grama Ragas with their number of Bhashas as.

	Ragas (15)		*Bhashas (73)*
1.	Takka	-	16
2.	Malavakaishika	-	8
3.	Kakubha	-	7
4.	Hindolaka	-	5
5.	Panchama	-	10
6.	Bhinna Shadja	-	9
7.	Souvira	-	4
8.	Bhinna Panchama	-	4
9.	Botta	-	1
10.	Malava Panchama	-	1
11.	Takka Kaishika	-	3

12.	Vesara Shadava	-	2
13.	Bhinna Tana	-	1
14.	Gandhara Panchama	-	1
15.	Panchama Shadava	-	1

15 Grama Ragas and 73 Bhashas derived from these Grama Ragas appear in the list. Furthermore the names of the Bhashas are also given by Matanga. His names of Bhashas are feminine whereas the names of the Grama Ragas are masculine. Some of the names of the Ragas appearing in 'Sangita Makaranda' occur in the list of Bhasha Ragas of Matanga, e.g., Gurjari, Saindhavi, Kolahala, Sourashtri, etc. Two Grama Ragas—Malava Kaishika and Hindola are in the general list of Ragas of 'Sangita Makaranda'. The most remarkable point in Raga description of 'Sangita Makaranda' is the absence of main seven Grama Ragas. The term Grama Ragas does not occur anywhere in 'Sangita Makaranda'.

Nanya Bhupala mentions almost similar number of Bhasha Vibhasha Ragas, i.e., 78 and he divides them into three types, namely—Mukhya, Deshakhya and Svarakhya, whereas Matanga mentions four types of Bhashas —

"भाषा चतुर्विधा प्रोक्ता मूलसंकीर्णदेशजाः
छायामात्राश्रयाः प्रोक्ता ग्रामरागे व्यवस्थिताः।"[11]

Nanya Bhupala classifies his Ragas into seven Grama Ragas and six Moola or parent Ragas giving rise to Bhashas —Deshakhya, Svarakhya, Uparaga, Mukhya, Kriyanga, etc. Nanya Bhupala accepts three Gramas with each Grama having its own Ragas, Bhashas and Vibhashas. The general Ragas evolve around five Geetis—Shuddha, Bhinna, Goudi, and Vesara, etc. Nanya Bhupala accepts six Moola Ragas as the parent Ragas of Bhashas and he believes that Matanga also followed the same principle of six Moola Ragas.[12] However, in 'Brihaddeshi' Matanga quotes Yashtika and follows him in accepting 15 Grama Ragas as the parent Ragas of Bhashas and Vibhashas.

सर्वभाषा स्वरूपैस्तु नियतैः क्वचित् मिश्रितैः।

युक्ताः समुपजायते ग्रामरागास्तु ते मताः।
ये च निःशेष भाषाणांमूल-रन्धाश्च हेतवः।
लोकेषु युक्ता बहुधा मूल रागास्तु ते स्मृता।"[13]

Bhashas are taken into account and discussed here because Ragas of 'Sangita Makaranda' similar to the Ragas of other authors, mostly come under the Bhasha and Vibhasha Ragas. Some of the Ragas of 'Sangita Makaranda' can be traced in Bharata Bhashyam too.

In 'Sangita Ratnakara', Sharngdeva enumerates five Grama Ragas adopting five Geetis.

पंचधा ग्रामरागाः स्युः पंच गीति समाश्रयात्[14]

Then he takes the Geetis one by one in their respective order and keeps them in Shadja Grama, Madhyama Grama and derives thirty Grama Ragas in all from the two Gramas. They are:

Gramas	*Geetis*	*No. of Ragas*
Shadja Grama	Shuddha	3
Madhyama Grama	Shuddha	4
Shadja Grama	Bhinna	2
Madhyama Grama	Bhinna	3
Shadja Grama	Goudi	2
Madhyama Grama	Goudi	1
Shadja Grama	Vesara	3
Madhyama Grama	Vesara	3
In both Gramas	Vesara	2
Shadja Grama	Sadharani	3
Madhyama Grama	Sadharani	3
Both Gramas together	Sadharani	1
	Total :	30

Then he names the Ragas, Uparagas—eight Ragas and 20 Upa-Ragas. He enumerates 15 parent Ragas of Bhasha according to Yashtika. His Bhashas are 96, Vibhasha 20, and four Antarabhashas. There are other classifications of Ragas too. They are Poorva Prasiddha and Adhuna Prasiddha, ancient 34 and prevalent at present 50, respectively. Then there are Bhashanga, Raganga and Kriyanga Ragas also. Sharngdeva finally settles down for 264 Ragas in all.

सर्वेषामपि रागाणां मिलितानां शतद्वयं
चतुःषष्ट्यधिकं ब्रूते शाङ्र्गी श्री करणाग्रणि।"[15]

The system of Raga classification of Matanga, Nanya Bhupala and Sharngdeva are described here to have some idea of the Raga system of their periods. Narada of 'Sangita Makaranda' rules out these systems, but he does not follow Narada of 'Naradiya Shiksha' and leaves out the Grama Ragas. His system of classification is vivid, unique and novel. Sharngdeva deals in Grama Ragas and follows Matanga and Nanya Bhupala at times but his "Adhuna Prasiddha Ragas" lets him down and shows the prevalent system of Ragas of his time. During his period the Grama Ragas have already become extinct and Vikrita notes have replaced the Murchana and Sadharana Svara system. Bhasha Ragas and Deshi Ragas became prominent during his time.

The other parallel system was Raga-Ragini system practised according to the Tantra traditions. The age old time theory got prominence and the above system might have been adopted, due to its more simple-to-follow rules. Now the question remains whether Bhasha became Bharya or vice versa. The parent Ragas (15) were, perhaps, reduced to six Moola Ragas and the Bhashas might have transformed into Bharyas and were attached to the six root Ragas; according to Nanya Bhupala and which was accepted by Matanga too.

These are some of the facts concerning the Raga system of the period starting from Matanga to 'Sangita Ratnakara'. 'Sangita Makaranda' is logically placed after 'Brihaddeshi', but it does not follow 'Brihaddeshi' in any way. The system of 'Sangita Makaranda' should be analysed in a more appropriate way, because it has its own principles, system and classification of Ragas besides the time theory and other dissimilar features.

His description of Ragas too is unique. He gives only the starting notes Ragas which denotes the importance of Murchanas in the formation of his Ragas.

Graha Svara

Graha stands for the word "to catch", 'to take' or 'to get' in Sanskrit. In music, 'Graha' means the note to be taken in the beginning of a Raga or the starting note of a Raga. Nowadays, the Shadja is the basic note of all Ragas and approximately all Ragas start with Shadja. Therefore the 'Graha' word lost its meaning of the past. The importance given to the 'Graha' note of Ragas in 'Sangita Makaranda' makes the work more conspicuous.

Narada mentions the starting note of the three types of Ragas — Sampoorna, Shadava and Oudava Ragas. This part of the work is meant to furnish the details of his Ragas (Lakshanam). The Raga Lakshanas given by Matanga, Nanya Bhupala and Sharngdeva are more elaborate and informative while Narada of 'Sangita Makaranda' gives only the starting notes of the Ragas. He takes Sampoorna, Shadava and Oudava Ragas, each as a separate lot and names the starting notes and the omitted note or notes of Shadava or Oudava Ragas. About the Ragas taken by him, he gives the singing time, starting note and naturally the omitted notes.

Giving importance to the starting notes without describing the Grama or Grama Ragas from which they are derived, creates an impression that the Ragas of his work depend upon the starting notes only. Probably, the Murchana system was more prominent at that time, and the Raga depended upon its starting note or the particular Murchana.

Different Murchanas created different Ragas was a generally accepted fact. That the same Murchana could produce various Ragas by changing its 'amsha' (prominent) note and other important notes like 'graha' and omitted notes, etc., was also a well-established fact, which applied to Jatis. In

'Sangita Makaranda', a selected number of Ragas is only described and many Ragas start on Shadja. Thirty Ragas are mentioned with their starting and omitted notes. Eleven Sampoorna Ragas, eleven Shadava and eight Oudava Ragas are given below :

Sampoorna Ragas

	Names	*Graha notes*
1.	Deshakshi	Madhyama
2.	Vasanta	Madhyama
3.	Shuddha Bhairavi	Madhyama
4.	Malavi	Gandhara
5.	Nata	Shadja
6.	Mukhari	Dhaivata
7.	Ahari	Madhyama
8.	Balahamsa	Gandhara
9.	Shuddhavasanta	Shadja
10.	Ramakriya (Shuddha)	Shadja
11.	Varatika (Shuddha)	Shadja

Four similar Graha notes (Shadja and Madhyama) of different Ragas indicate that the Ragas are based on all three Gramas. Another point to note is Panchama, Nishada and Rishabha do not appear as Graha notes, not at least in the list of Sampurana Ragas given in 'Sangita Makaranda'.

Shadava Ragas

	Names	*Graha note*	*Omitted note*
1.	Deva Gandhara	Gandhara	Nishada
2.	Neelambari	Gandhara	Nishada
3.	Shri Raga	Shadja	Gandhara

4. Shuddha Bahuli	Madhyama	Nishada
5. Shuddha Goula	Nishada	Dhaivata
6. Lalita	Shadja	Gandhara
7. Malava Shri	Shadja	Rishabha
8. Bhupala	Gandhara	Shadja
9. Padavanji	Nishada	Rishabha
10. Gundakri	Gandhara	Gandhara ?
11. Kuranji	Madhyama	Nishada

Narada ends the list of Shadava Ragas like this—

"संगृह्य नारदेनैव ग्रहस्वरमुदीरितम्।"

which means that these are given by him after proper compilation.

Oudava Ragas

Names	*Graha notes*	*Omitted notes*
1. Dhanashri	'Sa'	'Ri' and 'Dha'
2. Madhu Madhavi	'Ma'	'Ri' and 'Dha'
3. Gurjari	'Sa'	'Ri' and 'Dha'
4. Megha Ranji	'Ma'	'Dha' and 'Ni'
5. Velavali	'Ga'	'Sa' and 'Ri'
6. Ramakri	'Ga'	'Ri' and 'Dha'
7. Narayani	'Ni'	'Dha' and 'Pa'
8. Pali	Shadja	'Ma' and 'Pa'

The list of Sampoorna, Shadava and Oudava Ragas numbered 30 in all, appears with their starting notes and Varjya or omitted notes (in the case of Shadava and Oudava Ragas) as reproduced above with a concluding sloka as given below—

"एवं प्रधानरागाः स्युर्लक्षणोक्तं यथा क्रमम्।
अनन्ता सन्ति संदर्भा नाना देश्याः प्रकीर्तिताः।"

According to this above mentioned sloka, Narada has dealt with the main Ragas only. 'Sangita Makaranda' itself has many more Ragas which are not included in this list given above. Narada allots three kinds of castes to the Sampurna, Shadava and Oudava Ragas. He believes that Sampoorna Ragas come from Munis (मुनिजाः), Shadavas from Brahma or Brahmana (ब्रह्मजाः) and Oudava Ragas from Kshatriyas (क्षत्रजाः).

From the above list of starting notes of Ragas, the important points to be made are as follows:

1. Shadja, Gandhara, Madhyama, Nishada are mostly used as Graha notes. 'Dha' too appears only once.

2. 'Ri' and 'Pa' are not used as Graha notes.

3. Shadja is also omitted in Ragas, i.e., Bhupala and Velavali.

4. Madhyama is never omitted.

5. The adjacent notes which are not to be omitted in a Raga as a rule are also omitted by Narada of 'Sangita Makaranda' as in :

Megha Ranji	—	'Dha' and 'Ni'
Velavali	—	'Sa' and 'Ri'
Narayani	—	'Dha' and 'Pa'
Pali	—	'Ma' and 'Pa'

These omissions of adjacent notes are not permitted at present. Though Narada of 'Sangita Makaranda' has provided various types of Raga classifications and names about a hundred Ragas in all, but lack of proper description of Ragas makes it impossible even to imagine about the practical side of Ragas. Similarly, the descriptions provided by other authors of his time also does not throw any light on their practical side. Because, the music of those times, i.e., fifth to twelfth century has lost its ancient significance due to gradual changes in music with the passage of time and foreign invasions and influences.

Some Raga names appearing in 'Sangita Makaranda' either in the list of Graha notes or in the list of Pullinga (Masculine), Stri Ragas (feminine) and Napunsaka (Neuter) Ragas might be traced in 'Brihaddeshi', 'Bharata Bhashyam' and 'Sangita Ratnakara' with a slight difference in names, i.e., Malava for Malavi and so on. But the similarity ends with the names in many such cases of similar named Ragas. The descriptions are totally different. Some names of the Ragas given by Narada like — Bhairavi, Vasanta, Lalita, Narayani and Shri Raga are present even today but their forms have changed completely. The Sampoorna Ragas mentioned by Narada are not found in 'Brihaddeshi', 'Bharata Bhashyam' or in 'Sangita Ratnakara' in toto. Some of the Sampurna, Shadava and Oudava Ragas with their starting notes, etc., mentioned by Narada, which appear in other texts also, are recounted as follows:

Deshakshi—The first name in the list of Sampurna Raga is mentioned by Sharngdeva as 'Deshakhya' and it is a Shadava Raga.

Malavi Raga — (Sampoorna) appears in 'Sangita Makaranda' whereas in 'Brihaddeshi' and 'Bharata Bhashyam' it appears as Malava. In 'Bharata Bhashayam' Malava is a Shadava Raga while in 'Brihaddeshi' and 'Sangita Ratnakara' it appears as a Sampoorna Raga; a Bhasha of Takka Kaishika.[16]

The eleven Shadava Ragas appear in 'Sangita Ratnakara' either as Bhasha and Upanga Ragas or as Adhuna Prasiddha Ragas. *Lalita* and *Malavasari* are found in 'Brihaddeshi'.

Lalita : It appears as an Oudava Bhasha Raga in 'Brihaddeshi', while Nanya Bhupala opines that Lalita is a Sampurna Raga and quotes Kashyapa—

"सप्तस्वरास्तु ललिता गमक स्वरपेशला।"[17]

Matanga has given two Lalitas.[18] First Lalita is a Shadava Bhasha called Sankirna Lalita of Takka Raga omitting Ri, (according to the Alapa given in 'Brihaddeshi'). The second is an Oudava Lalita, leaving Sa and Pa notes. Nanya Bhupala also mentions that Panchama should be used less in Lalita.

Sharngdeva has given two Lalitas, one from Takka[19] and second as a Bhasha of Bhinna Shadja. Lalita of Takka is Oudava, omitting Ri and Pa. Second Lalita of Bhinna Shadja seems to be Sampoorna from the Alapa. Lalita of 'Sangita Makaranda' is a Shadava Raga omitting Gandhara. A few Ragas from the list of Ragas (Graha Svara) can be cited and compared with the Ragas of other works, similarly. For example:

Nata Raga: consisting of seven notes and starting with Shadja is not found in the available text of 'Brihaddeshi'. But Nanya Bhupala quotes 'Brihaddeshi' to support his Nata Raga,[20] which shows that the missing portion of 'Brihaddeshi' contained the Raga description which was available to Nanya Bhupala. Though it is described as a Sampurna Raga, the starting note Dha differs from 'Sangita Makaranda'. Sharngdeva regards the Nata as a Deshi Raga of Hindola. He does not disclose its Jati but starting note is accounted as Shadja.

Malavashri: This Raga is named by Matanga as Malavesari (मालवेसरी).[21] This appears as a Shadava Raga and as a Bhasha of Takka Raga. This Raga favourably corresponds with 'Sangita Makaranda's' Malavashri. Rishabha is the omitted note in 'Sangita Makaranda' while Matanga omits Panchama. Sharngdeva follows Narada of 'Sangita Makaranda' in the description of Malavashri.

In the Oudava Ragas, Gurjari and Belavali or Velavali can be traced from 'Brihaddeshi' onwards.

Gurjari: This is a Sampurna Raga according to Matanga[22] while in 'Sangita Makaranda' it is an Oudava Raga, omitting the notes Ri and Dha with its starting note 'Sa'. Matanga does not mention the Graha note, but gives the prominence to Gandhara and it is a Deshi Bhasha Raga. The published part of 'Bharata Bhashyam' does not mention Gurjari. In 'Sangita Ratnakara', the starting note and the prominent note is Ri and concluding note is Madhyama.[23]

Velavali : This is again an Oudava Raga, omitting 'Sa' and 'Ri' and starting with 'Ga' according to 'Sangita Makaranda'. Though it is not found in the available part of 'Brihaddeshi', Velavali of Matanga has been quoted by Nanya Bhupala. Velavali is Sampoorna and its starting note is Dhaivata.[24] Pratapa Velavali, an Upanga of Velavali is an Oudava Raga omitting 'Ri' and 'Pa'.

Ramakriti : It is an Oudava Raga of 'Sangita Makaranda' omitting the note 'Ri' and 'Dha' and starting with 'Ga'. It is described in 'Sangita Ratnakara' as Bahuli (बहुली पर्याय भूता रामकृति) Graha note is not given and it is a Shadava Raga omitting the note 'Pa'. It is derived from Raga Kolohala.[25]

From the above account of Ragas, it is clear that similar names of Ragas appearing in different works do not possess similar formation of notes or represent the same Ragas. The practical side of Ragas cannot be imagined or produced, though an Alapa or group of notes is given by the author to explain the Raga. But very often they are misleading as an Alapa of Shadava Raga has all the seven notes and vice versa. The notation is also impractical without providing any key signatures and the types of the notes. The discussion of Ragas mentioned above may drive the point home.

Narada of 'Sangita Makaranda' classifies the Raga into three groups. They are Pullinga Ragas — 'Masculine Ragas', Stree Ragas — (Feminine Ragas) and Napunsaka Ragas — (Neuter Ragas). The names of the Ragas are said to be unusual and termed as 'Vichitra' by the author himself. But some names of the Ragas of 'Sangita Makaranda' occur in 'Brihaddeshi', 'Bharata Bhashyam' and of course in 'Sangita Ratnakara'. They are discussed below in the respective order they appear in the list of Narada.

Masculine Ragas

1. Bangala	12. Shuddha Nati
2. Soma Raga	13. Malava Goula

3. Shri Raga
4. Bhupali
5. Chaya Gouda
6. Shuddha Hindolika
7. Andoli
8. Dombuli
9. Gouda
10. Karnataka
11. Phadamanji

14. Raga Ranga
15. Chaya Nati
16. Kolahala
17. Sourashtri
18. Vasanta
19. Shuddha
20. Sarang Bhairavi
21. Raga Dhvani

Bangala : This Raga is not described by Narada except its time of singing as morning. This Raga appears in 'Brihaddeshi' as 'Vankali' instead of Bangala. It might be the same Raga as that belonging to Bangala Desha- "बंगाल देश संभूता वंकाली".[26] It is a Sampoorna Bhasha Raga with starting note as Dhaivata.

In 'Bharata Bhashyam'[27] (published parts) the Raga Bangala is mentioned thrice. It surfaces as a Deshakhya, an Upa Raga and a Bhasha Raga, but its description is very vague and the quoted sloka of Kashyapa does not describe its Jati, note contents, or distinct properties. 'Brihaddeshi' is more elaborate about Vankali and there is another Raga named Mangali from Bangala, Sampoorna Raga.

'Sangita Ratnakara' describes Bangala as a Shadava Raga. Its starting note is Madhyama "ग्रहांशन्यासमध्यम:"[28]. It is a male Raga and appears in the list of 'Adhuna Prasiddha Ragas'; as a Raga in the 13 Raganga Ragas and in the list of nine Bhashanga Ragas as Karnataka Bangala. The significant point however, is the Ragas of male; female and neuter gender of 'Sangita Makaranda' are familiar Ragas and can be traced easily in other contemporary or later works. The classification only appears novel.

There are two more Bangalas, as the 'first' and 'second'

Bangala, in 'Sangita Ratnakara', with Shadja as their Graha note. First Bangala belongs to Shadja Grama, while the second Bangala is derived from the Grama Raga Kaishiki. They belong to famous Ragas (Adhuna Prasiddha Ragas) of present".

Soma Raga : 'Brihaddeshi' does not mention about this Raga but it appears in 'Bharat Bhashyam' under the name of Matanga, which confirms the extensive study of Ragas done by Matanga in his 'Brihaddeshi', which part is not available at present. It is treated as a masculine Sampoorna Raga, in 'Sangita Makaranda' Shadja is its Graha, Ansha and Nyasa note according to both Matanga and Nanya Bhupala.[29] Nanya Bhupala quote a number of Ragas from 'Brihaddeshi' which are not found anywhere in the present available text. Soma Raga is not mentioned by Sharngdeva. In 'Sangita Makaranda', Somaraga however, appears as a Suryansha Raga.

Shri Raga : This Raga is not present in 'Brihaddeshi' and Nanya Bhupala neither quotes Kashyapa nor Matanga in connection with this Raga. However in sloka no.199, it is described as appearing from Shadji Jati and is a Sampoorna Raga using less Panchama. The second sloka says that Shri Raga is derived from Takka Raga and is a melody of five notes omitting Ri and Pa. But 'Sa' is the starting (Graha), prominent (Ansha) and resting or ending (Nyasa) note in both versions.[30] Sharngdeva follows the first version of Nanya Bhupala's quoted sloka and accepts it as born out of Shadji Jati. This is the first Raga from the list of 'Adhuna Prasiddha Raga' of 'Sangita Ratnakara'. His Shri Raga uses less 'Panchama' and 'Sa' is the starting, prominent and ending note. Except Panchama's use **"स्वल्प पंचमम्"** it is supposed to be a Sampoorna Raga in 'Sangita Ratnakara'.[31] According to 'Sangita Makaranda', Shri Raga is Shadava omitting the note 'Ga' and its starting note is Shadja and it is a night melody.

Bhupali (Bhupala?) : On page 17 of 'Sangita Makaranda' while describing the Graha notes it comes as Bhupala which seems more appropriate as it is a masculine Raga. According to Narada, it is a Shadava Raga omitting the note Shadja and starting with 'Gandhara'. At present, the Shadja cannot be omitted. Bhupala is a 'Suryansha' or morning melody. This Raga does not appear in 'Brihaddeshi', 'Bharata Bhashyam' or in 'Sangita Ratnakara'.

Chaya Gouda and Gouda : Both Ragas appear as male Ragas in this work. Chaya Gouda is neither described by any other author nor any more description of this Raga is provided by our author except the vague comment, that all Gouda Ragas should be performed at noon.

Gouda Raga appears in 'Brihaddeshi' and 'Bharata Bhashyam'. Nanya Bhupala quotes 'Brihaddeshi', while describing the Gouda Raga. In 'Brihaddeshi' (the available portion), Goudi Geetis and its Ragas are mentioned. But Gouda Raga does not appear in the Ragas derived from Goudi Geeti. In 'Bharata Bhashyam', Nanya Bhupala quotes—

टक्करागेण सद्दशः पञ्चमेन विवर्जितः।
षड्जांश न्यास सम्पन्नो गौडः स्यात्त्रृषभग्रहः।।१६१।।
स्फुरितारव्य गमक निविडो गौडः...... ।६०।[32]

Gouda Raga omits the note Panchama like Raga Takka, Rishabha is the starting note, Shadja is the Ansha and Nyasa (ending) note; it is adorned with Sphurita named Gamaka. Our author mentions, Chaya and Karnata Gouda without mentioning the Graha or omitted notes. Supposedly Chaya Gouda has a Chaya (reflection) of Gouda and Karnata Gouda belongs to the Karnata desha.

Shuddha Hindolika — Most of the masculine Ragas, it seems, bear feminine names. As far as names of 'Sangita Makaranda' are concerned, they are not indicative of the gender. It might be the copyist's error or are unusual as Narada himself admits that his names are unusual (विचित्र). Otherwise the Raga should be named as Shuddha Hindolaka. The first general list of Ragas (53) includes Hendola. Narada does not describe Raga Hendola or Shuddha Hindolika.

But in 'Brihaddeshi', Raga Hindola is a very important Grama Raga of Madhyama Grama, with five Bhashas. Rishabha and Dhaivata are omitted, Shadja is its prominent (ansha) and ending note. Nanya Bhupala prefers to omit a single note and makes it a Shadava Raga with four Bhashas.[33] It belongs to Ma Grama Sharngdeva gives a similar description of Hindola.

This is about Hindola, but our author mentions Shuddha Hindolika here, which is not mentioned by anybody. Therefore no conclusions can be arrived at.

Often the Ragas mentioned in our work does occur in 'Bharata Bhashyam', where the Ragas from all the three Gramas are mentioned. 'Bharata Bhashyam' is an elaborate work comprising thirteen chapters, of which seven chapters are edited and published in two volumes. The second volume contains the incomplete seventh chapter on Ragas, though initially, the author has provided a list of Ragas belonging to all the three Gramas, the volume contains the description of Ragas related to Shadja Grama only that too, does not cover the entire Ragas of Shadja Grama mentioned by the author. Therefore, the Ragas not mentioned in the present volume-2 are not to be concluded as final omissions on the part of the author Nanya Bhupala.

Andoli : In 'Sangita Makaranda' Andoli appears as a Suryansha Raga and no more description is provided, except of its being a male Raga. Andhali and not Andoli is mentioned by Matanga as a Vibhasha of Panchama, Rishabha and Panchama are the prominent and concluding notes, respectively. The note Shadja is weak in this Vibhasha and Kakali Nishada is used. It is loved by Kinnaras.

Nanya Bhupala states that Andhali is a Vibhasha of Panchama and is related to Madhyama Grama. Sharngdeva opines that Andolika is a Vibhasha of the Bhasha Raga Dakshinatya of Shuddha Panchami. It is a Shadava Raga omitting 'Ga' and using 'Ni' rarely. Starting note is Panchama.

There are many authors who mentioned and described about these Ragas, but only selected ancient or a little later authors than Narada are given preference here. Though the names of Ragas may be similar, their lakshanas might have drastically changed with the times, e.g., ancient Bhairava is an Oudava Raga, while at present it is a seven noted Raga subjected to periodic modifications. Therefore the similarity in names of the Ragas are not to be taken account of. The time and period of the works, certainly are of importance to decide about the lakshanas of Ragas.

Nanya Bhupala is referred because he has dealt with the Ragas of all the three Gramas including Ga Grama similar to our author. Matanga is the earliest author on Ragas and 'Sangita Ratnakara' is the most popular, elaborate and important work in the field of music. Therefore, these three authors and their works are taken into consideration and given preference. Moreover, Narada of 'Sangita Makaranda' does not furnish any descriptive details of his Ragas, though such details taken from the three authors do not help in any way to reconstruct the Ragas of 'Sangita Makaranda' or provide any glimpse into the practical side of these Ragas, yet the similar names of Ragas might prove the antiquity and authenticity of the Ragas of the work.

It is obvious from the above account of Ragas of the three works that no author furnishes identical details without least difference; on similar Ragas. There are controversies, though they might be minute. The purpose of these statements of similar Ragas of different works is to provide the students and music lovers to form an idea of the Ragas mentioned in 'Sangita Makaranda' and an outline of these Ragas (similarly named ones) furnished by other authors.

Dombuli : This Raga appears in the general list of fifty-three Ragas, as a noon time Raga and again as a masculine Raga. Neither Graha note nor its Jati are mentioned. It is not mentioned even by other authors.

Phadamanji : This Raga appears as Padavanji, Pala-manjari and Phada Vanji. It is Suryansha Raga (morning melody). A Shadava Raga with six notes, Ri is omitted and the Raga starts on Nishada.

This Padamanji or Palamanjari, probably, appears as Prathama manjari in 'Brihaddeshi' and 'Bharata Bhashyam'. In 'Bharata Bhashyam' the name appears without any description due to earlier mentioned reasons.

In 'Brihaddeshi', Prathamamanjari appears as a Shadava Raga, omitting Rishabha and its starting note is Dhaivata. It is a Bhasha Raga, but it comes under masculine Ragas in 'Sangita Makaranda'. It is to be noted that Grama Ragas bear the masculine names in 'Brihaddeshi' and Bhasha and Vibhasha Ragas are treated as feminine Ragas (names). In our work, Narada does not speak about Bhasha, Vibhasha, Geetis or other types of general basic classification of Ragas. Matanga and his predecessors, i.e., Kashyapa, Yashtika, Shardula, etc., treats the Grama Ragas as masculine Ragas, by conferring masculine names and treating the Bhashas and Vibhashas as females affixing feminine names.

Sharngdeva includes the Prathamanjari in his current popular Ragas, though it is described by all the aforesaid ancient authors. Prathama manjari has Panchama as its Graha Ansha and Nyasa. It has Tara Ri and Dha and Mandra Ga.[34] There are many names of Ragas, which have changed slightly with times. As the description of Prathama manjari matches the description of Padamanji, it seems to be the corrupt version of Prathamamanjari.

Shuddha Nati : This Raga appears as a masculine Raga. It might be the Nata Raga. Nata is a Sampurna Raga, has Shadja as its starting note. It is not mentioned in 'Brihaddeshi', though a Raga named Nartha appears in it but the description is totally different.

Nanya Bhupala defines Nata as of Dhaivati Jati, it has Dhaivata as prominent, starting and concluding note. It is a Sampurna Raga. In 'Sangita Ratnakara', Nata is a Bhashanga Sampurna Raga with Shadja as its starting, prominent and ending note. It has a little similarity to Shuddha Nati of Narada.

Karnata Gouda : The Raga does not appear in 'Brihaddeshi', yet in the beginning of Deshi Ragas—a Sampurna Raga named Karnati occurs, which probably, belongs to the state of Karnataka. The Gouda Raga prevalent in south might be having the name of Karnata Gouda. There are other such names, viz., Karnata Bangala. Karnata Mishra Nati; that appear in 'Sangita Makaranda'.

Nanya Bhupala mentions one Andhra Gouda in Shadja Grama, which is not described.[35]

Sharngdeva is the only author, writes about Karnata Gouda as follows:

ज्ञेयं कर्णाटगौडस्तु षड्जन्यासग्रहांशकः।[36]

Karnata Gouda has Shadja as its thrice important note. In 'Sangita Makaranda', it is mentioned as night time, masculine melody.

Malava Gouda : It is a night time; masculine melody. It also appears as Malava Goula.

Raga Ranga : This Raga appears on page 15 as Ranji; a Chandramansha Raga and as Raga Ranga on page 16 as a masculine Raga. No other details are provided. Nanya Bhupala mentions it as Raga Ranjika.

Chaya Nati : It is a masculine Raga without any other details. In 'Sangita Ratnakara', it occurs as a Upanga Raga of Nata, described as:

छायानटा तु नट्टैव मन्द्र पंचम भूषितः।
नट्टोपाङ्ग निषादेन गान्धारेण च कम्पिता।।[37]

Shadja is the prominent and starting note of Nata according to Sharngdeva.

Kolahala : This is a very popular ancient Raga, prevalent from the period of Matanga. According to Matanga, it is a Bhasha of Takka Raga. It is an Oudava Raga, omitting the notes Panchama and Nishada, but the illustrated Alapa omits only Panchama in the text published by 'Sangita Karyalaya'. In 'Bharata Bhashyam', Kolahala is a Shadava Raga omitting the Panchama, but a Bhasha Raga according to Nanya Bhupala. In 'Sangita Ratnakara', Sharngdeva is of the same opinion, in addition to it he mentions Shadja as the thrice important, Graha, Ansha and Nyasa note. Another Kolahala mentioned by the author is a Takkanga Raga.[40] In 'Sangita Makaranda' it appears as masculine Raga.

Sourashtri : It appears twice in 'Sangita Makaranda', as a masculine and neuter Raga, which is rather erratic. No other details of the Raga is given, though it seems to be an ancient Raga. In 'Brihaddeshi'[41], it appears as a Bhasha of Takka Raga, of Sampurna Jati, starting note is Nishada. In 'Bharata Bhashyam'[42], it appears as Sourashtrika using Panchama scarcely, with the starting note as Nishada. According to Kashyapa, it is sung without Panchama. The illustration given by Matanga also omits Panchama.

Sharngdeva mentions two Sourashtri. The second one is from Takka Raga, omits Panchama and Sa is its thrice important note.[43]

Shuddha Vasanta : It appears in the list of Suryamsha Ragas (morning) and in masculine Ragas as well. It is a Sampurna Raga starting with the note Shadja. It seems to be a very important Raga, as it appears in all the lists given in 'Sangita Makaranda'. It does not appear in the available text of Brihaddeshi or in the published part of 'Bharata Bhashyam'.

Sharngdeva mentions that this Shuddha Vasanta is called as Deshi Hindola also.[44] It is, according to Sharngdeva, a Sampurna variety of Hindola, which is supposed to be an Oudava Raga. This Raga is included in the list of current popular Ragas of 'Sangita Ratnakara'.

Saranga Bhairavi : The correct word is Salanga (Salaga or Chayalaga) and not Saranga. The word Saranga is not used as the name of a Raga in 'Sangita Makaranda'. Saranga Bhairavi or Saranga Nata is a type of Bhairavi and Nata, which have some shadows of other Ragas, it seems. Narada describes about Bhairavi (Shuddha) as a Sampurna Raga, with a starting note — Madhyama. Bhairavi is supposed to be a remedial Raga for breaking the untimely singing of Ragas."

Raga Dhvani : The name Raga Dhvani appears as Nagadhvani in the general list, while in the masculine Ragas, it is mentioned as Raga Dhvani. Sharngdeva describes a Nagadhvani in 'Sangita Ratnakara'. Nanya Bhupala mentions a Raga Dhvani in his list of Madhyama Grama Raga and terms it as Deshakhya.

नट्टनारायणो रागो ध्वनि बङ्गाल एव च।"[45]

According to Sharngdeva, the Nagadhvani has Shadja as its starting, ending and prominent note, it is an Oudava type of Raga; notes of omission are Dha and Pa. With this Raga, Raga Dhvani, Narada concludes his list of Pullinga Ragas.

The list of 23 females Ragas is as follows :

1.	Tundi	13.	Velavali
2.	Turuslka Tundi	14.	Bahuli
3.	Malvari	15.	Gundakri
4.	Mahuri	16.	Ghurjari
5.	Pouraliki	17.	Varati
6.	Kambhari	18.	Dravadi
7.	Bhallati	19.	Hansi
8.	Saindihavi	20.	Goudi
9.	Salangakhya (Nata)	21.	Narayani
10.	Gandhari	22.	Ahari
11.	Devakri	23.	Megha Ranji
12.	Deshini	24.	Mishra Nata

The female Ragas seem to be more ancient as most of them appear in Brihaddeshi, but the names have some slight differences in spellings, e.g., Mahuri appears as Mahari in 'Brihaddeshi'. Many female Ragas are described by Sharngdeva too. It is a well-known fact that 'Sangita Ratnakara' describes the ancient system of music, comprising Murchana Jati and Grama Ragas and other essentials, which were not prevalent or practiced in his time. The Ragas described by him also seem to be of an earlier period. On the one hand, his Raga classification is similar to that of ancient authors like Durgashakti, Yashtika Matanga, etc., on the other hand, he describes a number of Vikrita notes and current popular Ragas, which present a totally different picture.

In 'Sangita Makaranda' the uniformity of the concept of a single school is maintained throughout the work. There are no discrepancies regarding the chronological order of the subject, expounded by Narada—Gandharva school of Music. It is a novel concept of music comprising the Deshi Ragas based on Murchanas. No deviation from the basic theme however, is found anywhere. This music system of Narada serves the spiritual purpose with a remedial measure for atonement of sins, appeasement of evil spirits, planets, and as a propitiation for deities to gain the worldly gains. Therefore, though the names of Ragas and their description may seem to be similar, they are basically different. Nevertheless, to get an idea about the Raga of the similar names is the aim of the following description of the Ragas.

Stree Ragas

Tundi and Turushka Tundi : Tundi is the main Raga and Turushka Tundi is its variety perhaps, the former might have been the ancient name of Raga Todi. We find Tundi, Trotika, Todika, etc., in some texts. Our author however, has not described it in any way except mentioning the category as follows.

They appear as female Ragas, and Tundi appears as the wife of Raga Phadamanjari. In 'Brihaddeshi', these Ragas are not mentioned. In 'Bharata Bhashyam', the name is mentioned as a Vibhasha of Madhyama Grama, without any description, in the second volume.

Sharngdeva describes Raga Todi as appearing from the important Grama Raga Shadava of Madhyama Grama. The importance of Shadava Raga is stressed by Matanga. It is one of the six Ragas (Grama) to be used in dramatics, according to Bharata — षट्सु रागेषु मुख्यत्वात् षाडवः[46]

The Raga Todi has Madhyama as its three important notes, it has Sa of upper octave, oscillating Panchama and lower Gandhara. He describes Turushka Todi in a single line—

तोड्यैव ताडिता गाल्पा तौरुष्की निध भूयसी।[47]

The Turushka Todi uses Ni and Dha frequently with scarce using of Ga. The notes are to be used with force just like Todi.

Malvari : The name is spelt with utter confusion. It appears as Malvari, Malahari and Manohari. Malvari does not appear in any other works. In 'Bharata Bhashyam', Mahlar appears as a Vibhasha Raga of Madhyama Grama, but the description is unavailable in the published vol. 2.

A Malhara is described by Nanya Bhupala and Matanga. Our Raga is nearer to Mahlar and Malhar is an entirely different Raga, so its description is not given.

In 'Sangita Ratnakara' Malhara and Malhari, both are mentioned in the list of 'current popular ragas'. In 'Sangita Makaranda' it appears as a female Raga and Manohari is mentioned as noon time melody. Malahari is the wife of Bhoopa.

Pouraliki : This Raga appears as Pourali or Pouraliki. This is an ancient and popular Raga mentioned four times by Matanga as — Bhasha of Bhinna Shadja, Bhasha of Takka, Bhasha of Malava Panchama, Bhasha of Hindola (Bhinna Pourali). Its Ansha note is Madhyama. It originates from the place called Pourali, so it is a Deshi Bhasha. Though, it is a popular ancient Raga, Sharngdeva does not describe it in the list of 'Poorva Prasiddha Ragas'. In 'Sangita Makaranda', besides being named as a female Raga, it appears as the wife of Bhairava. It is included in Shadja Grama by Nanyadeva without any description.

In 'Sangita Ratnakara', Pourali is mentioned as a Bhasha of Malava Kaishiki, Kallinatha—the commentator of 'Sangita Ratnakara' has described this Pourali on the lines of Sharngdeva. Kallinatha provides a number of Bhasha Ragas in the end of Raga Vivekadhyaya. There are many popular ancient Ragas, appearing in Kallinatha's list, which are not mentioned by Sharngdeva. These descrepancies create confusion about the period of a work. Therefore the names of Ragas cannot be taken as internal evidence.

Kambhari : This Raga is mentioned as the wife of Bhairava

and later as a wife of Megha Raga besides referred to as female Raga. Excluding this, there is no other description furnished in our work by Narada. This Raga appears four times with the same spelling, so it cannot be inferred as Khambaiti or Kamboji, the latter one is mentioned by Matanga. Kambhoji and Gopi Kamboji appear in the general list of Ragas in our work.

Bhallati: The name Vallati appears in 'Bharata Bhashyam'. This comes as a Bhasha of Roopa Sadharita —a Grama Raga of Sadharana Geeti based on Sadja Grama. According to Sharngdeva, Vallati is an Upanga Raga of Chevati, which is a Bhasha of Hindola. Shadja is its thrice important note (Graha, Ansha and Nyasa). In 'Sangita Makaranda', it appears in the general list of Ragas, and as a female Raga and the wife of Shri Raga.

Saindhavi : It seems to be a very ancient Raga, even mentioned by Bharata, and other ancient works. Matanga describes at least four Saindhavis belonging to different Grama Ragas. Some names of Ragas occur many times in a work, but their grammar differ in practical aspect, since they belong to different Gramas or Grama Ragas.

या इमा पुनरुक्ता.... ।
ता एव नामसाम्यतश्चोभया-ग्रामजाः स्मृताः
लक्षणालापरूपैस्तु भिद्यन्ते परमार्थतः ।।७६।।[48]

Nanya Deva believes that, though the names of two Ragas may resemble, they differ in notes Alapa and forms as they belong to different Gramas. Saindhavi or Pourali have identical name-sakes but according to the Gramas, Grama Ragas, Geetis, they differ considerably. These Ragas are derived from different Grama Ragas and Upa Ragas, Geetis, etc. Similar names of such Ragas or omission of certain Ragas in the work do not provide any clue or confirm about the period of a work. For example, Kamboji or Ghurjari is mentioned by Matanga. They are still prevalent, yet as far as practical side is considered, they may be totally different. In 'Sangita Makaranda', Narada names many Ragas which are still in practice like Nilambari, Saveri, Kamboji, Bahuli, Ghurjari,

Shri, etc., and many ancient Ragas which are now extinct. According to Matanga, Saindhavi belongs to Sindhu Desha, and a Sampurna Deshakhya Bhasha. It has Madhyama as its Ansha, Dhaivata as its Nyasa and Panchama and Rishabha should be used less. This Saindhavi is a Bhasha of Bhinna Shadja. There are other Saindhavis also, e.g., Saindhavi-Bhasha of Takka; Bhasha of Malavakaishika, Bhasha of Panchama, etc.

Gandhari : It is a famous ancient Bhasha of several Ragas — Bhinna-Shadja, Malava Panchama, Gandhara Panchama, Sourviraka, etc. A Sankirna Bhasha of Bhinna Shadja, has Dha as its starting and ending note. Dha and Ga combination is used much.[49] Another Gandhari of Souvira is a Sampurna Bhasha, has Nishada as its Ansha, Shadja as the concluding note and is used in Karunarasa.[50]

Devakri : It appears as a female Raga, and in the general list of Ragas as Deva Kriya. It again comes as the wife of Bhairava. Devakri or Kriya seems to be a Kriyanga Raga. The name list of Kriyanga Ragas provided by Nanya Bhupala and Sharngdeva endorse this view; the names of the Kriyanga Ragas conclude with Kri or Kriya, e.g., Gundakri, Ramakriya, Devakri, etc.

Bahuli : It appears many times in 'Sangita Makaranda' in the general list, as a Shadava Raga with an initial note Madhyama and omitting Nishada, as a noon time melody; as a female Raga and as the wife of Raga Bhupala. It always appears as Bahuli dvayam; two Bahulis, Shuddha and Salanga; excluding the list of female Ragas and when mentioned as a wife. In 'Sangita Ratnakara' Bahuli is supposed to be an alias for Ramakriti according to Kallinatha.

Varati : It is a very ancient Raga mentioned by Matanga as a Bhasha of Bhinna Panchama. It is a Shadava Bhasha with a weak Rishabha. Madhyama is its Ansha note and Dhaivata is the concluding note. Madhyama and Dhaivata are used in abundance. According to Matanga, it is a favourite melody of Vidyadharas.[51]

In 'Bharata Bhashyam', Varatika appears as a Vibhasha of 'Roopa Sadharita' in the list of Shadja Grama Ragas, and its description is not available. Its varieties — Karnata and Lata Varati are dissimilar. Nanyadeva quotes Matanga to describe these Varatis. Lata Varati seems to be Shadava and Karnata Varati is a Sampurna Vibhasha.[52]

Sharngdeva mentions Raga Varati as a Bhasha of Bhinna Panchama and includes it in current popular Ragas. He has followed the description of Karnata Varati of Nanya Bhupala sans the name. The same description appears as plain Varati. It is a Sampurna Raga, Shadja is the initial and concluding note, Dha is the prominent note. He does not mention about its Jati (sampurna).[53]

In 'Sangita Makaranda' Varati comes as a Sampurna Raga with the initial note as Shadja. It is a female, Chandramansha (night) Raga, a wife of Vasanta. Narada mentions many Varatis—Shuddha Varati, Naga Varati, Sarva Varati, etc.

Dravadi : It is also an ancient Bhasha of both Kaishiki and Hindola, described by Matanga. The Dravadi of Hindola has Panchama as its Ansha and Shadja as its concluding note. It is a Bhasha of Dravida region (south), supposed to be sung by a lost person to find the correct path.

The other Dravadi of Takka Kaishiki has Gandhara as its Ansha, and Dhaivata as concluding note. It too, belongs to the Dravida region.[54] Nanyadeva includes the Dravadi as a Deshakhya Bhasha of Gandhara Grama.[55]

Dravadi appears as a concluding Raga of Raga Vivekadhyaya in 'Sangita Ratnakara'. Sharngdeva describes Dravadi as the Vibhasha of Takka Kaishiki. Gandhara is the Ansha and Graha note and Dhaivata is the concluding note. It also appears in the list of current popular Ragas of 'Sangita Ratnakara'.

Dravadi or Dravatika is a Chandramansha Raga in 'Sangita Makaranda'. It is a female Raga and the wife of Raga Vasanta.

Hansi : Neither Matanga nor Nanya Bhupala has mentioned the Raga Hansi. A Raga named Rakta Hansaka is described by Nanya Bhupala according to Matanga which is not found in the present text of 'Brihaddeshi'.

In 'Sangita Ratnakara', it is mentioned with erstwhile popular Ragas as follows :

शंकराभरणो घण्टारवो हंसकदीपकौ।[57]

This appears in our work as a female Raga and is the wife of Vasanta Raga. There it appears as Hansi which is the correct name.

Goudi : Sharngdeva mentions Goudi (2nd) as consisting of Tara, Mandra Shadja and frequent Nishada note. It has Shadja as its three important notes and is a Bhasha of Malavakaishika. His description is according to Matanga. Yet in Brihaddeshi (available), we do not find this Bhasha. There is another Goudi too, which is the Bhasha of Hindola.[58]

The Goudi of Nanya Bhupala is also a Bhasha of Hindola and Malava Kaishiki. It appears as a Uparaga of Malava Vesari. No description is available in the present vol.2. In 'Sangita Makaranda', Goudi appears as a female Raga, the wife of Bangala. It is a noon time Raga.

Narayani : It is not mentioned in 'Brihaddeshi', 'Bharata Bhashyam', or 'Sangita Ratnakara'. At present, a Raga named Narayani is in practice, in Carnatic and Hindustani music. It is an Oudava Shadava Raga. In Aroha, 'Ga' and 'Ni' are omitted, while in Avaroha only Ga is omitted. It seems, that in ancient period, the dissimilar count of notes in Aroha and Avaroha is not allowed. The three types of Raga, Sampurna, Shadava and Oudava had respectively seven, six and five notes in both Aroha and Avaroha as a rule.

Narayani appears as a Suryansha, female Raga, the wife of Bangala Raga. It is an Oudava Raga omitting Dha and Pa, with initial note as Nishada.

Ahari : This Raga is not dealt by any other author except Narada. It is a Sampurna, Chandramsha Raga with Madhyama as its starting note, sung at night. It is the wife of Nata Raga. A Raga Ahari is still practiced in south. According to some, the singer of Ahari would not get his next meal in time.

Mishra Nati : This seems to be a mixture of various types of Nata Raga or some other Ragas mixed with Nata Raga. It does not appear in any other work. In our work it is a female Raga and the wife of Nata Raga, though the name seems to be erratic. The wives are mentioned as Salanga Nata (chaya), Natakhya (Mishra Nata) and Ahari.

After the female Ragas, Napunsaka (neuter) Ragas are enlisted, which are thirteen in number. Napunsaka Ragas seem to be those Ragas from which further Ragas are not derived.

They are as follows:

1. Kaishiki
2. Lalita
3. Dhannashi
4. Kuranjika
5. Sourashtri
6. Dravadi
7. Kaumoddaki
8. Ramakri
9. Saveri
10. Balahamsa
11. Samavedi
12. Shankarabharana
13. Shuddha

Kaishiki : It bears the name of a Jati and also of a Grama Raga arising of Madhyama Grama. Matanga defines it as a Bhasha of Panchama. It has Panchama as Nyasa, Madhyama as Ansha, and is weak in Nishada. It is a Sankirna Bhasha, the name Kaishiki occurs from the period of Bharata. But in 'Sangita Makaranda' it is referred to as a Napunsaka Raga, which supposedly do not have Uparaga oı Bhashas. Therefore, it cannot be a Jati or a Grama Raga.

In 'Bharata Bhashyam', Kaishiki appears as a Bhasha of Bhinna Geeti of Madhyama Grama.[59] Whereas in 'Sangita Ratnakara' Kaishiki appears as a Bhasha of Shuddha Panchama and is a Sampurna Raga. Panchama is its thrice important note. It is also known as a Bhashanga Raga by others.[60]

Lalita : This Raga has been already described as a Raga appearing in the general list of 'Sangita Makaranda'. Now it appears as a Neuter Raga. In 'Brihaddeshi' it appears as a Bhasha of Takka and Bhinna Shadja.

Dhannashi: In 'Sangita Makaranda', Dhannashi appears as an Oudava Raga, omitting Ri and Dha, with Graha note as Sa. In 'Bharata Bhashyam' Dhannashi is mentioned among the Gandhara Grama Ragas without any description. As already mentioned, the Raga Prakarana of Bharata Bhashyam is not published fully. It comprises some names of Ragas, Bhashas, Bhashanga, Vibhashas of all the three Gramas, and only a number of Shadja Grama Ragas (52) are described in the published volume.

According to Sharngdeva, Dhannashi is a Shadava Raga omitting the note Rishabha with Shadja as its Ansha and Graha note while Madhyama is the concluding note.[61]

Kuranji : Neither Matanga nor Nanya Bhupala has mentioned about this Raga. In 'Sangita Makaranda', Kuranji is described as a Shadava Raga, with 'Ni' as the note of omission and Madhyama as the starting note. In 'Sangita Ratnakara' a Raga named Gurunjika is mentioned in the list of past popular Ragas, without any description.

Kallinatha describes it as a Upanga Raga of Lalita. It is an Oudava Raga, omits 'Ri' and 'Ni' notes, Panchama gets the importance of being initial, concluding and prominent note. Kallinatha provides description of many ancient Ragas, which are only mentioned, but not described by Sharngdeva.[62] In our work Sourashtri has been described as a male Raga and Dravadi appears as a female Raga.

Shuddha : It is an ancient Bhasha Raga described by Matanga. Shuddha is a Bhasha of Bhinna Shadja. Dhaivata has its concluding and prominent note. It is an Oudava Bhasha with the omission of Rishabha and Panchama.[63]

It is a Vibhasha of Malava Kaishiki and Bhinna Shadja. It appears as a Vibhasha of Takka also. Panchama is the Ansha of this Vibhasha and Shadja is the ending note. It is to be sung at the end of the Bhashas.[64] It also appears as a

Vibhasha of Malava Kaishiki, which is Sampurna, has Ma as Ansha and Dha as concluding note. It expresses joy.[65] Nanya Bhupala enlists Shuddha in Shadja Grama Ragas without any description. Sharngdeva does not mention it. In 'Sangita Makaranda', no description is available except its reference as a neuter Raga.

Kaumodaki : Matanga, Nanya Bhupala or Sharngdeva have not mentioned about this Raga. A Kriyanga Raga of Shadja Grama, named Kumudakri appears in Bharata Bhashyam, without any details. In 'Sangita Ratnakara' Kumudaki is mentioned in the list of past popular Ragas, and Kamodika appears in the present popular Ragas.

Ramakri : It appears as a Kriyanga Raga of Shadja Grama in 'Bharata Bhashyam'. Ramakriti and not Ramakri or Ramakriya is however mentioned by Sharngdeva. That Ramakriti is a Shadava Bhashanga Raga of Kolahala, omitting the note Panchama. Its prominent note is Ma and concluding note is Sa. As a general rule, when a Graha note is not indicated, the Ansha or prominent note is taken as the initial note.

In 'Sangita Makaranda', Ramakri is a neuter Raga. Narada mentions Ramakriti as a night melody and an Oudava Raga, omitting Ri and Dha notes. Its Graha note is 'Ga'. Narada also mentions a Sampurna Raga named Ramakriya with an initial note 'Sa'. Whether three different Ragas—Ramakri, Ramakriti, and Ramakriya are given by the author, or one of them is is a misnomer, is incomprehensible.

Saveri : It is an ancient Raga found in 'Brihaddeshi' as per quoted verse in 'Bharata Bhashyam'. But, most of the Ragas (verses) quoted by Nanya Bhupala are not found in the available manuscript of 'Brihaddeshi'.

According to Nanya Bhupala and the quoted verse of Matanga, Saveri is a Shadava Raga omitting the Panchama. Dhaivata is the starting, concluding and prominent note. Nanya Deva describes it as a Vibhasha of Roopa Sadharita.[66] In the manuscript, it appears as Saravi, and while naming the Shadja Grama Ragas and their Vibhashas (Roopa Sadharita), the name Savari appears in the manuscript.[67]

Sharngdeva opines, that Saveri is derived from Raganti, which is a Bhasha of the Grama Raga Ka kubha. Panchama is omitted and Shadja is used sparingly. Madhyama is the Graha and Ansha note, while Dhaivata is the concluding note.[68]

In 'Sangita Makaranda', Saveri is a noon time melody and a neuter Raga without any other details.

Balahamsa : A noon time melody, that starts on Gandhara. This Raga is not mentioned elsewhere, it is a Sampurna Raga.

Samavedi : None of the three authors we refer to, till now, i.e., Matanga, Nanya Bhupala and Sharngdeva have mentioned this Raga. In 'Sangita Makaranda' it appears as a morning melody and a neuter Raga.

Shankarabharana : This Raga appears as a noon time melody and as a neuter Raga. No other details are available in 'Sangita Makaranda'. In 'Sangita Ratnakara', Shankarabharana appears in the list of Poorva Prasiddha Ragas (popular melodies of past) without any description

Thus the Ragas, which are mentioned in 'Sangita Makaranda' under the time concept, male, female and neuter Ragas and Ragas with their Graha notes— Sampurna, Shadava and Oudava types are explained with the help of 'Brihaddeshi', 'Bharata Bhashyam' and 'Sangita Ratnakara'. As already mentioned, many Ragas of this work appear in other works, e.g., Manasollosa, Sangita Raja, Sangita Parijata and works dealing in Carnatic music. Some of the Ragas (names) are practiced at present also, e.g., Saveri, Shankarabharana, Balahamsa in Carnatic music and Ghurjari, Todi, Shri Vasanta, Bhairava Bhupala, etc., in Hindustani music. The characteristics pertaining to the rendering of the similar named Ragas cannot be ascertained, as drastic changes have occurred and replaced the old system in all spheres. Music is not an exception to this rule. Moreover, 'Sangita Makaranda' belongs to an earlier period, and is based on a novel concept of Deshi Ragas. His system is entirely based on Murchanas and two Sadharana notes including regular seven notes of all the three Gramas. No other vikrita notes are used in this work, while in all the other later works many vikrita notes are mentioned.

The similarity ends with the name only. There are many Ragas bearing similar names like Narayani, Deshi, Gujari, Bhairava, Vasanta etc., which are still present. But the characteristics of the Ragas of past bearing the present names cannot be similar; at least the similarity cannot be ascertained.

Narada has not described about any other vikrita notes, other than two sadharana notes. Starting from 'Sangita Ratnakara', the later authors based their system on a number of vikrita notes. Ahobala has mentioned 29 notes in all; 7 shuddha and 22 vikrita notes. He leaves ten notes (vikrita) among them while describing the Ragas.

"इत्येतांश्च दशं त्यक्त्वा राग लक्षणभीरितम्
द्वादशभिर्विकाराद्यैः शुद्धैश्च सप्तभिः स्वरैः।"[69]

Whereas 'Sangita Makaranda' does not mention about vikrita notes, it mentions only two sadharana notes. Thus the Raga descriptions of Sangita Parijata and later authors are not applicable to the Ragas of 'Sangita Makaranda', just because of the similarity in the names. Sharngdeva also explains about 12 vikrita notes but his Ragas are based on Grama Ragas and Geetis. Vikrita notes are not used in describing the Ragas.

Nevertheless, 'Sangita Ratnakara' is the nearest work to 'Sangita Makaranda' and both have similarities as well similar verses at places.

Ahobala's list of Ragas bears many ancient names, even the names mentioned by Matanga as well as later names of his own period. His Bhimpalasi is similar to the present Bhimpalasi. Therefore the descriptions of Ragas which are not given by Narada, i.e., Nilambari, Shankarabharana and Malava Goula cannot be taken from Sangita Parijata, because that will not serve the purpose and provide any clue for these Ragas, as Ragas change with time as a rule.

Narada has classified the Ragas according to their time of singing. Then the three types of Ragas—Sampoorna, Shadava and Oudava with their starting notes. These classification are common and known to all. His special classifications of Ragas begins with three types of Ragas—male, female, and neuter Ragas. His treatment of Ragas are just like of human beings, hence his astrological and physical descriptions of notes are well justified.

After general classification of masculine, feminine and neuter Ragas, Narada proceeds with further classifications of special category. About the classification of male, female and neuter Ragas, no conclusions can be arrived at. The origin, purpose and qualifying factors which make them eligible for their category are also not known, neither described nor even mentioned. This may be the fertile imagination of the ancient authors and musicians, yet it does not seem proper to say that these classifications are meaningless jumbles decided by drawing lots. It is certain that it has something to do with the feelings and emotions; the Ragas are capable of creating. They create the atmosphere. Bharata has used Gandharva (music) in his dramaturgy to enhance the effect of dramatic situations and introduces the sentiments through music to the audience. Sometimes, the music (Dhruva) announces the entrance and exit of the main characters; it is used to normalise or prepare the audience to meet the dreadful or pathetic situations at another time. His notes Shadja, etc., carry emotional values, and he is followed by the later authors. Some notes are soft while others are harsh and hard. Speed too supplements in creating the required emotions. There are nine Rasas (eight according to Bharata) divided into three categories — soft and sweet, strong and hard and the neutral. As to that, the whole universe reflects only two factors — Male and female, Shiva and Shakti, Purusha and Prakriti. The softer, delicate and the beautiful things and subjects represent femininity while strong, superior, majestic and magnificient factors represent the masculine personae. In the same way Ragas also represent these two factors. In dance, there are Tandava and Lasya representing the male and female dances. This twofold dance also might be the basis of male and female Ragas. If Shringara, Karuna, Hasya Rasas, etc., are delicate and soft feelings and may be called as female oriented feelings, Veera, Roudhra, Adbhuta Rasas too are stronger feelings and purely masculine. Vibhatsa and

Bhayanaka Rasas too are strong feelings, but are neither sweet and appealing nor magnificent. None likes to witness these feelings, but they have dramatic value. They are not appreciated yet this does not diminish their importance in dramaturgy.

Bharata does not include Shanta as a Rasa in 'Natya Shastra'. It is dissimilar to Bhayanaka or Vibhatsa, but it has no dramatic value. Narada of 'Sangita Makaranda' includes Shanta Rasa in 'Sangita Makaranda' as his work deals in music only. Vibhatsa and Bhayanaka have nothing to do with music, but they are included by Narada with Shanta Rasa and the Napunsaka Ragas are supposed to cause these three Rasas. Rasas are different sentiments experienced by the human beings in various situations and circumstances. Shanta is the sentiment, where all the other sentiments merge and conclude. As Shanta Rasa ends all the feelings and no sentiments get started from it, this Rasa is handed over to neuter Ragas.

The properties of the nine Rasas are divided among the three classes of Ragas and named as Pullinga (Masculine), Stree (Feminine) and Napunsaka (Neuter) Ragas, which are acceptable to all the scholars.

Narada explains thus :

"रौद्रेऽद्भुते तथा वीरे पुंरागैः परिगीयते।
शृंगार हास्य करुणं (?) स्त्री रागैश्च प्रगीयते
भयानके च वीभत्से शान्ते गायन्नपुंसके।"

It is clear from the above statement that the Ragas are classified according to their emotional involvement. Atleast Narada has divided them according to the sentiments they create. First he has divided the nine Rasas into three types—male, female and neuter and then attributes them to the three types of Ragas as follows.

Roudhra, Adbhuta and Veera Rasas.—(Male Ragas) furiousness, marvellousness, heroism come under Masculine Ragas.

Shringara, Hasya and Karuna Rasas — (Female Ragas) love, mirth and pathos are created by the female Ragas. These Ragas should have soft notes with delicate note patterns.

Vibhatsa, Bhayanaka and Shanta Rasas — These sentiments are given to the Neuter Ragas as their share. These are hatred, fear and calmness.

Therefore, this type of classification might have been there from the time of Bharata, though not specifically named as Masculine, Feminine and Neuter Ragas. Matanga does not speak in these terms and his Deshi Ragas are not available, yet he names the Grama Ragas with masculine names and treats the Bhasha Ragas as females and names them accordingly. Narada of 'Sangita Makaranda' takes a step forward and categorises Ragas in three classes in clear terms as male, female and neuter Ragas. Narada says that these Ragas should be used as the situation demands, i.e., according to the Rasa to be used for that particular situation. Narada names Brahma as the supporter of these three types of Ragas — male, female and neuter. Brahma Himself has approved of these three types of Ragas.

In between, Narada mentions the thirteen names of Raganga Ragas as follows—

1. Madhyamadi
2. Malavashri
3. Shrika
4. Jaya Sakshika
5. Varati
6. Ghurjari
7. Gouda
8. Kolahala
9. Vasantaka
10. Dhanashri
11. Desa
12. Deshakya
13. Bangala

These thirteen Ragas are already described under other headings, excluding. Jayasakshika, Shrika and Madhyamadi.

Narada has given as many classifications as were prevalent in his time. Though Narada does not give any explanations about the classification, he enumerates all possible and feasible classifications of Ragas. The main and unique classification (not to be found in any other work except in Raga Sagara) of Raga-Ragini appears in the beginning. This classification is unique in the sense that it has eight Ragas and each Raga has three wives. The term Ragini does not occur in 'Sangita Makaranda'. Narada uses 'Pati' for the Ragas and 'Yoshita' for the Raginis. Ragini, the term, does not appear before the date of Ragarnava of fourteenth century, though the recognition of female Ragas must be much older in the music system of north India. According to many scholars, the bifurcation of Indian music system into two major systems — Carnatic and Hindustani took place after Sharngdeva. 'Sangita Ratnakara' is supposed to be accepted all over India and followed by all. In the same way, Raga-Ragini system is supposed to be related to north India only. 'Sangita Makaranda' is definitely an earlier work than 'Sangita Ratnakara' and it classifies the Raga under Raga-Ragini system. That indicates that Raga-Ragini system or a different system of Raga classification depending upon the nine sentiments and classified under male, female and neuter Ragas was in existence. This system which is recognised as a system belonging to north India, goes back to the period of Agamas and Tantric traditions, practised a little later or parallel to Vedic period. According to Tantra, the Nada itself is created by the togetherness of Shiva and Shakti (male and female). Though Narada does not explain all these, Matanga describes about this fact in the beginning of 'Brihaddeshi'. It has been already discussed earlier. Moreover Tantric practices mostly flourished in north India, in Kerala and a little in Karnataka. Raga-Ragini system is related to Tantra practices and its possibility of belonging to north India is more feasible. Its antiquity is more emphasised due to its said connection to Tantra.

If Sama Gana and Vedic chants are used to propitiate the Vedic deities, then this type of music with Ragas (male and female) is meant to please Shiva and Shakti around whom the Tantra cult has evolved.

Though the term Ragini appears very late, female Ragas

(with feminine names) were in practice from the time of Matanga — Saindhavi, Gandhari, Gurjari, Pourali, Dravadi, etc., as Bhasha Ragas. Neither Sharngdeva nor Nanya Bhupala mention about female Ragas, yet their Bhasha, Vibhasha and Antarabhasha bear the feminine names.

Major melodies or Grama Ragas are always treated as male Ragas and allotted particular seasons in which they should be sung. On the other hand, Bhasha, Vibhasha Ragas derived from the major Ragas or minor melodies do not enjoy this previlage. As already mentioned, Nanya Bhupala says that the time given to Gramas are applicable to Grama Ragas and Bhashas derived from them. Sharngdeva mentions the singing time of all major Ragas, but he leaves out the Bhasha, Vibhasha and the minor melodies. In 'Panchama Sara Samhita', of Narada, it is clearly explained thus—

"रागश्चेदालापेत् पूर्वं तत्पत्नीस्तदनंतरम्।
नान्य पत्नी प्रगातव्या नृपाज्ञयां न दूषणम्।"[70]

The author of 'Panchama Sara Samhita' mentions the time of Ragas in this sloka, i.e., says, that at first a Raga should be elaborated (Alapa) and then the Alapa of the Raga should be followed by the elaboration of his wife (Ragini or female Raga). No other Ragini, wife of other Raga should be sung after another Ragini's husband. He means to specify that a particular Raga should be followed by his own Raginis or wives while singing. Raginis or wives other than his own should not be sung just after him. But exceptions are there. By the king's order one can sing any Raga followed by any other Ragini.

In Indian music, there are atleast four systems of Raga classification from the ancient period till present. First is Gramas and Grama Ragas. Secondly, Ragas derived from Geetis based upon Grama Ragas. Thirdly, Ragas and their wives and fourth is the Mela system. There is yet another system in use, i.e., the Raganga system. All the other systems have some logic, rules and regulations, but Raga-Ragini system seems to possess no logical explanations or grammar in the formations of the system. However, there must be some rules and regulations which were lost with the time. It might be possible that they belong to Deshi type of Ragas, which have no proper rules. But even Deshi Ragas are governed by certain rules to avoid monotonous similarity. They must also have some form of order to distinguish them from each other. More or less, the Raga-Ragini system is based upon the time theory—seasons and the division of hours per day. The emotive value of notes a Raga consists of and the nine sentiments governing the three types of Ragas also play an important role in forming this type (system) of classification.

"In 'Panchama Sara Samhita', it seems, the term "Ragini" appears for the first time, because in the Asiatic Society of Calcutta, the manuscript of 'Panchama Sara Samhita' bears a colophone — dated 1440 A.D., 1362 Saka."[71] The year is mentioned in coded Sanskrit words.

Yet another striking fact is that all the works attributed to Narada or to the name of Narada are similar in one way, i.e., in Raga classification. They follow the male-female classification. The works belong to different periods and authors—Naradas; are also different. It seems that they follow some old system expounded by some original Narada which is not available at present. This music system of Raga-Ragini might belong to a school of music of Narada. Hence all the authors following the school of music of Narada have adopted the pen name of Narada as well. The works of Narada of different periods make improvements in the old system, according to the demands of their time, though basically the works are of a similar system.

In the first work of Narada— 'Naradiya Shiksha', only seven Grama Ragas, Gandhara Grama with its seven Murchanas are given.

Narada of 'Sangita Makaranda' goes a little further and gives the notes of Gandhara Gramas, male, female and neuter classification of Ragas, Purusha and Bharya or Yoshita Raga classifications.

'Raga Sagara', which is attributed to Narada and Dattila combined, follows the same classification of Raga which is unique and found in 'Sangita Makaranda', only eight Ragas having three wives each. The published version of 'Raga Sagara' is not available. Its manuscript is in a very precarious condition and is kept in the Madras Government Library.[72] The work 'Raga Sagara' begins with the names of eight male Ragas and then leaves it abruptly and quotes some verses from 'Svaramela Kalanidhi', 'Sangita Ratnakara' and Sharngdeva is given more importance. The work looks like an old work with patches of new in between. It has the Raga classification of Ragas, their wives, daughters and sons not exceeding three in number. There are Mitra Ragas, messenger Ragas (female) Dooti Ragas. Every male Raga has a female messenger Raga.

Next in order comes 'Panchama Sara Samhita' ascribed to Narada again. The term Ragini appears in 'Panchama Sara Samhita'; with contemplative and meditative verses given to each Raga and his Raginis. In this work, the 8 Ragas and 24 Raginis are not mentioned. The system of 6 Ragas with 36 Raginis is explained. In this work, the singing time of the Raga is given more elaborately and stress is laid upon the point that the Raginis are to be sung after their own Ragas.

Supposedly a later work attributed to an author Narada is Chatvarimshachatta Raga Nirupanam. It deals with 140 Ragas, as their growing number cannot be adjusted in six Ragas and six Raginis each, this Narada introduces sons and daughters-in-law. Ragas also grow in number. Ten Ragas are mentioned instead of eight or six. Each Raga has five wives and four sons and four daughters-in-law making the total 140 in all. The name of the work also indicates the same.

First of all, the names of the male Ragas are given with their meditative verses. Though, the Raga Nirupanam is placed as the latest work among Narada's other works, (by O.C.Ganguli) it seems a little later work than 'Panchama Sara Samhita'. In this work, the relationship of sound (Tantra tradition) called Bijakshara 'अ', 'प' and 'ई' with the deities are mentioned in Gana Prakarana. It has not been discussed elaborately, as it is beyond the scope of work.

The Raga-Ragini system of 'Sangita Makaranda' it seems,

is based on the divisions of the day and night. There are eight praharas or yamas in twenty-four hours, each consisting of three hours. It is called Ghadi (घड़ी) in vernacular. The eight male Ragas might belong to eight praharas and their wives follow them. This is according to ancient Indian system which was followed all over India in the past. The temples followed these time divisions to perform their daily rituals of worship and even at present the daily religious ceremonies and rites are done according to the divisions — Yama (जाम) of the day. They are divided into two parts, of four praharas each, beginning from sunrise—6 to 6 in the morning and 6 to 6 from the evening after sunset. The eight Ragas probably represent, these eight praharas are based on time theory only. The number of Raginis being three again confirms this concept as they represent the three hours of a prahara.

The second classification of six Ragas with six or five Raginis probably is based upon the six seasons of India—Grishma, Varsha, Hemanta, Shishira, Sharada and Vasanta each consisting of two months, or sixty days. Now the number of Raginis is divisible in these sixty days, each Ragini having 10 to 12 days of its own. Perhaps, Narada of 'Sangita Makaranda' does not give importance to this later classification of six Ragas and 36 or 30 Raginis.

The first classification of eight Ragas with their twenty-four—Raginis is given below :

Ragas		*Wives*
1. Bhupala	—	Velavali, Malahari, Bahuli.
2. Bhairava	—	Devakriya, Pourali, Kambhari.
3. Shri Raga	—	Kambhoji, Bhallati, Kuranjika.
4. Pada Manjari	—	Deshi, Manohari, Tundi.
5. Vasanta	—	Varati, Dravadi, Hansi.
6. Malava	—	Gunda Kriya, Ghurjari, Goudi.
7. Nata	—	Sarang Nata, Natakhya, Ahari.
8. Bangala	—	Narayani, Gandhari, Ranji.

The male-female Ragas together make thirty-two in all.

"स्त्री पुंस रागमाख्यातां द्वात्रिंशद्राग संमतिः।"[73]

The three names of the wives of Nata Raga do not sound correct. They should be Salangakhya and Mishra Nata. These two names are given in the Stree Ragas and the wives mentioned by Narada are taken from the twenty-four Stree Ragas only. This classification of 32 Ragas is not found anywhere except in 'Raga Sagara', as mentioned earlier. They are as follows:

Raga		*Wives*
1. Bhairava	—	Devakriya, Megha Ranji, Kuranji.
2. Bhupala	—	Bilahari, Malahari, Bhandi.
3. Shri Raga	—	Andali, Bhallati, Sahuli.
4. Padamanjari	—	Deshi, Mukhari, Lalita.
5. Vasanta	—	Ramakriya, Barali, Gouli.
6. Malava	—	Gunda Kriya, Gurjari, Palika.
7. Bangala	—	Kalyani, Ahari, Saveri.
8. Nataka	—	Ghanta Rava, Kambhoj, Shakarabharana.[74]

The names of the eight male Ragas are same, while names of their respective wives differ. These classifications of eight Ragas and three wives each are unique and occur only in these two works.

There is a novel idea explained in this work 'Raga Sagara', about the three wives. The three wives can be divided again into three types of Ragas—Sweeya, Parakeeya and Samanya(स्वीया, परकीया और सामान्या). Sweeya stands for Shuddha Ragas. Parkeeya is Salaga Raga, a Raga with a shadow of another Raga. Samanya is a Sankara or mixed Raga.

"स्वीया परकीया च सामान्या च त्रिधा मता।
शुद्धा स्वीया इति प्रोक्ता सालगा परकामिनी।
सामान्यो संकर प्रोक्तारो कोहलेति निगद्यते।"[75]

The mention of the name Kohala might be to make it authentic or there might be some ancient work authored by kohala.

There are many other novel ideas about the time theory and sentiments too. The popular Raga-Ragini classification familiar to all appears after this peculiar classification. This widely used classification of six Ragas with their six wives according to Shivamata is mentioned by Narada of 'Sangita Makaranda' with their names. The other classification of six Ragas and five wives each is left out by Narada. The six Ragas are as follows with their wives.

Raga	Wives
1. Shri Raga	— Goudi, Kolahali, Dravati, Andolika, Madhavi, Deva Gandhari.
2. Panchama	— Shuddha Nata, Saveri, Saindhavi, Malati, Troti, Kaumodaki.
3. Megha Raga	— Sourashtri, Kambhari, Bangali, Madhu Madhavi, Devakri, Bhupali.
4. Nata Narayana	— Vallabha, Madhavi (repetition) Vidagdha, Abhisarika, Triveni, Mega Ranji.

Though Vasanta and Bhairava Ragas are mentioned in the list of six Ragas, the Raginis are not found as the original manuscript is damaged and probably could not be deciphered by the copyist. Because, in the available manuscript also the place is left blank for the sloka no. 79.

Narada has classified the Ragas according to their singing time, three types of Ragas according to the number of notes and Raga-Ragini classification and so on. Now there is another novel classification which is applicable to all times i.e., according to the quality or applying technique of the notes in a Raga. They are Muktanga Kampita, Ardha Vikampita and Kampa Vihina. Kampa means vibrating, unsteady shaking and trembling. This Kampa applies to the notes used in a Raga.

Muktanga-Kampita—Raga which has notes those are shaking and are shaken purposely as the part of the Raga, is called Muktanga Kampita. This categorisation is still applicable and can be compared to the present 'Raganga', which distinguishes a pair of Ragas with the same scale. Bhairava and Kalingada are differentiated by the shaking (Andolit) notes 'Ri' and 'Dha' of Bhairava. In the same way, Adana has plain notes, while the 'Ga' and 'Dha' of Darbari Kanhara are unsteady and trembling.

Ardha Vikampita : The notes are not shaking or unsteady all the times. They are only half unsteady as the Muktanga Kampita.

Kampa Vihina : The Ragas in which notes are steady and never shake are called as Kampa Vihina.

The rules of these three Ragas regarding their notes-shaking or steady should not be contradicted. According to Narada the singer and the listener will be destined to face the greatest sin of being a Brahma ghatin, for negligence of their part. Kampavihina should not have shaky notes and Muktanga should not have steady notes.

Narada explains the merits and boons of singing the three types of Ragas Sampoorna, Shadava and Oudava Ragas, before the above classification.

Sampoorna Ragas are capables of granting longevity, religious attainments, intelligence, wealth, a good harvest and fruits to the singer and listeners of the Ragas. He means that the Sampoorna Ragas should be used to get these attainments mentioned above.

'Shadava Ragas', he changes the expression and explains about their usage. They should be used to describe the war, beauty, grace, separation and to praise to anybody. Oudava Ragas win the upper hand. They are powerful enough to ward off enemies, illness, fear and misery, poverty and planetary positions, causing mishaps. They also destroy vanity of passions and ill effects of poisons. The village deities are appeased by singing Oudava Ragas.

Therefore, Oudava Ragas are always preferred by earlier authors.

This is all Narada says about the Ragas. He concludes this third pada of Sangitadhyaya with some general hints of do's and don'ts, which are important enough to be neglected. The neglect of these simple enough rules may cause calamities.

The whole music is personified as the Trinity — Brahma, Vishnu and Shiva. Brahma is Pranava, Vishnu is the Tala and Nada is Shiva Himself. Therefore, music should be treated with full respect and devotion.

The singer should first decide the tempo of Tala (लय) then after producing the correct Nada, he should start singing the song. What Narada means to explain is very practical. By 'Nada', he means the pitch and voice application. To give a good performance, the singer should first fix his measure of Tala and apply the voice. Then only he should start singing. Music should be listened to in this fashion only. To ignore this simple rule has no parallel sin. Tuneless singing, playing the instruments and listening make the listener miserable. Narada always makes the listener responsible for the mistakes of singer. Listeners only make the singer to give out his best performance. Listeners should possess full knowledge of music and should not ignore or neglect or show leniency to the tuneless and incorrect singing of the singer. Ignorance on their part makes a good singer sore at heart as their labour and knowledge of music are lost on them. Nowadays the listeners are not very particular about these facts and have no knowledge of even the basics of music, which is the cause of the degeneration of classical music.

Narada names some of the defects of singers and the consequences of listening to such defective music.

Apasvaram — misplaced notes hard on ears.

Kunadam — defective sound

Shrutiheenam — tunelessness (lower than the accurate tone).

Shruti Adhikam — higher than accurate tone.

The ignorant person who listens to such music with tuneless or highly pitched misplaced notes and unbearably harsh voice falls in hell and stays there for long. According to Shastras, this type of defective singing causes misery, sorrow, poverty and even curtails the life span. This is not all, the listeners who encourage this type of singing reap all the above consequences. If the listener is a king, he may lose his kingdom in addition to all the ill-effects mentioned above. The king who knows all these Shastras about music and listens accordingly will get wealth, health and longevity.

In ancient India, it was customary to conclude all the treatises on any subject, mainly related to religion with a promise of boons, good results and spiritual attainments by going through the treatises and respecting the rules and regulations laid in them. Music is certainly one of the most spiritual subjects and it is the personification of God Himself. There is always the advice to follow the rules to the letter, to be suitably rewarded, failing which a catastrophy will fall on him. This concluding part of the treatise is called "Phala Shruti" (फल श्रुति) and the reader should not avoid this part.

But about music, whatever has been said by Narada is correct and applicable to all ages and places as well. Music is supposed to be a universal language. It can appeal only by its perfection and sweetness. Its soothing and healing effect is destroyed by defective singing—tunelessness, tonal defects; and harsh unmusical sound will create tension only. Healing by music and its medicinal properties are widely discussed at present. To be successful in restoring physical and mental health, music used for the purpose should be perfect in every way.

Ragadhyaya, though it is not named as such by Narada of 'Sangita Makaranda' has many important, unique and remarkable points which are not found in many treatises.

First of all, Narada begins at the beginning — the time theory or the singing time of Ragas. He has allotted particular time of the day and night to the Deshi or minor Ragas, which are not done by Matanga, Nanya Bhupala and Sharngdeva, though the time of particular 'savanas' was there from the Vedic period. Bharata does not deal in Grama Raga or Ragas of any sort though his sloka "मुखे तु मध्यम ग्राम" names five Grama Ragas. But he does not describe them and he is more concerned about Dhruvageetis and dramaturgy. He mentions only about the time which should be presented by the particular Dhruva.[76]

Narada has classified the Ragas according to their time of singing. They are Suryansha, Pratahkala, Madhyanha, Chandramansha and then divides the Ragas giving them exact praharas or Yamas of the day and night.

The Ragas are again divided into three general types, Sampoorna, Shadava and Oudava — seven noted, six noted and five noted Ragas with their starting notes and omitted notes; in the case of Shadava and Oudava Ragas.

The Ragas are described with starting notes, omitted notes and the time of singing, but this does not apply to all Ragas. Only the selected Ragas (basis unknown) are treated like this. There are many Ragas starting on the same note and omitting the same notes which prove that three Gramas are used by Narada. The Ragas are based on Murchana system. In Bhupala, Shadja is omitted which shows Shadja's unimportance. Grama Ragas and Geetis are not mentioned. Another unique point is in five noted Ragas he has omitted two adjacent notes, which is possible only in Murchana system, i.e., 'Sa' and 'Ri' in Velavali, 'Ma' and 'Pa' in 'Pali' which is not permitted at present.

The Ragas are based on Murchana systems. Obviously, Narada has used all the three Gramas for his Ragas, as he has not given any other particulars of his Ragas in this work

'Sangita Makaranda'. Many of his Ragas do not resemble in all the points to the Ragas of Matanga, Nanya Bhupala or Sharngdeva except in name, so there might have been another ancient extensive work of Narada which is not extant.

'Bharata Bhashyam' of Nanya Bhupala is the only work which uses all the three Gramas. He follows Narada in many places and mentions Grama Ragas, Bhasha, Vibhasha, Raganga, Kriyanga besides many other types of Ragas based on all the three Gramas. He mentions Dhanyasi as a Raga of Gandhara Grama, but unfortunately the complete work has not been published. The second part contains only some of the Shadja Grama Ragas, as such the Ragas of 'Sangita Makaranda' cannot be compared with the Ragas of 'Bharata Bhashyam' which seems near to 'Sangita Makaranda'.

'Bharata Bhashyam' follows 'Sangita Makaranda' in many topics but it does not mention the masculine, feminine and neuter Ragas. After the starting notes of Ragas, Narada names the three types of Ragas — Pullinga, Stree and Napunsaka Ragas based on nine sentiments. Masculine Ragas express Veera, Roudhra and Adbhuta sentiment. Feminine Ragas are used for Shringara, Karuna and Hasya Rasas. Vibhatsa, Bhayanaka and Shanta are expressed by Napunsaka Ragas.

Two types of Raga-Ragini classifications are discussed. Eight Ragas and three Raginis each, are based on eight praharas and three hours of a prahara.

Six Ragas and six Raginis are based upon six seasons and twelve months.

Another scheme of Raga classification follows; based on the application of notes-shaking, half-shaking, and steady, i.e. Muktaṇga Kampita, Ardhavikampita and Kampavihina. That is the last classification but the names of Ragas, which come under these categories, are not mentioned.

The practical side of music is also well advocated and the listeners also are advised to have thorough knowledge of music, so that they can encourage the faultless traditional music.

In the fourth pada of 'Sangitadhyaya', Narada again stresses that there are only 32 Ragas including Sampoorna, Shadava and Oudava Ragas which confirms his preference for the Raga classification of eight Ragas with three wives each, amounting to 32 number. There might be endless variety of Ragas relating to various places, countries and circumstances that enumerate 500 Sampoorna Ragas, 200 Shadava Ragas and 100 Oudava Ragas, but main Ragas are thirty-two.

REFERENCES

1. *Sangita Makaranda*, p. 14.
2. *Ibid.*
3. *Bharatiya Sangita Ka Itihasa*, p. 28.
4. *Chandogya Upanishad.*
5. *Natya Shastra*, Chapter 32, p. 373.
6. *Bharata Bhashyam*, part II, p. 150.
7. *Ibid.*, part II, p. 226.
8. *Ibid.*
9. *Sangita Ratnakara*, vol. II, sl. 39, p. 37.
10. *Brihaddeshi*, p. 26.
11. Ibid., p. 25, September, 1975.
12. *Bharata Bhashyam*, part II, p. 228.
13. *Ibid.*, p. 229.
14. *Sangita Ratnakara*, vol. II, p. 3.
15. *Ibid.*, p. 18.
16. *Ibid.*, p. 131.
17. *Bharata Bhashyam*, vol. II, p. 264.
18. *Brihaddeshi*, p. 21.
19. *Sangita Ratnakara*, pp. 120-21.
20. *Bharata Bhashyam*, vol. II, sl. 193-94, p. 276.
21. *Brihaddeshi*, p. 27.
22. *Ibid.* pp. 23, 25 and 27.
23. *Sangita Ratnakara*, vol. II, p. 77.

24. *Bharata Bhashyam*, vol. II, p. 297.
25. *Sangita Ratnakara*, vol. II, pp. 96 and 106.
26. *Brihaddeshi*, October, 1975, p. 27.
27. *Bharata Bhashyam*, vol. II, p. 261.
28. *Sangita Ratnakara*, vol. II, p. 96.
29. *Bharata Bhashyam*, part II, p. 281.
30. *Ibid.*, part II, p. 280.
31. *Sangita Ratnakara*, vol. II, p. 77.
32. *Bharata Bhashyam*, vol. II, p. 267.
33. *Ibid.*, vol. II, sl. 56-57, p. 233.
34. *Sangita Ratnakara*, vol. II, p. 96.
35. *Bharata Bhashyam*, vol. II, sl 31 and 42, p. 231.
36. *Sangita Ratnakara*, vol. II, sl. 156, p. 113.
37. *Ibid.*, p. 107.
38. *Brihaddeshi*, p. 146.
39. *Bharata Bhashyam*, vol. II, p. 239.
40. *Sangita Ratnakara*, Chapter 2, p. 81.
41. *Brihaddeshi*, p. 141.
42. *Bharata Bhashyam*, vol. II, p. 259.
43. *Sangita Ratnakara*, vol. II, p. 119.
44. *Ibid.*, p. 8.
45. *Bharata Bhashyam*, vol. II, p. 236.
46. *Brihaddeshi*, p. 80.
47. *Sangita Ratnakara*, Chapter 2, p. 105.
48. *Bharata Bhashyam*, vol. II, p. 236.
49. *Brihaddeshi*, vol. 10, p. 195.
50. *Ibid.*, vol. 10, p. 175.
51. *Brihaddeshi*, sl. 127, p. 175.
52. *Bharata Bhashyam*, vol. II, pp. 232 and 295-96.
53. *Sangita Ratnakara*, vol. II, p. 75.
54. *Brihaddeshi*, pp. 179 and 189.
55. *Brihaddeshi*, vol. II, sl. 77, p. 236.
56. *Sangita Ratnakara*, chapter 2, p. 131.
57. *Ibid.*, p. 16.

58. *Ibid.*, vol. II, pp. 125-26.
59. *Bharata Bhashyam*, vol. II, p. 276.
60. *Sangita Ratnakara*, vol. II, p. 198.
61. *Ibid.*, p. 85.
62. *Ibid.*, p. 147.
63. *Brihaddeshi*, vol. II, p. 146.
64. *Ibid.*, p. 167.
65. *Ibid.*, p. 149.
66. *Bharata Bhashyam*, vol. II, p. 292.
67. *Ibid.*, p. 232.
68. *Sangita Ratnakara*, vol. II, p. 292.
69. *Sangita Parijata*, p. 200.
70. *Fundamentals of Ancient Indian Music and Dance*, p. 9.
71. *Ragas and Raginis*, p. 43.
72. The transcript of *Ragasagara* is with the researcher.
73. *Sangita Makaranda*, p. 19.
74. *Raga Sagara*, Transcript, p. 18.
75. *Ibid.*
76. *Studies in the Natya Shastra*, p. 173.
    "The entrance song is to be sung to indicate anything happening in the fore-noon and the exit. Song may be used to indicate anything happening by day and night."

8

Prakirnaka

This chapter is named as Prakirnaka, because it covers miscellaneous subjects related to music which appear in the fourth pada of 'Sangitadhyaya'. The present chapter of this work deals in Mridanga Lakshanam, instruments, Vaggeyakara Lakshanam and merits and demerits of musicians.

The chapter starts with Mridanga Lakshanam—definition of a Mridanga. Mridanga is a percussion instrument which resembles —Pakhavaj, Khol, Madul, Dholak in shape and in principle. It has two sides covered with skin and played on both sides by both hands.

This is the most ancient percussion instrument used to keep time. Now Narada of 'Sangita Makaranda' provides a novel idea which indicates the affiliation of this work to Tantra Shastra. Tala is said to be originated from Shiva and Shakti, but here Mridangam itself represents the principle of Shiva-Shakti combination according to Narada. He says that right side of Mridanga represents Rudra (Siva) and the left side stands for Uma (Shakti). Therefore the sound produced by Mridanga consists of physical properties of both Shiva and Shakti—sweetness and majesty. Nada, according to Tantra, is produced by the combination of Shiva-Shakti. All matters, living and non-living including the whole universe are created by Shiva and Shakti. They cannot be, and should not be separated from each other. This is the main principle of Tantra. Now, Narada says that the sound produced by right side (Shiva), creates ill-health, while the sound of left side gives poverty. This shows that Mridanga should be played on both sides for prosperity and health. The sounds of both sides of the Mridanga should be equal. The sound should be in tune, clear and sweet. This sort of sound produced by a well tuned Mridanga pleases the listeners as it gives them longevity, wealth, etc. According to 'Sangita Makaranda', music leads to spiritual and worldly attainments. It gives unforseen (अदृष्ट) attainments, according to the ancient authors. Mridanga is named as 'Mardala' by Narada. Starting the Vadyadhyaya in 'Natya Shastra' Bharata says :

"मृदङ्ग पणवानाञ्च दर्दुरस्य तथैव च
गान्धर्वञ्चैव वाद्यञ्चं स्वातिना नारदेन च।"[1]

Bharata opines that Narada and Svati has described about Mridanga, Panava and Dardura, etc., (percussion instruments) in their works. Bharata is indebted to Narada for his Gandharvam, Dhruvas and now to the percussion instruments as mentioned earlier.

In 'Sangita Makaranda' another unusual fact is mentioned about the sound quality of both sides of the Mridanga. Narada says:

स्त्री ध्वनि पुरुषाकारः स्त्रयाकारश्चैव पुंस्वरः।
आयुर्लक्ष्मीहरौ नित्यमश्राव्यौ तावुभौ ध्वनि।[2]

Narada expresses simply that male form with female sound and female form with male sound—both should be discarded and should not be listened as both of them are capable of destroying life and wealth. It appears that it might be applicable to human beings too. Because, he mentions about female and male forms instead of sides. Usually left side of a Mridanga has a deep sound, while the right side is tuned to the required pitch. But according to Narada, the right side of Mridanga should produce a deep and resounding male like sound and left side should have sweet and high pitched sound. These two sounds should be tuned in such a way that the sound produced by both sides should blend and match well. According to Narada, no side should become prominent or left aside even for a beat. He says that the sound of a single side will cause ill-health or poverty. Therefore both sides should be played equally and simultaneously. Besides Mridanga, Narada has enlisted at least 14 names of percussion instruments. They are :

1. Dardura	7. Dakka	13. Udu
2. Panava	8. Damaru	14. 15. 16.
3. Jharjari	9. Mandra	Three types
4. Pataha	10. Madhu	of Gunja
5. Mukharika	11. Jharjara	17. Kataka
6. Alinga	12. Dindima	18. Karana

These names are not found in 'Natya Shastra' or in 'Sangita Ratnakara', Narada is supposed to be an authority on percussion instruments, according to Bharata, and there might have been some ancient work of Svati and Narada which is not available at present.

In the present available 'Sangita Makaranda', it seems that there are verses included from outside works at places. There are many passages, which do not coincide with the principles of Narada and they are certainly added afterwards.

'Sangita Ratnakara' describes Mardala and its structure and the technique of playing it. Sharngdeva gives a list of 22 percussion instruments with short description. He has given more scientific details of making a Mridanga. Sharngdeva identifies Mridanga as Mardala only and he uses the word Mardala for all his description.

Narada of 'Sangita Makaranda' too gives the instructions to make a Mridanga. His Mridanga is unique because he wants equal sides for his Mridanga. In 'Sangita Makaranda' Narada takes the spiritual side at first instance and later on in the fourth pada of Nrityadhyaya he describes the structure of a Mridanga. Narada prefers sandalwood only which should be soft, defectless and beautiful without crookedness, deformity or holes.

"चन्दनं सुकुमारं च सुवृक्षं च मनोहरम्
वक्र कोटरवर्ज्यं हि आनयेद्देवदारुकम्।"[3]

The Mridanga described by Narada is 32 inches in circumference in the middle. Its height is 68 inches (अंगुलि पर्व). Both sides are faces of the Mridanga and are of 16 inches in diameter. They are covered with circular shaped skin. The right and left sides represent Shiva and Shakti respectively. The leather straps that fix the side skins are 36 in numbers, which represent the 'Chanda' and the knots of the straps that hold the skin covers on the sides represent Trinity—Brahma, Vishnu, and Maheshwara. Therefore the Mridanga should be handled with respect and devotion. Mridanga should be played after salutation with both hands, keeping the Mridanga horizontal on the surface, right side should be played with two fingers and left side with the palm. 'तद्धितोटय' should be played by five fingers. That is the starting of playing a Mridanga even today. The sound produced by both sides bestows various boons to the listeners, i.e., victory in the battle, expansion of kingdom and issues, etc. But listening to the separate sound of one side will produce ill-effects only. Illness will result from the sound of right side and poverty from the sound of left side. Both sides should produce an equally matched sound.

The description of Mridanga of 'Sangita Makaranda' leaves an impression of the antiquity of the work. The Mridanga of Narada has equal sides, while the Mardala of Sharngdeva has a larger right side and smaller left side. Therefore it may not produce the same kind of sound and it seems a developed version of Mridanga. At present, the left side is larger than the right. Narada stresses the point of playing both sides of Mridanga at the same instance and both sounds should be heard simultaneously.

In 'Sangita Ratnakara' the description of Mardala is given with instruction to make a Mardala. Its description comes under 'Mardala Lakshanam' in the Vadyadhyaya.[4]

Instruments : Narada has named percussion and stringed instruments. Only two wind instruments are mentioned.

Mridanga is the only percussion instrument described by Narada. He has not described stringed instruments. Sharngdeva has named 22 percussion instruments and 11 stringed instruments, while Narada has named 18 (19 ?) stringed instruments and 18 percussion instruments.

The names of stringed instruments given in 'Sangita Makaranda' are as follows.

They are eighteen in numbers according to Narada but they are actually nineteen Veenas. Nine Veenas of a type and ten Veenas of another type.

1. Kachchapi
2. Kubjika
3. Chitra
4. Vahanti
5. Parivadini
6. Jaya
7. Ghoshavati
8. Jyesta
9. Nakuli

These are said to be (nine) Veenas of similar type.

Another type of Veenas are ten in number.

1. Mahati
2. Vaishnavi
3. Brahmi
4. Roudri
5. Koormi
6. Ravani
7. Saraswati
8. Kinnari
9. Sairandhri
10. Ghoshaka.

Narada does not provide any description of these Veenas except the above said two categories. These are differentiated by the position of the strings :

दशवीणा समाख्याता विन्यास भेदतः
षट्त्रिंशदगुली वीणा विस्तारः षड्भिरंगुलैः।"[5]

Nanya Bhupala mentions that Mahati Veena had twenty-one strings on which three Gramas can be played and Narada Muni was the only one who is able to play it, which again confirms the use of Gandhara Grama in 'Sangita Makaranda', though whether the author of 'Sangita Makaranda' is the

Muni, mentioned by Nanya Bhupala is uncertain. But the fact of being a follower of Narada's School of Music and the description of Gandhara Grama with its Murchanas, confirm the use of Gandhara Grama played by original Narada Muni in 'Sangita Makaranda'.

"एकविंशति तन्त्रिकां नारदो वादयन्मुनिः
अत्रव्यक्तास्त्रयो ग्रामाः स्फुटाः सप्तस्वराऽपि।
त्रि ग्राम संख्याभिस्तन्त्रीभिः महतीति या।
नारदो वादकस्तस्या नापरो दिवि विश्रुतः।।"[6]

The point to be noted is the name 'Mahati' which is mentioned by Narada of 'Sangita Makaranda' only. This name of the Veena is not mentioned by anybody else. Even Sharngdeva does not name this important Veena of twenty-one strings. Vipanchi Veena of 'Natya Shastra' is not mentioned in the above list of Narada. Mattakokila is also not included in the list. The list of Narada again confirms the antiquity of the work. His Veenas are not to be found in any other work, except for one or two of the list. But they are not unfamiliar though. They appear from the Vedic period but not as a group, and in one place and period. They are mentioned here and there, one or two at a time. Many Vedic Veenas became extinct with time.

In 'Natya Shastra' Chitra and Vipanchi are main Veenas and Kachchapi and Ghoshaka are their subordinates. In the percussion instruments — Bheri, Pataha, Dindima, Panava, Dardura, Bhanda, Gomukha and Alinga are given. The shapes are said to be like Gopuchcha Haritaki, etc. The names of the percussion instruments are somewhat similar in both 'Natya Shastra' and 'Sangita Makaranda'. Some more names, i.e., Jharjhari, Madu, Dakka, etc., appear in 'Sangita Makaranda'.

In 'Sangita Ratnakara' eleven stringed instruments are mentioned and they are :

1. Eka Tantri
2. Nakula
3. Tri Tantrika
4. Chitra
5. Veena
6. Vipanchi

7. Matta Kokila
8. Alapini
9. Kinnari
10. Pinaki
11. Nisshanka Veena

Among these Veenas, Kinnari, Chitra and Vipanchi are the only similar names in 'Sangita Ratnakara' and 'Sangita Makaranda'.

The fourth pada of Sangitadhyaya mainly describes the merits and demerits of musicians and characteristics of Vaggeyakara.

Gayakalakshanam : Narada of 'Sangita Makaranda' describes the entire characteristics of the Vaggeyakara and the merits of the singer under this heading "अथ गायक लक्षणम्"

Narada begins with Vaggeyakara's characteristics, but does not mention it as such. His description of the Vaggeyakara is similar to that of Vaggeyakara Lakshanam of Sharngdeva. The slokas are approximately similar. Sharngdeva has devoted almost a chapter to the types of voice, merits and demerits of voice, musicians, Vaggeyakara and other practical side of music.

This topic, excluding Vaggeyakara is dealt by all ancient authors but in brief. The slokas from 22-40 of 'Sangita Makaranda' contain the description of Vaggeyakara (22-32) and merits of a singer (33-40). 'Sangita Makaranda' does not describe the demerits of a musician as is presented in 'Sangita Ratnakara'. The verses from 22-40 appear in 'Sangita Ratnakara' too almost word by word. In 'Sangita Makaranda', the text is full of grammatical errors and misspelt words. It is difficult to decide whether 'Sangita Ratnakara' lifted them from 'Sangita Makaranda' or someone (copyist) extracted it from 'Sangita Ratnakara' and interpolated them in the present work. Both arguments are tenable. Sharngdeva is more elaborate and describes the merits and demerits of musicians, types of voice and its defects and merits which are not dealt by Narada. Narada has only described about Vaggeyakara and merits of musician and leaves all other topics related to the subject. A remarkable point to note is the description of Vaggeyakara, his types, musicians, his merits and demerits, which are more or less similar, appear in Manasollasa of Someshvara, whose name is mentioned by Sharngdeva in the list of ancient scholars. Someshvara describes about the types of voice too, in a similar way; he is certainly a predecessor to Sharngdeva.

Sharngdeva has adopted the types of voice Kafaj, Pittaj, Vataj, etc., from 'Brihaddeshi' and with a slight alteration of headings he has presented it as his own. In 'Sangita Makaranda' we find many novel ideas and unique systems not found in any other work. Therefore, it might be possible that Vaggeyakara lakshanam, (though it is not titled as such) is his original subject which is presented by Sharngdeva in a polished way.

Narada also mentions the ten merits of singing, accepted by Narada of 'Naradiya Shiksha' and Bharata and other ancient authors, which are not mentioned by Sharngdeva in his Prakirnakadhyaya.

In 'Sangita Makaranda' the characteristics of Vaggeyakara begin without any prelude or introduction, under Gayaka lakshanam. Only the concluding sloka says that these are the qualities of a Vaggeyakara. The 28 qualities of Vaggeyakara are identical to the Vaggeyakara lakshanam of 'Sangita Ratnakara', so they are not discussed here. Uttama, Madhyama and Adhama Vaggeyakara and Kuttikara are also defined in 'Sangita Makaranda' just like 'Sangita Ratnakara'. Again in continuation of the topic Vaggeyakara, the merits of musicians are given in 'Sangita Makaranda', which again are identical to Sharngdeva's Gayana Lakshanam. In this context, the much discussed sloka with the name 'Mahamaheshvara' about music with defects occurs. This sloka confirms the fact that it has been copied from 'Sangita Ratnakara', by the copyist, because the author would not commit such a visible error. It cannot be proved beyond doubt how far the copyist has copied from 'Sangita Ratnakara'.

The merits of musician and good singing are defined by almost all the authors, ancient and later ones. In 'Sangita Ratnakara' it has taken a much developed form.

The properties and merits of good music are described by Narada of 'Naradiya Shiksha' in these words.

गानस्यतु दशविधा गुणवृत्तिस्तदस्तद् यथा--
रक्तं पूर्णमलंकृतं प्रसन्नं व्यक्तं विक्रुष्टम्
श्लक्षणं समं सुकुमारं मधुरमिति गुणाः।"[7]

Then he describes the ten qualities and defines each quality.

Raktam — It means tunefulness, to produce similar voice like Veena and Venu (the accompaniments). The voice should merge with the flute and Veena.

Purnam — The word means perfection or fullness. The music should be perfectly in co-ordination with metre, note, tune and lyrical side and words should be well pronounced and division of syllables should be well adjusted to music.

Alamkritam — It means ornamented or decorated. The musical quality should be the same in all the three registers.

Prasannam — It means the voice of the singer should be clear and effortless and without any strain.

Vyaktam — The meaning of the song should be clear and pronunciation of words should be expressive and syllables of the words should be pronounced and divided carefully.

Vikrushtam — To pronounce the words, their syllables and letters clearly in the upper register or high pitch.

Shlakshanam — The word means smooth, delicate or polished. When the musician blends the different layas, upper and lower notes, long and short syllables with a smooth tone, it is called shlakshanam. Blending smoothly is termed as Shlakshanam.

Samam — It means equal. The starting and ending notes of the songs are always fixed. When these are handled according to the rules it is called Samam.

Sukumaram — This indicates the delicate and musical application of voice and pronunciation of the words effortlessly without harshness.

Madhuram — It means sweetness. Natural sweetness of the song pronounced by a happy and sweet voice.

In 'Naradiya Shiksha' these ten demerits of songs are named without any description. They are :

1. शंकितं	8. स्थान विवर्जितम्
2. भीतं	9. विरसं
3. उद्‌धष्टं	10. विश्लिष्टं
4. अव्यक्तं	11. विस्वरं
5. अनुनासिकं	12. विषम आहतम्
6. काकस्वरं	13. व्याकुलम्
7. शिरसिगतं,	14. तालुहीनं।[8]

The meanings of the above demerits are easy to follow, so no need to describe these in detail.

In 'Natya Shastra' Bharata gives much importance to the merits of music and singing. Abhinava Gupta has also done full justice to the subject. The 33rd chapter begins with this verse:

"गुणात् प्रवर्त्तते गानं दोषं चैव निरस्यते।"

and is fully devoted to the subject of merit and demerits of music. The chapter is named as "Guna Dosha Vichara". Bharata names only six merits of voice. They are :

घनः, श्रावकः, स्निग्धः, मधुरः, अवधानवान्, त्रिस्थान शोभीः

He describes them also.

Ghana — Tuneful and continuous voice without any break.

Shravaka — Voice which can be heard well from a distance, high pitched and clear is shravaka.

Snigdha — Voice which is neither dry nor harsh but smooth.

Madhura — Pleasing to the hearts is called Madhura and which does not slip while singing the difficult phrases.

Avadhanavan — Who is always cautious about the accuracy of notes is called Avadhanavan.

Tristhana Shobi — A voice which is sweet and melodious in all the three registers.

Bharata names five demerits as well, they are—

कपिला, अव्यवस्थित, संदष्ट, काकी, तुम्बकी।

Kapila — A voice which is full of phlegm and becomes tuneless due to that.

Avyavasthita — The tone which is not accurate, always less or higher than the basic pitch is called 'Avyavasthita', which means unsteady.

Sandashta — If the singer sings with the help of the teeth or by grinding the teeth is called Sandashta.

Kaki — One who does not stay on a note for long and takes very short notes like a crow is called Kaki.

Tumbaki — Tumbaki is a singer with nasal voice.

Bharata has mentioned these five defects in musicians which should be avoided. Abhinava Gupta in his commentary says:

.......न तूत्कृष्ट दोष योगे तु तद्गानमेव न किंचित् गर्दभभाषितम् हि तत्।[9]

Thus this subject of merits and demerits of singer are described by many ancient authors, though Vaggeyakara was not defined by them. It seems to be a later addition. In 'Brihaddeshi' four types of sounds (Dhvani) are mentioned: Vataj, Pittaj, Kafaj and Sannipataj.[10] This classification appears in 'Sangita Ratnakara', as Shabda Guna Dosha. Matanga does not describe the merits and demerits of musicians or about a Vaggeyakara.

Sharngdeva deals with this topic elaborately, i.e., merits and demerits of musicians and music. He has mentioned fifteen merits and eight demerits of voice. He has covered this subject by describing Shabda, Gayana and Sharira Guna Dosha.

Narada of 'Sangita Makaranda' after describing a Vaggeyakara's pre-requisites, classifies the three types of Vaggeyakara — Uttama, Madhyama and Adhama (best medium and worst). In the same way after describing the musician's merits, he explains about five types of musicians — Shikshakara, Anukara, Rasika, Ranjaka and Bhavaka. Narada does not mention the demerits of musicians here. He only opines that one who follows the traditions and has the merits is praised as the best musician. A musician who has no defects but has less merits is a medium singer. A musician who has defects is the worst. Here the controversial sloka quoting the name Mahamaheshwara occurs :

महामाहेश्वरेणोक्तः सदोषो गायकाधमः ।[11]

Matanga too has used this adjective Maheshvara for Kohala in his 'Brihaddeshi'.

"षड्जं वदति मयुरः..... ।
तथा च आह कोहलः महेश्वरः ।[12]

This is already discussed earlier. Here, at this stage it is only discussed to throw light on the singing of music which is full of defects.

Narada mentions the ten qualities of singer and his voice which are similar to that of 'Naradiya Shiksha'.

"व्यक्तं पूर्णं प्रसन्नं सुकुमारं अलंकृतम्
समं सुरक्तं श्लक्ष्णं च निकृष्टं मधुरं तथा
दश्यैते स्युंगुणानं ते (?) तत्र वक्ता (व्यक्तः) स्फुटः स्वरः ।"[13]

Slokas from 42-46 are descriptive of these ten qualities.

Vyaktam: is natural and clear pronunciation of Shrutis.

Poornam: is perfect coordination of metre, melody, language and notes.

Prasannam: is good and meaningful expression.

Sukumaram: is the even voice production.

Alankritam: capability to sing in all the three octaves effortlessly.

Saman: is the exact or accurate placement of the notes, syllables and letters in the proper laya and tala.

Suraktam : is the merging quality of the voice with the tuneful and sweet instrumental accompaniments like veena and flute.

Shlakshanam: is a smooth voice production without harshness throughout the singing, a facile and flexible voice.

Vikrushtam: is misspelt as Nikrushtam. Here Narada quotes Bharata and says according to Bharata to sing in high pitch is called Vikrushtam.

Madhuram: pleasant voice which attract and give pleasure to the audience.

Though Narada mentions the demerits amounting to ten in number, the text of 'Sangita Makaranda' is full of errors in that particular place so it is impossible to make out or even guess the names. The names which seem legible are as follows but they are still doubtful:

Shrutikala Virodhi, Sandigdham, Gatashramam

Gramyam are some of them. The demerits are not explained either.

This chapter gives us an idea of the instruments of the period of 'Sangita Makaranda' and Mridanga in the percussion instruments is especially described. Narada's approach to this instrument is unique. The description is novel as well as spiritual. Though Veenas are not described, yet they are also supposed to represent Shakti in a way. Mridanga represents both Shakti and Shiva, Trinity (Brahma, Vishnu and Maheshwara)and other deities also.

The Vaggeyakara lakshanam holds many principles from the merits of musicians of ancient authors. They are presented by both Narada and Sharngdeva. The merits of musicians are also similar in both works. But the whole subject of merits and demerits of musicians and other qualities regarding voice, and Vaggeyakara was there in earlier ancient works. Later authors only developed the ideas and presented the subject in a new garb. Therefore, it cannot be said that 'Sangita Makaranda' or 'Sangita Ratnakara' have copied slokas after slokas from one another or from ancient authors. Narada gives both ancient and prevalent qualities of musician to show the difference or to respect the old principles of 'Naradiya Shiksha' and 'Natya Shastra'. As far as Narada of Sangita Makaranda is concerned, his slokas about Vaggeyakara and the merits of musician seem original and Sharngdeva might have borrowed the idea and systematised it with more developments. His Shabdabheda is ample proof of this because he has borrowed it from Matanga's Dhvanibheda except the name. Narada has atleast mentioned the name of Bharata for his ten names of qualities of musician. Similarly, as already mentioned, the Vaggeyakara lakshanam is mentioned by Someshvara in his 'Manasollosa', which has a definite priority over 'Sangita Ratnakara'. It proves that Vaggeyakara lakshanam was there even before the period of 'Sangita Ratnakara' in some ancient work, which is not available now. Or we may assume that our 'Sangita Makaranda' was the earlier work upon which Someshvara based his chapters on music.[14]

REFERENCES

1. *Natya Shastra,* Chapter. 34, p. 464.
2. *Sangita Makaranda,* p. 21.
3. *Ibid.,* p. 48.
4. *Sangita Ratnakara,* vol. 4, p. 596.
5. *Sangita Makaranda,* p. 22.
6. *Bharata Bhashyam,* part I, pp. 167-68.
7. *Naradiya Shiksha,* p. 19.
8. *Ibid.,* p. 22.
9. *Natya Shastra,* Chapter. 33, p. 307.
10. *Brihaddeshi,* p. 22.
11. *Sangita Makaranda,* p. 21.
12. Brihaddeshi, *Sangita,* 1975, p. 5.
13. *Sangita Makaranda,* p. 25.
14. *Manasollosa,* vol. III, sl. 20-25, p. 3.

9

Nrityadhyaya

The chapter named as Nrityadhyaya by Narada contains very little about dance. In the beginning of the chapter, Narada gives the description of Natyashala (dancing hall), sabha (spectators), sabhapati (chief guest of the audience) and other participants and the scholars among the audience. These are somewhat original and novel ideas not to be found in 'Natya Shastra'. 'Sangita Ratnakara' and 'Samayasara' of Parshvadeva. 'Abhinavadarpana' of Nandikeshvara has presented some of the topics mentioned above.

In 'Sangita Makaranda' more details are given about the prominent spectators forming a forum for the performance. Nrityadhyaya commences with the auditorium and a description of Sabha or court. By sabha, Narada means the Royal Court and courtiers. He has described the scholars, poets, Bhatas (waged singers), musicians, comedians, historians, astrologers, physicians, Pouraniks (mythologists) and Sabhapati (leader of the court).

Natyashala is described by Bharata in Chapter II of the 'Natya Shastra'. Bharata has explained about three types of theatres—Rectangular, square and triangular. He has given the sizes of the theatre and seating arrangements. The Natyashala of Narada described in 'Sangita Makaranda' is a little different in measurements. It is a square theatre of 86 Hastas — one Hasta is equal to one and a half feet.[1] The theatres of Bharata are of three sizes —large, medium and small. The large is of 108 Hastas, medium of 64 and small is of 32 Hastas. 'Sangita Makaranda' describes the theatre as follows.

षडशीति हस्तमात्र चतुरस्रत्र समन्विता।
चतुर्विंशतिकस्तम्भ नाना चित्र समन्विता।[2]

In 'Natya Shastra' the square Natyashala is given as of 32 × 32 Hastas. This theatre of Narada seems bigger than the medium theatre of Bharata and smaller than the large theatre of Bharata. But the number of pillars seems to be the same, i.e., 24 in both theatres of Bharata and Narada. The stage also differs in size from Bharata. Narada prefers a stage (Vedika) of 24 Hastas in the centre of the theatre. The theatre of Naradas has four entrances. Narada has described the decorations of the theatre also. The pillars should be painted with vivid beautiful pictures. The doors are to be decorated with silk, gems and other decorations like flags and flowers. In the middle of the theatre there should be a vedika (platform) of 24 Hastas. Everything of the theatre should be well decorated and perfumed with incences and scents. Then the throne should be put and the flowers and fruits and other auspicious things should be placed in front of the throne and the king should be seated on it. Thus the theatre of Narada is a royal auditorium. He again advises to follow the instructions regarding the theatre and everything as per his advice without fail to avoid any mishaps.

In the 'Abhinava Darpana', more or less the same description of Sabha is given.

In 'Sangita Ratnakara' and 'Sangita Samayasara' the royal court is described as the performing place. In the same way, Sabhapati is the king and his merits are described by them. But the approach of Narada is unique, though his Sabhapati is also the king and the spectators are the scholars of the court. His performances take place in a special theatre built for this purpose and a separate throne is placed and special decorations are made to witness the performance. 'Abhinava Darpana' of Nandikeshwara only comes near to the description given by Narada. Narada wishes to have a scholarly forum of audience to witness the performance. First of all, he describes the ideal Sabhapati and his qualities, to judge and appreciate the performance. The success of a performance always depends upon the audience. A programme of a much high standard will fail miserably if the audience has no knowledge of the subject. Narada prefers a court full of scholars and intellectuals from all walks of life. Nandikeshwara has described the ideal sabha in this sloka with a beautiful simile.

"सभा कल्पतरुर्भाति वेदशाखोपजीवितः।
शास्त्र पुष्प समाकीर्णो विद्वद्भ्रमर शोभितः।"[3]

In this sloka he has compared the sabha with the heavenly tree (Kalpa Taru) having Vedas as its branches and Shastra as its flowers and the scholars as the bees on the flowers. This shows the standard of cultural programmes of those days.

Narada describes the sabha, court or the forum. He says that a sabha should have nine intellectuals or types of scholars. They are—

1. Vidwan (Scholar)
2. Poet (Kavi)
3. Bhata (a waged singer)
4. Musician
5. Comedian
6. Historian
7. Astrologer
8. Vaidya (Physician)
9. Pouranik (Mythologist)

He lays stress that barring physician and astrologer the

important seven parts (Sapatanga) of the court are also formed by these learned men. Then Narada defines these nine learned scholars with their characteristics. As these are not included in any other work on music; in the 'Natya Shastra' or in 'Sangita Ratnakara', they deserve notice. The definitions of the nine main characters of the court are as follows:

Vidwadlakshanam : 'Vidwan', stands for a scholar. A scholar is one who wins his place in any type of gatherings, able to present correct arguments and establish his points, who is capable of making quick witty remarks and repulse the attacks and arguments produced by his rivals and is an authority on all subjects and faculties of learning. Again a scholar has a keen interest to entertain, and is an adornment of any noble court. When it is said that a scholar should be well versed in all subjects, music and dance naturally are covered by the statement. In the past it was customary, that every scholar got recognition by travelling to all the countries and attending the courts of that country and presenting his talents in front of the king surrounded by his group of scholars and other talented people of his country. The scholars of that particular court used to compete and defeat the new comer. He got recognition only if he could surpass all the scholars who had challenged his knowledge. None was accepted as the best of his profession without proving his worth by giving trials in the court and defeating the existing talents of that court. Hence the nine main important talented professionals of art and culture are the part of a well-organized court.

Poet (Kavi) : He should be pious, gentle, intelligent, humble, knowing the other arts, scholarly, good in composing sweet verses with a knowledge of Rasa, emotional, of a noble family (high born) and handsome. A poet should have a thorough knowledge of metre and grammar and the quality to understand the qualities of other people. These qualities are necessary for a good poet to impress the people and to make flawless poetry, correct in metre, rhetorics. He should be well informed. Impatience and dishonesty make the composition cheap and distorted. Arts always reflect the mind and emotions of the artists. Therefore, the artist should possess, noble qualities, a good character and personality to impress the people.

Bhata : He is a hired singer who sings to praise the king only. He knows the family tree of the king. Narada defines a Bhata as one who is a linguist and knows the history and lineage of the royal family well enough to sing about it whenever the occasion demands. He should be capable of composing different types of prabandhas.

Gayaka Lakshanam : A favourite musician of the king is described as one who entertains the people with all the three types of Ragas: Oudava—five noted; Shadava—six noted and Sampoorna—seven noted Ragas, who has a well modulated steady voice which does not change very often and is always sweet and identical. Here, Kaku Varjita means the voice should be defectless and without any type of affectation and under tones.

Parihasaka Lakshanam : He may be termed as the jester of court. He should know all the proverbs, phrase, puns and witty intelligent remarks to suit the situations, at any time. Parihasaka should be able to make people laugh with his intelligent and humour—laden talks. He should be imaginative and creative to produce humour as the occasion demands as well as ready witted.

Itihasagya (Historians): They are also the important part of the court. In any country, the historians play an important role in preserving the past historical events for the future generations. They are also important to assess a performance for its historical validity and to justify of the facts presented in the performance (drama). But Narada attributes the knowledge of music to him as well "साक्षाद्गीत वाद्य विचक्षणाः" i.e., perfect in practical music and instruments.

A historian should be capable of explaining the facts of puranas and should know the history well.

Jyotisha: He is the astrologer who knows the auspicious time for starting any work or journey. He has high principles, is a good thinker and advisor, who knows about the planetary positions well. He is highly respectable like the teacher of the Devas (Brahaspati). Though an astrologer is not related to music in any way, yet he is the part of the court.

Vaidya (Physician) : He is no way concerned with music or cultural programme, but a king and his court cannot forego a physician. A king had his own physician, astrologer, historian and so on. Even today the practice of having a President's physician, specialists and national artists of all arts continues. In 'Sangita Makaranda', the physician's qualities are discussed elaborately. He should be a specialist in diagnosing the diseases and curing all diseases caused by poisons or past karmas, by supernatural powers, i.e. ghost, witches, etc., by natural elements—cold, heat or airborne diseases and the diseases caused by the imbalance of three Dhatus — Kapha, Pitta and Vayu. The physician might be well versed in all the three samhitas and should be a scholar. He should be able to cure all the known, unknown and unheard diseases. This description almost covers all the natural and supernatural diseases.

Pouranika Lakshanam :[4] He is a mythologist who has studied the Puranas well. He should be adept in referring to or quoting the subsequent Puranic event, to satisfy the people and provide authenticity to any form or part of the performance or condemn it. He should be well versed in the Vedas and be able to deliver a speech with many examples and parables from the Puranas. He must know all the Shastras. Hence a Pouranika also plays an important role in deciding the merit and authenticity of a programme. This description helps to understand the formation of a royal court of those days. The efficiency of the nine main characters of the court lacks in nothing. They are the cream of their profession. Every king had to judge the real merit and worth of an artist, a scholar or any professional man impartially and had to honour him and reward him accordingly with presents. Hence all these scholars and artists of a high order were declared as the gems of the court and were employed by the court. This description is not found in any other work on music as these characters are not concerned with the actual performance. They are the part of the audience belonging to a special category.

After discussing the court with the learned people from all the branches of knowledge, Narada comes to the Chairman of the court. Here the chairman is the king. In ancient times the king was used to be a master of all arts and was trained in all the 64 arts from childhood. Narada describes the Sabhapati in four lines of a sloka and proceeds to the seating arrangements of the audience under the same heading "Sabhapati Lakshanam". It is as follows:

"अनेक शृंगार विचित्र रूप:
सर्वज्ञचातुर्य रसान्वितोऽसौ।
संगीतसाहित्यकलानुरक्तो
निर्मत्सरो वाक्सुगुणैरूपेत:।।[5]

Narada says that the Sabhapati should be well adorned with all the ornaments and should be adept in estimating every type of emotional values and should have an endless knowledge of all subjects. Sabhapati should be interested in literature, arts and music. He should be devoid of jealousy. He should speak with ease and the speech should be of a high quality, and language should be good.

These are the minimum qualifications a chairman should possess to judge any performance of the outside artists of other countries. In the 'Abhinava Darpana', the same type of characteristics of Sabhanayaka are given.

श्रीमान् धीमान् विवेकी वितरण निपुणो गान विद्या प्रवीण:
सर्वज्ञ: कीर्त्तिशाली सरसगुणयुतो हावभावेष्वभिज्ञ:
मात्सर्यद्वेषहीन: प्रकृतिहित: सदाचारशीलो दयालु:।
धीरोदात्त: कलावानभिनयचतुरोऽसौ सभानायक: स्यात्।"[6]

Sabhapati Lakshanam is given in 'Sangita Ratnakara' also.[7] But as usual he is more elaborate, and dedicated six slokas (334 to 339) to describe Sabhapati. The description though elaborate contains the points mentioned by Narada and Nandikeshwara.

In the 'Sangita Samayasara' of Parshwadeva, the author has described the Sabhapati as Bhupati or the king :

भूपतिः संगीतगुणदोषज्ञः सर्वभाषाविचक्षणः।
प्रियवाग्वादमध्यस्थः पारितोषकदायकः।।
सत्यवादी च शृंगारी मार्गदेशीप्रभेदवित्।
धीमान् सर्वकलाध्यक्षः तदध्यासितभूपतिः।।

However all these characteristics mentioned by various authors illuminate the attributes, an impartial and learned judge should have. It is always natural for the people to follow and accept their leader's judgement and sometimes the masses are susceptible to fall for mediocre performance of a person of their own country. At that time, it is the duty of the chairman (king) to take an impartial decision and approve the best. Very often the king himself excels in a form of art and is the author of reputed works, e.g., Nanya Bhupala, Someshwara and Mansing, etc. Hence, broad mindedness without jealousy was necessary for the kings to appreciate music of others than music of his own country.

Therefore, the role of Sabhapati justifies the characteristics mentioned by Narada of 'Sangita Makaranda' as every art and attainment of any individual or a group presentations of local artists or outsiders are performed in front of the king to get his approval and applauded by the audience.

Music is mainly a performing art and as such it should have listeners and critics to encourage the artist. Therefore the critics themselves should be without defects. They should follow the rules and regulations laid down by Narada. Sabhapati should be well versed in all the arts to detect the weak points and praise the exceptional qualities.

'Sangita Makaranda' is more concerned with music than dance and drama. It gives more importance to Ragas and its division than Jati and Dhruva music.

The formation of court or seating arrangements in the court is another topic which is mentioned by various authors. Narada also describes the positions of all the courtiers under the same topic Sabhapati Lakshanam.

The Sabhapati is to sit on the simhasana (throne) flanked by mythologists, Bhatta etc. on the left side and by ministers and priests on the right side. Backside of the throne should be guarded by the treasurer, scholars, poets and relatives should sit near the king. The astrologer, physician, sooth sayers, praise singers, etc., are to be seated on the right side of the king. Narada repeats the position of ministers and Bhata once again and says that the ministers and commander-in-chief should sit on the left side of the king. The royal ladies should sit beside the king. The ladies are also described as beautiful, intellectually well accomplished adept in arts, literature, music, dance and politics.

This description of the court appears in 'Sangita Ratnakara' also.[8] His description is more systematic and order of position or the ranks is more practical, because of his practical knowledge of the real court.

Thus the forum for presenting the programme is fully formed with learned people who know their subjects well.

Narada mentions about the Nata-Vishesha (special). This Nata should know all the four types of Abhinaya and all languages. He should possess the knowledge of ethos, sentiments and the value of proper time, place and chronological order of events so as to compose the accurate and correct sequences. Nata Vishesha seems to be the main Nata, who controls and guides the performance.

Without mentioning any other participants, Narada describes the Ghargharika, who wears a waist girdle named Gharghara, which serves as a bell type Ghana instrument. The Ghargharika sports a twitch of hair on his otherwise shaven head. His whole body is rubbed with white ash. He is very agile and nimble limbed and has a knowledge of all the Talas. He dances to entertain the elite. In the 'Sangita Ratnakara' the same type of description occurs, and that is more expressive. The Ghargharika is called as Perani.[9] He seems to be the mimic dancer with jingling bells which keep the time.

Narada does not describe about the director, sutradhar, vaitalika, etc., but he gives a brief delineation of the artists in a sloka (28) and then describes in length about the female participants which is not relevant to the subject—music. The artists are supposed to be positioned behind the curtain and they should be well dressed and be adept in their professions, i.e., keeping the Tala, playing the Mridanga, etc.

This first chapter of Nrityadhyaya explains the methods of giving Pushpanjali by the beautiful female participants with a verse praising Lord Shiva. The same verse appears in the beginning of the work and other verses are also added to it.

This chapter contains the description of the nine gems of the court, theatre plan and measurements, court formation and seating arrangements, Sabhapati Lakshanam, etc. The descriptions given by Narada are not to be found in any work of music.

Another important point to note is Narada is only concerned with music and dance and his courtiers of the court also have the knowledge of music and dance. Dramaturgy is not his subject and it is clearly shown in many ways. Nritya or dance also comes as a secondary subject. Though he has devoted equal chapters to dance, three parts of the Nrityadhyaya are concerned with Tala and the description of theatre, court and courtiers, etc.

REFERENCES

1. *Studies in Natya Shastra*, p. 185.
2. *Sangita Makaranda*, p. 27.
3. *Abhinava Darpana*, p. 82.
4. All these descriptions of the above mentioned nine scholars of the court are given in *Sangita Makaranda*, pp. 27-29.
5. *Sangita Makaranda*, p. 29.
6. *Abhinava Darpan*, p. 82.
7. *Sangita Ratnakara*, vol. IV, p. 394.
8. *Ibid.*, p. 395.
9. *Ibid.*, pp. 384-85.

10

Tala

In Indian music, the Tala is a unique, indispensable component which cannot be compared with the rhythm cycles used in Western music. The peculiarity of Indian Tala lies in its cyclic movements. It has a fixed number of beats for each type of Tala. The number of beats is arranged in a cycle. In Hindustani classical music the various types of Talas have fixed Boles.[1] e.g., Teen Tala has the following Boles :

1	2	3	4	5	6	7	8	9	10	11	12	13	14	15	16
धा	धिं	धिं	धा	धा	धिं	धिं	धा	धा	तिं	तिं	ता	ता	धिं	धिं	धा

In the same way, other Talas also have a fixed type of Bole, varying according to beats of the Tala. While accompanying a musician, Tabla player has to play the Boles of that Tala, though he can improvise in between. Yet, he has to return to the same cycle of Boles again for the convenience of the musician, because the musician has to arrive at the Sam or beginning point of the Tala with the help of Boles. But, in Carnatic music, the Mridangam player has many options as the Talas of Carnatic music have no fixed Boles. They depend on only signs shown by hand. There are fixed number of beats only for every Tala and loose Boles like Din, Tat, Taka, Dhimi, Takila etc. comprising even and odd aksharas. The Mridangam player has to arrange the Boles into the number of beats of a Tala according to his own imagination. He is not bound to any Boles to show a particular Tala. More often, the Mridangam player uses the Boles to suit the words of a song. As there is no fixed Bole for the starting (Sam) of a Tala in Carnatic music, it should be shown with the gesture of a hand. Even while a Mridangist plays a solo, Tala should be shown by the signs of hand by somebody which are fixed for each Tala. The Carnatic music singer cannot follow the Mridanga by listening to the Boles as his north Indian counterpart does as there is no fixed Boles for any Tala in Carnatic music. Therefore, the Kriyas (ancient gestures of hands to keep time) are still in practice in Carnatic music.

Tala, an important part of the music, is described by all the authors on music. 'Naradiya Shiksha' and 'Brihaddeshi' do not discuss about Tala. As for 'Brihaddeshi', it is incomplete (available manuscript) and many portions of 'Brihaddeshi' are missing. Bharata and Dattila have described about Margi Talas. Deshi Talas are not mentioned by Bharata and Dattila. In 'Sangita Makaranda' five Margi Talas are mentioned which are originated from the five faces of Sadashiva accordingly. Again similar to the Svara description, Narada has given colour, caste and Vedas of five Talas. Narada has mentioned 101 names of Deshi Talas with the description, 10 Tala Prabandhas 10 Pranas of Tala.

Deshi Talas are said to be 108 in number inclusive of five Margi Talas. In 'Sangita Makaranda' 101 Talas are only mentioned and in the first instance, Narada has given less than 100 names and while describing, the number exceeds 101 Talas. 'Sangita Ratnakara' mentions 120 Deshi Talas. But in Bharatarnava, 112 Talas are mentioned and described. In 'Sangita Samayasara' 101 Talas are mentioned but only a few are described. Dattila, Matanga (?) and Nanya Bhupala follow Bharata and they describe Margi Talas in the context of Geetaks and Dhruva Geetis. Nanya Bhupala has described Deshi Ragas and Deshi Talas go with the Deshi Ragas. But it seems that he has not described them. His Taladhyaya is not edited and published yet. Dr. A.K. Sen in his work 'Bharatiya Talon Ka Shastriya Vivechan' gives this information about the Tala of Nanya Bhupala on the basis of the manuscript—

तालों की चर्चा, भरत का अनुकरण करते हुए कहा है—
युग्मायुग्मौ इति ख्यातौ द्वौ तालौ ब्रह्मनिर्मितौ।
युग्मश्चंचतपुटो इति ज्ञेयो अयुग्मश्चाचपुटः स्मृतः।।

"इस ग्रन्थ में भरत की मान्यताओं का ही विवेचन विस्तार से हुआ है।" ताल विषयक चर्चा पत्र क्रमांक १४१, १५८, १५६, १७६, तथा १७७ पर उपलब्ध है।[2]

According to Nanyadeva, each of these five Margi Talas has hundreds of types, i.e., Chachaputa has 520 types and Chanchatputa has 4930 different varieties.

Narada's Taladhyaya is peculiar in many ways. First of all his description of the two sides of a Mridanga is novel. The Mridanga sound is also distinguished as male, female sound related to right or left side. His five Margi Talas come out of the five faces of Lord Shiva, which is again not mentioned by any other works except in Oumapatam. Then he has given Tala Prabandhas, which are composed by mixing more than two Talas. He has given the ten pranas. The Talas are not classified as Margi or Deshi Talas by Narada. He names the Margi Tala as Pancha Tala and mentions the term Margi under the title "अथ देशी क्रिया":

Narada has described the usage of Dhruvaka, Sarpini, etc., the signs of Talas shown by hands. According to Narada, the Pancha Talas are of divine origin and he does not classify them as Margi Talas.

Pancha Talotpatti Prakaranam

Generally, Lord Shiva is accepted as the founder of dance and laya. Tala naturally comes under Him. The five Talas are described as :

1. *Chanchatputa:* This Tala emanates from the Sadyojata face (East facing) from which Rigveda also appeared. The colour of the Tala is milky white, and it is Brahmin by caste and it is called as Gopuchcha.

2. *Chachaputa :* This Tala arises from the south sided face-Vamadeva (Shiva) from which Yajurveda is said to have

appeared. It belongs to Kshatriya caste, and is saffron coloured and it is named as Pipilika.

3. *Shatpita Putraka* : This Tala has originated from the face-Aghora (Shiva) facing the west side. Atharva Veda also emanated from this west sided face. The colour of this Tala is golden and it is named as Muraja. It is Vaishya by caste.

4. *Sampadveshtika* : This Tala appears from the north sided face of Shiva from which Sama Veda appeared. It is called Gandharva and is pearl or crystal coloured. It is called Rigama and used by Rishis (sages). This is a little bit confusing as Narada says "गांधर्वमिति संज्ञ" and "रिगमा इति संज्ञा" for the same Tala. Gandharvam might be its caste.

5. *Udghatta* : It has originated from the upper face of Shiva which generated the Shastras and Agamas. It is blue coloured and belongs to various castes (नाना जाति). It is called Yati or Samayati.

These are the five main Talas, which originate from the five faces of Rudra.[3]

Narada names the one hundred and one Talas without stating their types — Margi or Deshi. He says that listening to the names of those names will erase all the worst sins. He says that Narada and Nandikeshwara too have approved the power of Talas in destroying the effect of the worst sins. Five sins which cannot be erased are — stealing of gold, adultery, murder of Brahmin, habit of drinking and helping to commit these sins. These five sins named as 'पंचमापातक' are expiated by listening to the names of Aditala, etc., numbering one hundred and one Talas. Listening to the names of Talas grants other boons also, like expansion of kingdom, name, fame, good issues and defeat of the enemy.

Though Narada has mentioned the number of Talas named by him to be 101, yet he has given only 90 names including four types of Kankala Talas.[4]

While describing the Tala, Narada has given more than 101. These names of Talas are given in Bharatarnava of Nandikeshwara. He has given 112 talas including four types of Kankala and Varna Talas. Adi Bharata and other works in Tamil and Sanskrit mention 108 Talas only. They are identical to 'Bharatarnava' and 'Sangita Makaranda's' names of Talas. The Tala names are mentioned by Vasudeva Shastri and Dr. A.K. Sen as well in their works. In 'Sangita Makaranda' and 'Bharatarnava' the description and the list of names of the Talas are same. These Talas are extinct at present and they were more or less applicable to Abhinaya or dance which are not discussed in detail. These Talas had particular arrangements of Ganas (गण) and Matras and used to be shown by fixed gestures and signs of the hand. These Talas are given under Nrityadhyaya, they are more related to dance than to music. However, there are Prabandhas of Matanga, Sharngdeva bearing the Tala names, e.g., Simha Leela, Gajaleela and Charchari, etc. Therefore, it should have been applied to music too.

A novel subject related to Tala is the Tala Prabandhas, given by Narada. These are Talas comprising more than two Talas.

Narada has given ten types of Tala Prabandhas. These Prabandhas are described in the third pada of Nrityádhyaya. Seven Prabandhas are only intelligible and the other three are not so clear. There in the beginning, Narada has mentioned Adambara, Shabdambara and Arekha Talas of Nandikeshwara. But the starting sloka gives the impression of describing prastara of Aditala, etc.[5] The ten Tala Prabandhas are given below with the names of the Talas, which form the Prabandhas.

1. *Tribhangi* : It comprises three Talas—Rajatala, Vanamali and Rangadyuta.

2. *Chaturmukha*: This Prabandha has Ekatala, Kankala, Chatustala, and Dombuli. By listening to this Prabandha enemies are destroyed.

3. *Pancha Tala Prabandha* : Vijaya, Jaya, Ananda, Jayashri and Jayamangalam—these five Talas form Panchatala prabandha. This prabandha has power to give success and happiness.

4. *Shat Tala Prabandha* : Chanchatputa Chachaputa Shatpitaputraka, Pratyanga, Gajaleela, Shattala (?) form this prabandha.[6]

5. *Martanda Jayada* : This Prabandha has Madana, Utsava, Lakshmisha, Krida, Keerti, Rati and Simhalila.

6. *Ashtamangala* : This Prabandha consists of eight Talas namely — Kandarpa, Bindumali, Samatala, Nandana, Raja Vidhyadhara, Jampa, Vishama and Kanduka. This prabandha relieves from the influences of evil planets.

7. *Nava Tala Prabandhakam* : Udbhata, Simhanada, Abhanga, Viravikrama, Sharabha leela, Simha-Vikridita, Pratapa Shekhara, Simha Vikrama, and Raya Narayana, these nine talas form this Navatala Prabandha.

8. *Dasha Roopa Prabandha* : This Tala takes ten Talas into its fold and bestows fame and good reputation. The Tala names are as follows — Abhinandana, Krida, Mallatala, Dombuli, Kudukkaka, Pratimantha, Makaranda, Charchari, Parikraman and Hamsanada.

9. *Ekadasha Tala Prabandha* : This prabandha has eleven Talas. They are—Nandi, Tritiyaka, Laghu Shekhara, Varnamatta, Charchari, Varnatala, Dwitiyaka, Utsava, and Madana.

10. *Dwadasha Tala Prabandha* : This Prabandha comprises the following Talas—Vanamali, Rajachudamani, Varna tala, Pradipaka, Rangabharana, Udghatta, Rati, Kirti, Nanda, Vikrama, Lakshmisha, and Utsava.

These types of Tala Prabandhas are not mentioned in any other work. But, there are musical prabandhas, i.e., Talarnava, Panchatalshwara, etc., mentioned in 'Sangita Ratnakara' which consist of more than one Tala. In Carnatic music, the compositions set to a number of Talas is called Suladi. In ancient Greek rhythm, this type of mixed rhythms is found.[7]

These ten Tala Prabandhas are used for dance as well as music. These Prabandhas might be the origin of the refined Prabandhas based on compound Talas of later period. The

Matra and Gana description of these Tala Prabandhas are also given by Narada. The third, fourth and fifth Prabandhas are given in the slokas no. 14-18 on page 40, i.e., the ten Prabandhas are scattered.

According to Narada, playing and listening to these Tala Prabandhas will grant success in every sphere of life.

Narada has given seven suladi Talas and twelve Angatalas and their descriptions too.

The Anga Talas

1.	Yakshapati	7.	Vadhya Jhampa
2.	Vadya Vibhrama	8.	Brahmanda
3.	Mara Tala	9.	Raya Kolahala
4.	Matha	10.	Maha Shani
5.	Brahma Tala	11.	Tinabheri
6.	Geeta Jhampa	12.	Vadhya Gajankusha[8]

These are the twelve Anga Talas with description.

After describing the 101 talas, ten Talaprabandhas and Anga Talas, Narada comes to Tala Shabda Nishpatti and ten Pranas of Tala. The definition is similar to all other works, and nothing is special in it. He says Tala represents both Shiva and Shakti and bestows worldly and spiritual attainments and then describes the ten Pranas as follows :

Kala (काल): It is the first prana (essential) of Tala, which stands for time. Tala is based on time measures or units, which form the measured rhythm-Tala. The smallest unit of 'Kala' is called as Kshana, which is the time consumed to pierce 100 lotus leaves, kept one over another, with a needle.

8	Kshanas	=	1	Lava
8	Lavas	=	1	Kashta
8	Kashtas	=	1	Nimesha
8	Nimeshas	=	1	Kala

2	Kalas	=	1	Anudruta
2	Anudrutas	=	1	Bindu
2	Bindus	=	1	Laghu
2	Laghus	=	1	Guru
3	Laghus	=	1	Pluta

Bharata does not follow this chart of Kala which denotes general time. According to him, a Matra is equal to the time taken to pronounce five short letters. Laghu is equal to one Matra.

Marga : After the Kāla (time), Narada describes about the term Marga. Literally 'Marga' means a way, path, method. Here it is applied as a way to govern the count of time units in a Kalā (कला): a time measure comprising two Matras in its normal state. Now a Matra in a Tala might be defined as the time taken to utter five short letters. These Matras control the tempo of the Tala—rhythmic cycle. Generally, Margas are threefold Sharngdeva adds one more Marga—named Dhruva. The three main Margas accepted by all authors are Chitra, Vartika and Dakshina. Our author Narada mentions six Margas. They are as follows:

Dakshina : It is the slowest Marga comprising a Kalā of eight Matras.

Vartika : This Marga has four Matras in a Kala and is of medium tempo.

Chitra : Chitra has the Kalā comprising two Matras which is the fast tempo. Narada adds three more Margas, each one is of double speed than the preceding one.

Chitra Tara : This has a single Matra in a Kalā.

Atichitratara : It comprises of a Kalā of half of a Matra or a Druta.

Atichitratama : The fastest tempo of a Tala consisting of only Anudruta: one-fourth of a Matra.

The point to note is that Narada does not mention the term Margi even while he describes the five Margi Talas, their materialisation evolution, etc. He uses the term Margi, while elucidating the Kriyas of Tala, describing the Matra to be used in Margi Talas. Matra is defined as follows:

लघ्वाक्षराणां पञ्चानां मानमुच्चारणे हि यत्।
तत् परिमाणं परिज्ञेयं मार्गस्तालैस्ततो बुधैः।।

This verse comes before the description of Kriya—one of the ten Pranas of Tala. In the Kāla (time), Narada names Laghu instead of Matra. Moreover, the 'Kala' denotes the general time used to form hours and Praharas, etc., which are not applicable to the time measure of Tala in music.

Kriya : It means 'work', to work, action and verb (grammar). But in Tala, the term Kriya is used for the actions used to keep the time units of a Tala by hands. The specific time units— mostly Matras are shown by the measured movements or clappings of the hands. They are eight in both Margi and Deshi Talas. Kriyas are twofold—Nisshabda and Sashabda.

Sashabda Kriyas of Margi Tala : Tala, Shamya, Dhruva, Sannipata. Dhruva is the first Sashabda Kriya according to Sharngdeva. But in this work it comes as the third Kriya. These Sashabda Kriyas are sounded beats and are known as Pata Kalā also.

Nisshabda Kriya : Avapa, Nishkrama Vikshepa and Pravesha. These are known as Kalas(कला), while Sashabda Kriya produces sound with the palms, clappings, snapping the fingers, etc. Nisshabda Kriyas are actions without producing sound; movements of hands, gestures related to fingers, drawing them inwards and spreading out, etc.

Deshi Kriyas are also eightfold. The first Kriya named Dhruvaka is a sounded beat whereas others are unsounded beats. They are—Sarpini, Krishya, Padmini, Visarjita, Vikshipta, Pataka and Patita. These Deshi Kriyas are called Matras and are to be used in the three Margas—Chitra, Vartika and Dakshina.

Anga : Anga stands for limbs, parts of a body. Here it is related to Tala, as the parts forming a rhythmic cycle—Tala. Tala or the rhythmic structure is formulated by various time units; these time units are called as Angas. They are fivefold according to Narada. They are :

Anudruta, Druta, Laghu, Guru and Pluta.

Narada names the presiding deities of these Angas except for Anudruta.

Druta has Shambhu as its presiding deity. Laghu has the daughter of Adripati, i.e., Parvati, Gouri and Shri both are the deities of Guru. The Trinity—Brahma, Vishnu and Maheshwara, are the deities of Pluta.

Anudruta is the smallest unit in the Tala units. It is only 1/4th of a Matra, half a Matra is called Druta, Matra has two Drutas and four Anudrutas. Two Matras or Laghus make one Guru and three Matras make one Pluta.

These five units have four synonyms each—

1. *Anudruta*: Ardhachandra, Vyanjanam, Charu Nasikam, Avyaktam.

2. *Druta* : Ardhamatram, Vyomam, Valayam, Bindu.

3. *Laghu* : Vyapakam, Hrasvam, Matra, Saralam.

4. *Guru* : Dvi Matram, Vakram, Deergham, Kala.

5. *Pluta* : Trayam, Trimatram, Deeptam, Samodbhavam.

The Angas are represented by these signs or symbols:

Anudruta	-		-	1/4th matra
Druta	-	O	-	1/2 matra
Laghu	-	|	-	1 matra
Guru	-	S	-	2 matras
Pluta	-	S	-	3 matras

This description is given in the end of the third part of Nrityadhyaya.

Graha : The word Graha means to catch, or to start. In Tala, Graha indicates the starting point of Tala in the sequence of a song. Generally, it is well known, that Tala or the beats of a Tala (on Tabla) start from a specific pre-decided point of a song. The Tala, starts either with the song or after or before the starting of the song. These are called Grahas, they are threefold.

Sama Graha : The song and Tala start simultaneously. The starting point of song and Tala coincides, then it, Sama Graha.

Nita or *Atita :* Atita means 'past'. When the starting point of a song is already over and Tala joins after some pause, it is named as Atita or Nita.

Anagata Graha : Anagata means not arrived. When the Tala precedes the song it is called Anagata. The latter two Grahas add beauty and stress of the rhythm.

Jati : In colloquial language, Jati indicates the caste, class or type. Tala is also categorised into Jatis according to the number of beats—odd or even and a mixture of both odd and even number of beats. Our author Narada adds one more Jati—Khanda Jati, which consists of many divisions presented by a number of Laghus replacing the bigger time units, i.e., Guru and Pluta.

The Jatis are four according to Narada. They are :

Trayashra : It has an odd pair of beats; Matras or odd number of Kalās (Kalā = two matras).

Trayashra Jati Tala has three Kalas in its original and initial state and can be expanded upto ninety six Gurus by multiplying each forward number with two. 3|6|12|24|48|96| गुरु त्रयं समारम्य द्विगुणं द्विगुणं क्रमात्

Chaturashra Jati : As the name suggests, this Jati has even numbered pairs of beats, i.e., four Kalās or Gurus (eight matras). It can be expanded upto 128 Gurus similarly.

4|8|16|32|64|128. गुरु द्वयं समारम्य द्विगुणं द्विगुणं क्रमात्

Mishra Jati : When the odd and even numbered Talas are combined in various ways, the Mishra Jati Tala materialises.

Khanda Jati : As already mentioned Khanda Jati Tala consists of numerous divisions—Khandas, and the Tala consisting of a number of Laghus is called as Khanda Jati Tala. Khanda stands for small divisions, here laghu or a single Matra represents the Khanda. The definition of Khanda Jati Tala given by Narada is as follows :

तदालैश्चतुरस्र जातीनां खण्डाः विभागा भविष्यन्ति
तत्र तदा खण्डार्था ताला इति ख्याता जायन्ते।

Here in 'तदा लैः, लैः stands for Laghu.

Laya : It is the tempo or speed of the Tala. The interval between two beats are the governing factor of the tempo of a rhythmic cycle. This Laya is threefold. The natural normal speed which is used in speech or action is Madhya Laya, viz., neither fast nor slow; it is medium, slower than Madhya Laya or to be more specific half of the Madya Laya is Bilambita Laya. Druta Laya is the double (fast) of the Madhya Laya. Thus the three Layas are—Druta (fast), Madhya (medium) and Biambita (slow).

Kala : It is equal to a Guru comprising two Matras or Laghus. But it is not consistently constant in terms of its unit counts. According to Margas, it changes its count of Matras. It takes eight, four, two Matras in Dakshina, Vartika and Chitra Margas respectively.

Yati : Various combinations of the above mentioned three Layas are named as Yati.

Samayati : When a single Laya is maintained throughout the Tala without any change in tempo, it is termed as Sama Yati.

Shrotovaha : The systematic alteration of Layas from fast to slow tempo is Shrotovaha.

Gopuchcha : Exactly opposite to the Shrotovaha Yati. Variety of Layas produced from changing slow to fast. This definition is according to 'Sangita Makaranda'. Narada says that when Druta, etc., are changed in their respective order, i.e., Druta Madhya and Bilambila, (though he does not say it in as many words or uses the names of three Layas) and the opposite order of Druta, etc., forms the Gopuchcha Yati. It has to be clarified because other authors have a different view.

Prastara : Narada explains the importance of Prastara. He says that there are countless Talas in practice, all of which are not described in this work. Therefore, to understand them, nineteen easy methods are named, which will be of great help to understand and derive new Talas. Prastara is one of those methods.

Prastara means expansion. It is more or less like an equation or simplification. It consists of several specific steps to be performed to replace the bigger units by the smallest unit —Drutas. The Prastara ends when all the units of a Tala are changed into as many Drutas. But the important factor is the number of steps and specific rules to be followed while doing a Prastara. A Guru cannot be changed into four Drutas, which is its value in Drutas, in three steps. It is done as given below:

1st step	S
2nd step	II
3rd step	OOI
4th step	OIO
5th step	IOO
6th step	OOOO

Similarly a Pluta has to pass through 19 steps to be represented by Drutas. After Drutas the Prastara ends.

Thus Narada of 'Sangita Makaranda' has dealt the topic Tala in a very elaborate way. Its inclusion in the Nrityadhyaya suggests the connection between the 101 Talas and Nritya. Various Prabandhas bearing similar names of the Talas are also mentioned in the works dealing in Prabandhas like

'Brihaddeshi', 'Sangita Ratnakara', etc. The special and unique feature of the subject Tala dealt in this work is the inclusion of Pancha Talotpatti, the description of 101 Talas, ten Tala Prabandhas, Anga Talas and six Margas in the ten Pranas of Tala, etc. The six Margas instead of commonly mentioned three Margas are unusual as his five types of Nada, Mridanga description and analogy of music and Brahma Veena. There are various such unusual features scattered throughout the work.

The fourth part of Nrityadhyaya also adds up to the exceptionally extraordinary treatment of the subjects in this work—'Sangita Makaranda'. Though, the four parts are devoted to Nritya (dance), first part comprises the description of the Natyashala, chairperson (king) courtiers, seating arrangements, important personalities, i.e., scholars, artists, etc. Two parts are devoted to Talas and the last part consisting of 43 slokas explains about Nritya.

The first ten slokas describe the Mridanga, thus only thirty-three slokas speak about actual dance—the postures, gestures of hands, rotation of body, head, etc.

But the names of the poses are very uncommon, and Narada names them as Natibhava, which is more accurate and justifiable. Because all the Bhavas or postures including hand gestures and signs are accompanied by steps, movements of waist, body, gaits and movements of eyes. The names, specified for the actions of dance are also not used by anybody else. The author has mentioned five single-handed and equal number of double handed gestures.

Samyuta (both hands) Hastam : Arekha, Sarini, Samprasari, Samagaikam and Kaivalam.

Asamyuta Hastam (single handed): Chaturam, Kuvalam, Dhritahastam, Anuranam and Parikramam.

The eight Bhramarikas (rotations) are named. They are —Kurudayi, Chitrataram, Chitrakali, Ghanaravam, Nagabandham,Chakrabhramari, Atichakrabhramari, and Vidyutabhramani.

Narada then mentions nine positions of the heads — Botavani, Chiguru, Samagatram, Viragatram, Vishamakam, Ardhagatram, Viragatram (repetition), Phanivalam and Chitibotavani.

He concludes the poses with four Charanams. They are Chitram, Atichitram, Vindanti, and Samam.

These adds upto thirty-one only. But Narada says that thirty-three Natibhavas acceptable to all the scholars adept in dance and Shastras, are explained by him.

The names except Chakra, Vidyuta, Bhramari are not mentioned in any work on dance. Hence the names do not serve any purpose and no comparative study is possible.

CONCLUSION

After a thorough study of 'Sangita Makaranda', there are many remarkable points worth considering. Here I am again throwing light on these points step by step.

'Sangita Makaranda' is a short work on music comprising two Adhyayas each with four parts. It is an independent and complete work and not a compilation of quotations of Narada. No work has been done so far on 'Sangita Makaranda'.

This work has a name of its own and consists of many unique and independent views of the author which are not found in any other work. There are many short works similar to 'Sangita Makaranda' like 'Dattilam', 'Oumapatam', 'Sangita Choodamani', 'Veena Lakshanam', etc. Therefore, the size of this work does not contribute to its being a compilation as suggested by M.R. Kavi. In 'Sangita Makaranda' many other general slokas without any serious subject matter or facts also appear. They need not be memorised by students of music. Therefore it is not a compilation of Narada's or any other authors' quotations of music. Indeed it is a complete work based on an ancient work of original Narada.

The text of the work is full of grammatical errors as well as corrupt terms and names of Murchana, Ragas, etc. As there is only one manuscript at present, it is very difficult to edit the text. The manuscript of 'Sangita Makaranda' now available is the copy of the original manuscript, which might have been in a very precarious and damaged condition. Therefore, the copyist copied some verses from 'Sangita Ratnakara' and copied other verses full of errors (as he understood them) from the damaged original manuscript of 'Sangita Makaranda'. Because some verses make no sense at all.

Narada is a general name adopted by many authors of various works on music. However, the author Narada does not give any indications to place him in a definite period. The name of Narada indicates that the author is a follower of the music system found by the Narada.

The time of the work or the author of 'Sangita Makaranda' has not been fixed till now. I have placed 'Sangita Makaranda' in between seventh and tenth century at the latest after giving ample internal and external evidences with reasonable and logical arguments.

'Sangita Makaranda's' priority over 'Sangita Ratnakara' is proved by the Gandhara Gramas and its arrangement of notes quoted by Sharngdeva as of Narada.

The names of the musicians and scholars (Matru Gupta of 550 A.D.) given by Narada proves that the work is not earlier than the sixth century. Other principles of his system of music fix the time not later than ninth or tenth century. Mahamaheshwara's name appearing in 'Sangita Makaranda' pushes it forward in time. This has been fully discussed. The main argument being the exclusion of Abhinava Gupta's name in the list of musicians and scholars. It could have been mentioned by Narada, if he was to announce the name of Mahamaheshwara and that too for a much ordinary fact which does not need anybody's support. This was the main objection raised by scholars for placing it before Abhinava Gupta, (tenth century A.D.) the objection being cleared by the above justification, I have placed 'Sangita Makaranda' in seventh to tenth century.

Gandhara Grama with its Murchanas has been discussed and its usage in his Raga has been confirmed.

His Ragas are based on Murchana system only as he has given only Graha (starting note) Svara. His usage of three Gramas is confirmed by the similar starting and prominent note of more than three Sampoorna Ragas. There are many more such Ragas. Narada has not even mentioned Grama Raga, Geetis, or Dhruva Gana. His main Raga classification system is eight Ragas with three wives each. This is based on eight praharas of the day and night and the three hours of a prahara. The second Raga classification of six Ragas and six Raginis each are based on six seasons of the year. Narada is more concerned about music, dance comes next to music only and dramatics is not his subject.

The description of court with the nine important scholars or prominent personalities shows that Narada's music is meant for learned scholars who know about music and can appreciate it. The work as a whole reflects the spiritual inclination of Narada and his Tantric approach to the subject. Every term and subject represent the Shiva-Shakti elements including the Mridanga.

Narada is very much keen to train the listeners also. He never leaves them alone. The benefits and sufferings are equally divided among the musicians and listeners accordingly. His Talolpatti Prakaranam again confirms the Tantra element in him and his work. His Tala seems to be an independent part from music and is not treated as accompaniment only.

This work is more religious, spiritual and ritualistic. We frequently come across the attainments by listening to the names of terms (Tala) and correct tuneful music with Ragas in their allotted time which confirms the above statement. The only drawback of the work is that the subjects are not arranged properly and in a systematic way. The definitions appear in the last, while the subjects are discussed earlier.

On the whole 'Sangita Makaranda' is a very important work and it is a link between 'Brihaddeshi' and 'Sangita Ratnakara'. It has many novel and unique principles about the music of past, though it would not be of any great help as far as practical side of music is concerned.

REFERENCES

1. Boles — certain sign words produced by Tabla to show the divisions of Tala and they are fixed for each particular Tala.
2. *Bharatiya Talon ka Shastriya Vivechan*, p. 317.
3. *Sangita Makaranda*, p. 33.
4. See Appendix 5.
5. *Sangita Makaranda*, sl. 6-13, p. 39 ; sl. 19-32, pp. 40-41.
6. *Ibid.*, sl. 17, p. 40.
7. The Rise of Music in the Ancient World — Greek Rhythm.
8. *Sangita Makaranda*, pp. 42-43.

APPENDIX 1

The names of eighty four Tanas

अग्निष्टोमोऽत्यग्निष्टोमो वाजपेयोऽथ षोडशी।
पुंडरीकोऽश्वमेधश्च राजसूयश्च सप्तमः ।। १०६ ।।

इति षड्जहीनाषाडवताननामानि। स्वरसृष्टि (?)
तृड्बहुः.+ सुवर्णश्च गोसवश्च महाव्रतः।
विश्वजिद् बहुयज्ञश्च प्राजापत्यस्तयैव च ।। १०७ ।।

इतिऋषभहीनषाडवताननामानि।
अश्वक्रांतो रथक्रांतो विष्णुक्रांतस्तयैव च।
सूर्यक्रांतो गजक्रांतो वलतीनामवज्रकौ ।। १०८ ।।

इति पंचमहीनाषाडवता (न) नामानि।
चातुर्मासिकसंज्ञश्च शस्रश्चैवकोत्थकस्तथा।

सौत्रामणिश्च पित्रा च उद्भिद्यागश्च सप्तमः ।। १०६ ।।
इति निषादहीनषाडवताननामानि।
इति षड्जग्रामे षाडवताननामानि अष्टाविंशतिः।
सावित्री चाद्यसावित्री सर्वतोभद्र एव च।

सर्पो यजनसंज्ञश्च तथा वैकुंठवायनः ।। ११० ।।
इति मध्यमग्रामे षड्जहीनताननामानि।
अग्निचिद् द्वादशाहश्च उपांशुः सोम एव च।

अश्वप्रतिग्राहोद्वहीस्तथाभ्युदयं इत्यपि (?) ।। १११ ।।
इति ऋषभहीन (तान) नामानि।
सर्वस्वदक्षिणो दीक्षा सोमः समिधसंज्ञकः।

स्वाहाकारश्च नूनश्च तथा गोदोहनस्तथा ।। ११२ ।।
इति गांधारहीनताननामानि। इति मध्यमग्रामे एकविंशति षाडव
(तान) नामानि। इत्येवमुभयग्रामाश्रिता (हये? न्ये) कोनपंचाशताननामानि।

इडख्यः पुरुषमेधश्च श्येनो यज्ञ इषुस्तथा।

अंगिराः कंससंज्ञश्च षड्जग्रामेऽपि चौडवाः ।। ११३ ।।
(इति) षड्जपंचमहीनताननामानि।
अग्निष्टोमोऽथ दर्शश्च नांदी वै पूर्णमासिकाः।
अश्वप्रतिग्रहो रात्रिस्तथा कौभरतो मतः ।। ११४ ।।
इति गांधारनिषादहीनताननामानि।
सौभाग्यकश्च शारीरी शारिकृत पुष्टिकृत तथा।
वैनतेयो भवेदेव उच्चाटनवशीकृतौ ।। ११५ ।।

इति पंच(म) ऋषभहीनताननामानि। इति षड्जग्रामे
औडुवितताननामानि एकविंशतिः।
त्रैलोक्यमोहनो धीरः कंदर्पबलशासनः।

शंखपूगो गजच्छायो रौद्रोऽसौ विष्णुविक्रमः ।। ११६ ।।
(इति) मध्यमग्रामे धैवतऋषभहीनौडुवितताननामानि।
भैरवः क्रामदश्चैव आकुष्टोऽब्जश्च पालकः।

सृष्टिकृद वर्षकांतारः सप्तमो रक्षितः स्मृतः ।। ११७ ।।
इति मध्यमग्रामे औडुवितताननामानि चतुर्दश। उभय–
ग्रामिक्यौडुविताः पंचत्रिंशद् भवंति। षाडवा औडुविताश्च
मिलित्वा चोभयग्रामिकास्तानचतुरशीतिर्भवंति।

APPENDIX 2

Kashyapa : This sage is referred to by Matanga in his 'Brihaddeshi' seven times, Abhinava Gupta, two times, by King Nanyadeva two times. He is mentioned as one of the authorities in 'Sangita Makaranda' of Narada and by Sharngdeva in his 'Sangita Ratnakara'. "There are two works—Laghu Kashyapa and another Brihat Kashyapa, the latter being similar to Brihaddeshi".[1]

Vishwakarma: Vishwakarma is generally connected with architecture and carpentry. Alain Danielow mentions the name Vishwakarma and places him in the first period, i.e., that extending from prehistoric ages to the Mahabharata-Purana period. "The main teachers in probable succession Brahma, Prajapati, Kashyapa, Brihaspati, Vishwakarma...."[2]

According to A. Mcdonnel, Vishwakarma is an ordinary designer or builder.[3] The following is an account in a thesis by Damodaran Nambiyar.

"The term Vishwakarma is expressive of two distinct significations. Vishwakarma is the son of Bhuvana, a well-known Vedic seer and Vishwakarma is numerically identical with God as the creator of the Universe ....."[4]. In puranas it has been stated that Vishwakarma is the son of Tastra and the chief architect of the building.

Some hymns are dedicated to Vishwakarma in Rigveda. Therefore though Vishwakarma is not related to music yet he deserves mention as the Creator of the Universe. As in Tantra Shastra it is accepted that the Universe evolved from Nada,

Vishwakarma the Creator of the Universe may also be related to the Nada and thus to music.

Vayu: This name is given in the list of 'Sangita Makaranda', and 'Sangita Ratnakara'. There is no information about him in any authoritative work. "Certainly Vayu's part is very great in any myth of the origin of Sangita Shastra. It is also likely that the name Vayu refers to the Vayu Purana which says something of music."[5]

Bharata : Bharata is well known for his work 'Natya Shastra'. The name Bharata in the list assures it being written by some Narada other than the Narada of Naradiya Shiksha. Narada and Tumburu are the names of Gandharvas who are the founders of Gandharva Veda.

Visvavasu : He is also a Gandharva and as such he enters the list.

Kubera : He is the God of Wealth and a son of Shiva. "He hides like his treasures in the depths of the Earth listening to the music of the artists and is the horse riding genii, like the Gandharvas and the Kinnaras."[6]

Ravana : He was very adept in Sama Gana. With his Sama Gana and Veena playing he used to please Lord Shiva. He is associated with a particular Veena. He is a mythological figure in the Ramayana.

Shanmukha : Also called Guha was an old writer of music. Sri Krishnamacharyar states thus, "the original work of Shanmukha is lost, Sangraha Choodamani is said to form the part of Skanda Purana, composed by Shanmukha. In three chapters it deals with the origin of music and musical tones ..... . At best it must be reproduction of the lost views of Shanmukha.

REFERENCES

1. *Some names of early Sangita Literature.*
2. *The Ragas of North Indian Music*, p. 12.
3. *Vedic Mythology*, p. 11.
4. *Naradiya Purana —A Critical Study*, pp. 46-47.
5. *Some names of early Music Literature.*

APPENDIX 3

श्रुतियों के नाम

संगीत मकरन्द		भरत भाष्यम्		संगीतसमयसार मन्द्र सप्तक	
१.	सिद्धा	१.	तीव्रा	१.	मन्द्रा
२.	प्रभावती	२.	कुमुद्वती	२.	अतिमन्द्रा
३.	कान्ता	३.	छन्दोवती	३	घोरा
४	सुप्रभा	४	मन्दा	४	घोरतरा
५	शिखा	५	दयावती	५	सौम्या
६	दीप्तिमती	६	रसिका	६	सुमना
७	उग्रा	७	रौद्री	७	पुष्करा
८	ह्लादी	८	क्रोधी	८	शंखिनी
६	निर्विरी	६	वज्रिका	६	नीला
१०	दिर	१०	प्रसारिणी	१०	उत्पला
११	सर्प सहा	११	प्रीति	११	मण्डना
१२	क्षान्ति	१२	मार्जनी	१२	सानुनासिका
१३	विभूति	१३	क्षिति	१३	घोषवती
१४	मालिनी	१४	रक्ता	१४	लीन नादा
१५	चपला	१५	संदीपनी	१५	आवर्तनी
१६	बाला	१६	आलापिनी	१६	रणदा
१७	सर्वरत्ना	१७	मदन्ती	१७	गम्भीरा
१८	शान्ता	१८	रोहिणी	१८	दीर्घतारा
१६	विकलिनी	१६	रम्या	१६	नादिनी
२०	हृदयोन्मलिनी	२०	रंजनी	२०	मन्द्रजा
२१	विसारिणी	२१	उग्रा	२१	सुप्रसन्ना
२२	प्रसूना	२२	क्षोभिणी	२२	निनदा

	संगीतसमयसार मध्यसप्तक		संगीतसमयसार तारसप्तक
१	नादान्ता	१	ईश्वरी
२	निष्कला	२	कौमारी
३	गूढ़ा	३	सवराली
४	सकला	४	भोगवीर्या
५	मधुरा	५	मनोरामा
६	गली	६	सुस्निग्धा
७	एकाक्षय	७	दिव्यांगा
८	भंग जाती	८	सुललिता
९	रस गीती	९	विद्रुमा
१०	सुरंजिका	१०	महार्का
११	पूर्णा	११	शंकिनी
१२	अलंकारिणी	१२	राका
१३	वांशिका	१३	लज्जा
१४	वैणिका	१४	काली
१५	त्रिस्थाना	१५	सूक्ष्मा
१६	सुस्वरा	१६	अति सूक्ष्मा
१७	सौम्या	१७	पुष्टा
१८	भाषांगी	१८	सुपुष्टिका
१९	वार्तिका	१९	विस्पष्टा
२०	सम्पूर्णा	२०	काकली
२१	प्रसन्ना	२१	कराली
२२	सर्वव्यापनिका	२२	विस्फोटा

APPENDIX 4

CHART 1

The Cries of Animals and Birds Representing the Seven Notes (Svaras)

SEVEN NOTES (SVARAS)

Authors	*Shadja*	*Rishabha*	*Gandhara*	*Madhyama*	*Panchama*	*Dhaivata*	*Nishada*
Narada (Naradiya Shiksha)	Mayura (Peacock)	Gava (Cow)	Aja (Goat)	Crouncha (a bird)	Kokila (Cuckoo)	Ashva (Horse)	Kunjira (Elephant)
Matanga	"	Chataka (a bird)	"	"	"	Dardura (Frog)	Gaja (Elephant)
Narada (Sangita Makaranda)	"	"	"	"	"	Ashva (Horse)	"
Nanya Bhupala	Shikh-andina (Peacock)	Rishabha (Ox)	"	"	"	Sapti (Horse)	,, ,,
Sharang Deva	Mayura (Peacock)	Chataka	"	" –	"	Dardura	"

CHART 2

The Particulars of Swaras given by Narada of 'Sangita Makaranda'

SWARAS

Particulars	*Shadja*	*Rishabha*	*Gandhara*	*Madhyama*	*Pachama*	*Daivada*	*Nishada*
Colour	Padmabha	Pinjra	Swarna	Kundi	Sita	Pita	Karbura
Islands	Jambu	Shaka	Kusha	Krauncha	Shalmali	Shweta	Pushkara
Rishis	Daksha	Attri	Kapila	Vasishta	Bharagava	Narada	Tumburu
Deities	Vahini	Brahma	Sarada	Sarva	Srinatha	Bhaskara	Ganeswara
Metres	Anushtub	Gayatri	Trishtup	Brihati	Pankti	Ushnig	Jagati

CHART 3

The Particulars of Swaras given by Narada Sangita Makaranda.

SWARAS

Particulars	*Shadia*	*Rishabha*	*Gandhara*	*Madhyama*	*Pachama*	*Dhaivada*	*Nishada*
Gotra	Jamadagni	Atreya	Gantama	Vasishta	Srivatsa	Parashar	Shalankaya
Stars (Nakshatra)	Shatabishak	Chitra	Dhanishta	Makha	Uttara	Poorva Ashada	Anuradha
Rasi	Kumbha	Tula	Jhasha	Sinha	Kanya	Dhanu	Vrischika
Lords of Rasis	Sani	Bhrigu	Sasi	Surya	Budha	Guru	Mangal
Rasas	Adbhut and Vira	Raudra	Santha	Hasya	Sringara	Vibatsa	Karuna

APPENDIX 5
101 TALAS
Pages 35-39 : Sangita Makaranda

१ चंचतपुट
२ चाचपुट
३ षट्पिता पुत्रक
४ सम्पद्वेष्टिक
५ उद्घट्ट
६ आदिताल
७ दर्पण
८ चर्चरी
९ सिंहलील
१० कन्दर्प
११ सिंहविंक्रम
१२ श्रीरंग
१३ रतिलील
१४ रंगताल
१५ परिक्रम
१६ हंसलील
१७ वर्णभिन्न
१९ राजचूड़ामणि
१९ प्रत्यंग
२० गजलील
२१ प्रिभिन्न
२२ वीरविक्रम
२३ रंग द्यूत
२४ राजताल
२५ सिंह विक्रीडित

२६ वनमाली
२७ वर्णताल
२८ रंग प्रदीपक
२९ हंस नाद
३० सिंह नाद
३२ मल्लिकामोद
३२ शरभलील
३३ रंगाभरण
३४ तुरंगविल्ली (लील)
३५ सिंह नन्दन
३६ जय श्री
३७ विजयानन्द
३८ प्रति ताल
३९ द्वितीयक
४० मकरन्द
४१ कीर्तिताल
४२ विजय
४३ जयमंगल
४४ राज विद्याधर
४५ मण्ठ
४६ जयताल
४७ कुडक्कक
४८ निसारिणी
४९ क्रीड़ा
५० मल्ल ताल

५१ दीपक
५२ अनंग लील
५३ विषम
५४ नान्दी
५५ मुकुन्दक
५६ एकताल
५७ कंकाल
५८ चतुस्ताल
५९ दोम्बुलि
६० अभंग
६१ राय भंकाल
६२ मधु शेखर
६३ प्रताप शेखर
६४ जग झम्प
६५ चतुर्मुख
६६ झम्प
६७ प्रतिमण्ठ
६८ तृतीय
६९ वसन्त ललित
७० रति
७१ करुणा
७२ षट ताल
७३ वर्धन
७४ वर्ण यति
७५ राय नारायण

७६ मदन
७७ पार्वती लोचन
७८ गारूगि
७९ श्री नन्दन
८० जय
८१ लीला विलोकित
८२ ललित प्रिय
८३ जनक
८४ बद्ध
८५ लक्ष्मीश
८६ राग वर्धन
८७ उत्सन
८८ ललित
८९ त्रिभंगी
९० कोकिल प्रिय
९१ निःसारूक
९२ श्रीकीर्ति
९३ बिन्दुमाली
९४ सम ताल
९५ मट्टिका
९६ द्विमट्टिका
९७ वर्णमटिका
९८ अभिनन्दक
९९ काल बन्धन
१०० झल्लक
१०१ उद्वीक्षण

BIBLIOGRAPHY

English Works

A Classical Dictionary of Hindu Mythology and Religion, Geography, History and Literature, John Dowson, M.R.A.S., Trubner's Oriental Series, London, 9th ed., 1957.

A Companion to Sanskrit Literature, Sureshchandra Banerji, Motilal Banarsidas, Ist ed., 1971.

A Cultural History from the Vayu Purana, Devendar Kumar Patil, Motilal Banarsidas, 1973.

A History of Sanskrit Literature, V. Varadachari, Allahabad Ram Narein Lal, 1952.

A Study of Dattilam, Mukund Lath, Impex India, New Delhi, 1978.

A Treatise on Hindu Music, Arun Bhattacharya, K.P. Bagchi and Company, Calcutta, 1978.

Early History of Deccan, Bhandarkar, B.D.R. Institute, Poona, 1983.

Fundamentals of Ancient Indian Music and Dance, Suresh Chandra Banerji, L.D. Institute of Indology, Ahmedabad, 1976.

History of Classical Sanskrit Literature, Krishnamachariyar, Oriental Book Agency, Poona, 1937.

Hindustani Music and its Physics, B.G.H. Ranade, IInd edition, 1951.

Hindu Music from Various Authors, S.M.Tagore (compiler), Choukhamba Sanskrit Series, Varanasi, III ed., 1965.

Music, its Form, Function and Value, Swami Prajnananda, Munshi Ram Manohar Lal Publishers Ltd. Ist ed., 1979.

Melodic Types of Hindustan, N.K. Bose, Jaico Publishing House, Bombay, 1960.

Kudumiamalai Inscriptions, Journal Oriental Research, Madras, Vol. 7., 1933.

Music of Hindostan, A.H. Fox Strangways, Oxford Clarenden Press, 1965-67.

Naradiya Purana—A Critical Study, A thesis of Damodorn, Nambiar University of Poona, 1968.

New Catalogues Catalogorum, Vol. 10 - Na, Nya, Dr. Kunjunni Raja (ed.), University of Madras, 1978.

Principles of Tantra, Introduction by Arthur Avlon, and S.B.K. Majumdar, Ganesh and Co., Madras, 1960.

Ragas and Raginis, Amiyanath Sanyal, Orient Longman Private Ltd., Calcutta, 1959.

Ragas and Raginis, O.C. Ganguli, Nalanda Publications, Bombay, 1948.

Story of Indian Music, O. Goswami, Asia Publishing House, 1961.

Studies in Natya Shastra, G.H. Tarlekar, Motilal Banarsi *das,* Varanasi, Ist ed., 1975.

The Ragas of North Indian Music : Their Structure and Evolution, N.A. Jairaj Bhoy, Faber and Faber, Queen Square, London.

The Music of India, H.A. Popley, IInd ed., Calcutta, 1950.

Some Names of Early Sangita Literature, Bulletin, 1956-57.

Role of Sanskrit in the Development of Indian Music, S.S. Janaki, Journal of Music Academy, 1985.

The Ragas of North Indian Music, Alain Danielu, London, 1968.

Sanskrit and Hindi Works

Agni Purana Vishayanu Kramani, Dr. Ram Shankar Bhattacharya, Bharatiya Vidya Prakashan, Varanasi.

Adbhuta Ramayanam, Maharashi Valmiki, Ram Kumar Rai, (Ed. & Tr.) Prachya Prakashan, Varanasi , 1982.

Abhinava Darpana, Nandi Keshwara, Manmohan Ghose (ed.), Firma K.L. Mukhopadyaya, Calcutta, 1957.

Bharata Bhashyam — Part I, Nanya Bhupala, Ist ed., Khairagarh, (M.P.), 1961.

Bharata Bhashyam—Part II, Ist ed., 1976.

Brihaddeshi, Matanga, Sangita Karyalaya Hathras, IInd ed., 1962.

Bharata Kosha, Ramakrishan Kavi.

Bharatarnavam, Vasudeva Shastri (Ed.).

Dattilam, Dattila, Sangita Karyalaya Hathras, 1960.

Natya Shastra, Gaekwad Series, Chapters 28-36.

Naradiya Shiksha, 1960.

Naradiya Mahapurana, Khemraj Krishna Das, Venkatesh Press, Bombay.

Pancha Tantram, Vishnu Sharma, Pandit Pustakalaya, Kashi, 1973.

Sangita Pari Jata, Aholbala, Sangita Karyalaya, Hathras.

Sangita Ratnakara, Shringi, Ist Chapter, Ist ed.

Sangita Ratnakara Vols. I-II, Adyar Kala Kshetra, 1973.

Sangita Samaya Sara, Shri Kund Kund Bharati, Ist ed., Delhi, 1977.

Sangita Darpan, Hathras, 1962.

The Narada Pancharatra, K.M. Banerji, (Ed.), Bishop's College Press, 1865.

The Institute of Narada, Asiatic Society of Bengal.

Vikramanka Deva Charitam, Subhash Publications, Calcutta.

Bharatiya Sangit Ka Itihas, S.C. Paranjape, Choukhamba, 1985.

Bharatiya Talon Ka Shastriya Vivechan, Dr. A.K. Sen, Academy Press, 1973.

Sangita Shastra, Vasudeva Shastri.

Manuscripts of *Sangita Makaranda, Panchama Sara Samhita, Chatvarinsha — Chatta Raga Nirupanam, Sangita Narayana, Raga Sangara*, etc.

Index